Hans-Georg Ziebertz

Religious Education in a Plural Western Society

Empirische Theologie

herausgegeben von

Prof. Dr. Dr. h. c. Johannes A. van der Ven
(Katholische Universität Nijmegen)
Prof. Dr. Dr. Hans-Georg Ziebertz
(Universität Würzburg)
Prof. Dr. Anton A. Bucher
(Universität Salzburg)

Band 11

LIT

Hans-Georg Ziebertz

Religious Education in a Plural Western Society

Problems and Challenges

To Judith

in honor
Jan 2005

Hans-Georg

LIT

Bibliographic information published by Die Deutsche Bibliothek
Die Deutsche Bibliothek lists this publication in the Deutsche
Nationalbibliografie; detailed bibliographic data are available in the
Internet at http://dnb.ddb.de.

ISBN 3-8258-6692-0

© LIT VERLAG Münster – Hamburg – London   2003
   Grevener Str./Fresnostr. 2   48159 Münster
   Tel. 0251-23 50 91   Fax 0251-23 19 72
   e-Mail: lit@lit-verlag.de   http://www.lit-verlag.de

Distributed in North America by:

Transaction Publishers
New Brunswick (U.S.A.) and London (U.K.)

Transaction Publishers	Tel.: (732) 445 - 2280
Rutgers University	Fax: (732) 445 - 3138
35 Berrue Circle	for orders (U. S. only):
Piscataway, NJ 08854	toll free (888) 999 - 6778

Content

Preface 7

Part I : Social Contexts of Religious Education

1 Challenges of Religious Education 11

Problems of Perception ...11   Postmodern Society and the Presence of
Plurality...13   Plurality as a Challenge...14   Growing up in Plurality...18
Religious Education in the Context of Religious Plurality...25

2 Religious Education in a Multicultural Society 33

Concepts of Pluralism...34   Comparison of the Concepts of Pluralism...38
Concepts of Pluralism and Religious Education...41   Challenges...46

Part II : Reflecting on the Goals of Religious Education

3 Religious Didactics as a Reflection of the Process of
Religious Learning 53

Religion and Didactics...53   Theory and Practice...56   Religious Learning
Processes: Reflections, Plans, and Answers...59   A Record of Religious
Learning...61   Learning for Life...64

4 Religious Education as an Opening of the Religious
Dimension of Reality 67

The Religious Dimension in the Modern Context...67   What is Religion?...69
Religion and Faith as a Fertile Tension...77   Opening up the Religious
Dimension of Reality...79

5 Functions and Objectives of Religious Learning 83

The Transcendence-Reference in Education...83   Goals of Different
Concepts of Religious Education...86   Dimensions of Objectives...89
Objectives of Religious Education...92

6 Identity as Narrative and Process 95

Endogenous Identity?...96   Erik Erikson's Concept of Identity...96
Identity from Interaction...97   Narrative Pluralistic Identity...99   Identity
in Religious Education...103

Part III : Religious Education and the Plurality of Religions and Values

7 Religion, Religiousness, and Inter-religious Learning 109
Pluralism in Worldviews and Inter-religious Learning...110   Dialogical
Theology...112   Treatment of Differences and Changing of Perspectives...115   Open Questions...120

8 Teaching Ethics in a Plurality of Values 123
What makes the teaching of ethics so difficult?...123   The Plurality of
Values and Norms: Problem and Challenge...125   Models for Teaching
Ethics...128   Sense of Judgment within the Horizon of the Christian
Tradition...136

Part IV : The Dimension of Space

9 Educational Space Inside and Outside of School 145
Developing Space as an Exercise for the Teaching of Religious Education...146   Education in the Space of School...146   The Individual's Body
as Space...149   Bringing Tradition to Life: The Sacred Space...152
Transcending Everyday Life - Virtual Space...154   Conclusion...157

10 Religious Education and the Public 159
What does *Public* mean in Religious Education?...160   Culture...163
Media...167   Politics...172   Outlook...175

Part V : Religious Education as a scientific discipline

11 Methodology: The Empirical Orientation of Practical Theology 181
The Material Object of Empirically Oriented Practical Theology...181
Methodology: Hermeneutics, Empirical Orientation, and Ideological
Criticism...185   Quantitative and Qualitative Orientation in Constructivist
Perspectives...187   General Functions of Empirical Research in Practical
Theology...192

References 197

Acknowledgments 203

The Author 203

Preface

Plurality is a decisive characteristic of the modern Western world, existing in Western culture, sciences, economies, and politics. Plurality also exists with regard to religion. When plurality is spoken of, not only the historically established religions such as Christianity, Islam, and Judaism are meant; we also encounter plurality in the religious attitudes of people. Their beliefs and practices can have religious character without having to understand themselves within the context of a religious community – religion is not to be found only in the churches anymore. Plurality also exists within each religion. When one speaks of Christianity, he must precisely identify which of the approximately 300 Christian denominations he means. Yet plurality reigns even within one specific church. For example, the Roman Catholic Church, which is especially hierarchically governed, is a reflection of plurality. In some situations, Catholics in Holland, Poland, or the Scandinavian Diaspora have fewer commonalities than an intellectual Catholic and a Swedish Lutheran. Religion today exists in the context of societal and cultural plurality and must find its place there. At the same time, plurality exists within every religion.

Religious Education in school is education in an official space. It has plurality not only as a theme, but from the beginning, it must also design and establish its concepts from the multiform nature of plurality. Religious Education must be "plurality-capable." This is the task this book sets for itself. Some concepts of Religious Education recommend a neutral, objective treatment of religious themes in the face of plurality. Others think that there is no Archimedean point from which religion can be neutrally observed. Religion is fundamentally evocative and uncovers an existential dimension. The ideas and reflections in this book uphold the latter position. Religious Education serves to give the rising generation the skills needed to speak about the religious dimension of reality. Ecumenical and inter-religious candidness exists in knowledge of one position and in the ability of students to bring this knowledge into discussion. This is not just a matter of two phases: first, religious instruction and second, religious dialogue. Rather, religious learning processes are constitutive at their beginning – already characterized by plurality. In encountering and interacting with what one considers to be strange, alien, and other, he begins to ponder the question of who he himself is. The construction of an individual religious identity is linked with the unfamiliar.

The first section of this book reflects on the premises of Religious Education. The second section turns to the pedagogical question of the goals of Religious

Education. The third section takes up two themes that are particularly affected by Religious Education: the diversity of religions and the diversity of world-views. The fourth section expounds on the problems of the dimension of space. The fifth section considers the methodological question of how Religious Education can be approached scientifically. Naturally, the ideas and reflections in this book are not wholly and purely objective. The Catholic perspective of a German scientist will be recognizable in these reflections, which might be indigenous in a different religious tradition or in a different context. Nevertheless, most questions addressed in this book are not specific to a religious tradition. They are relevant to other countries and to other religious contexts in analogous ways. So let these ideas be an international contribution to the consideration of the question of how, under the conditions of the modern, Western, plural world, Religious Education can be conceived and established.

I should like to acknowledge my gratitude to Grant Lovellette from USA, a student in Würzburg in 2001/2002, whose skills as editor, native speaker and writing instructor were vital in bringing this book to publication.

Part I

Social Contexts of Religious Education

1

Challenges of Religious Education

Religious Education does not take place in one particular field. Religious Education lessons are given by a teaching body consisting of members of this society and take place in the public institution of school. Religious Education lessons are attended by pupils who have been born into this society. From the society and its culture emanates a basic molding of character, and thus the questions arise as to what the basic social requirements for religious learning processes might be and which challenges for religious learning ensue.

In this chapter, we discuss the difficulty of reaching an adequate diagnosis of present time. We examine dimensions of the modern, as well as of the postmodern society. Subsequently, we consider a specific characteristic of this postmodern society – plurality – and which particular problem areas characterize growing up today. These reflections make it clear that we can no longer simply talk about "the youth in general." We conclude this chapter with comments concerning the topic of school education in plurality.

Problems of Perception

An attempt to shoot a time photo as reliable evidence about the present social conditions of Religious Education requires a preliminary remark. Although we all live in the same world, we each perceive this world differently. The world is different for different people. What is designated below as contemporary society's challenging of didactics of Religious Education is the upshot of a perspective with which others may well disagree. Let us attempt to clarify the matter in hand. When modern society is discussed in theological or ecclesiastical texts, we often come across the comparisons *nowadays* and *in the past*. The idea goes something like this: in the past, the basic conditions were better for living a Christian life and for introducing young people to the Christian faith. Society was more receptive to Christianity, and Christianity represented by the churches was, on the whole, more sociably acceptable. References to Christianity in the political, cultural, and economic spheres (a social market economy) were common practice. On the other hand, nowadays we are dealing with a time in which many people are classed as anti-religion, and many others at least as indifferent towards religion. A personal, decisive, public confession of the Christian faith is an exception today. The adolescent generation is now only in part (more precisely, in an ever diminishing part) socialized in and dedicated to a church.

This assessment is supported both biographically and historically. The generation born between the two World Wars that have lived after the ecclesiastical Spring (Vatican II, 1962) can hardly reach any other conclusion when looking rationally at the current situation of Christianity, faith and society. Even to those who do not perceive decline and the end of the Christian West, evidence of serious social change is still very clear. Suiting the methods of teaching Religious Education to the times will depend upon an awareness of the relativity of this experience: the decline of church life in the modern world. Young people between 20 and 25 years of age who study Theology and Religious Education only come across "everything was better earlier" attitudes in literature or perhaps h ear a bout t hem f rom t heir p arents o r t heology p rofessors. This a pplies even more so to school pupils between the age of 6 and 19 years. They have all grown up in circumstances in which the norm is that when the neighbors park their car at church every Sunday morning, they then go off for a jog rather than off to worship. Children and teenagers will not judge this as either negative or positive, since, based on their own life experience, they cannot employ any historical means of comparison. The fact of the matter is (and must be accepted) that some people identify more, some less, and some not at all with religion or church-represented Christianity. If the older generation decides that this lack of religious identification is indicative of an indifference to religion, the younger generation c annot c omprehend w here t he p roblem l ies b ecause i n their v iew, there is no problem. The younger generation takes the postmodern situation of ideological plurality for granted. They enjoy freedom of worship and do not expect a decision for or against to have any impact of social consequence. Plurality is normality.

These findings are important in relation to the teaching of Religious Education. The success of a learning process also depends upon how it succeeds in understanding the *lebensweltlich*[1] requirements or the pre-conditioning of the pupils. If teachers generalize their own assessments of the world, they run the risk of further complicating matters and compromising education. For the younger generation, there is no one point in time 20, 30, or 40 years ago that was normative in the sense that it could be used to evaluate what might have improved and what might have become worse since that normative time. The present and the future are what matters. Methods of teaching Religious Education must add opportunities and formulate objectives that take into account the current conditions that adolescents experience. The way Christian religiousness is to be experi-

---

[1] *Lebensweltlich,* adj. Derived from the German *Lebenswelt*, meaning the subconscious, pre-conditioned socio-cultural way of viewing the world and life.

enced today and in the future cannot be derived from the past. It is necessary to find new ways to communicate the religious dimensions of reality clearly and make the language of Christianity more accessible.

Postmodern Society and the Presence of Plurality

What lies at the heart of the problem of our time? The term *postmodernity* is now on everyone's lips and exists in all academic areas. It inevitably deals with an enigmatic concept. A reappraisal of what is currently meant by *post-modern* cannot and must not be carried out here. We cannot avoid this concept, however, if we are to attempt to illuminate the social requirements of religious learning processes.

In his analysis of the present, "Postmodern Modernity," Wolfgang Welsch demonstrates that postmodernity can only be fully understood in relation to modernity (Welsch 1994; see also Cahoone 1996). In economic terms, modernity is generally understood as the gradual decline of agrarian societies and the rise of industrial societies. In political terms, it is seen as the collapse of the feudal power structures of the Middle Ages and the emergence of societies with comparably more democratic parameters. The Enlightenment marked an historical caesura in the arts and sciences. The emphasis on reason and rationality and the proclamation of the autonomous individual created a new concept of *being in the world*. In the 19th century, the idea of modernity became an ideology and target. As an ideology, it stood for unstoppable progression, the Industrial Revolution, a trust in technology, and a concentration on economic progress (ecology was not yet a subject in public domain). It led to a high respect for (and sometimes an overestimation of) the human ability to make anything possible and to dominate the world. Traditions were valued less if they did not conform to the old norm and if they keep up with pace of progress. They were fought against and ridiculed if they did not comply with the dictates of progress. In particular, the Catholic Church experienced this tension, and between 1850 and 1950, it repeatedly attacked that which represented modernity. An added motivation must have been its loss of influence over public opinion and personal morality during the same period. Not until the Vatican Council II (1962-1964) was a Church-world relationship based on partnership achieved.

Modernity is to some extent a collective term for the phenomenon outlined above. Neither has it come to an end, nor is it justified to talk about a new era of postmodernity. Indeed, there are conceptual schemes of postmodernism in which development targets are set for Politics, Economy, Law, and Culture. In the context of this chapter, the term *postmodernity* should principally be spoken of in an analytical-descriptive manner. Accordingly, various definitions of postmodernity explain it as modernity's critical self-reflection or as the enlightenment of modernity about itself (Welsch 1994). What is meant here is that the postmodern view sees both sides of the coin, i.e. the good and the bad side of modernity; it includes both a positive reference to dynamism of modernity just as much as it does a negative reference to the concomitant losses. Today we recognize that the attempt to control nature has lead not only to an improved life style, but also to the exploitation of natural resources, the possibility of nuclear contamination, the cloning of human beings, etc. Many people have profited from scientific and technological progress, but the promise of progress has not been universally realized. There is a neglected periphery. For most people in the Global North, life is going well, but this improved way of life has not been granted to everyone – not to some people in the Global North and not to many people elsewhere. Many fall through the cracks and struggle to survive. Wealth and justice are not distributed evenly; in reality, the gaps between the haves and the have-nots are widening. On one side, many human values are legally safeguarded in many countries' constitutions, but at the same time, modernity's claim of humanity's humanism has been discredited by many disastrous wars. How can we trust this "higher education" of man if it did not prevent the atrocities at Auschwitz? This and similar experiences act as obstacles in the path of an uncritical stance on modernity. What is clear is that there is no way to go back to premodernity. A critical reflection on modernity seems to be needed since pessimism about modernity is not a concept upon which educators can build a plan for teaching.

Postmodernity has many causes and influences, and there are at least as many ideas about what the term *postmodernity* actually means (cf. Ziebertz 1999b). One of the most prominent advocates of postmodern thought, Jean-François Lyotard (1984), sees the core of postmodernity in heterogeneity. Others speak of radical plurality. This plurality concerns worldviews and life orientations as much as it does styles and schools of art, architecture, etc. Advocates of postmodern thought believe that variety can no longer be traced back to one common root. Unity and homogeneity are signs of the past.

Plurality as a Challenge

Naturally, the scope and validity of such diagnoses of the present are questionable. What is not contestable, however, is that plurality is a crucial characteristic of the present world, whether the present be labeled as either modern or as postmodern. Radical plurality is obviously a problem for most religions, although this problem extends beyond religion. How should the religions deal with plurality if they claim a more or less exclusive approach to the ultimate truth (Ziebertz 1996)? In order to set things out in concrete terms for the Christian didactics of Religious Education, we must decide how we can plausibly talk about Christ as the universal redeemer if plurality is the structural basis of our society and if other religions make the same claim. Does dynamism arise from plurality, a dynamism that, at the end of the day, promotes a type of *anything goes* mentality? Under these circumstances of pursuing Christian religious upbringing, will it not become more and more difficult to make this claim? Indeed, there are objective conditions that are more or less advantageous, but it also depends on the attitude one has towards those conditions. Lecturers of Religious Education must develop a rational relationship to plurality that implies not just seeing plurality as a problem, but moreover seeing it as an exercise to be carried out and a challenge to be met (in depth: Schweitzer/Englert/Schwab/ Ziebertz 2002). Three aspects must be briefly addressed here.

The Irreversibility of Plurality

At least for the near future, we must act on the assumption that plurality is irreversible. Postmodern theoreticians can hardly be contradicted when they point out that the conception of the world of the Middle Ages, a world of unity in which vaulted Christian conceptions of the world molded all aspects of life, has irrevocably dissolved into nothing. Modernity has lead to a move towards autonomy of different sectors of society; politics, economics, law, medicine, and culture are no longer subject to the control of religion but rather establish themselves according to their own rules. Religion has become a just another academic subject to be studied alongside all the others. From the perspective of plurality as a problem, this development could be regrettable. Understanding plurality as a challenge involves discussing the influence of the universal force in forming our notions of our lives and the world around us. This universal force and Christianity's claim to redemption must be discussed in learning processes in such a way that adolescents learn to integrate a religious view of the world into their conceptions of the world and daily life. The development of the ability to integrate attitudes towards life in the individual is a tribute to individualization. Postmodern thought makes it clear that we can only strive towards homogeneity under the conditions of plurality. Pupils must bring their choir-ego, their football-ego, their pupil-ego, and their particular forms of speech and thought into contact with their religiousness-ego. The religiousness-ego cannot be asserted against the others, but it must be brought into communication with the others. For the planning of religious learning processes, this means that Religious Education teachers must take into consideration the necessity of such integration processes in the pupils. The process of integrating religiousness into the plural of perspectives on life can be made easier if a *lebensweltlich* context is achieved in class communication. Today, a competence in didactics of Religious Education alone cannot exhaust the aspects related to the knowledge of a discipline. It also involves a familiarity of the worlds of children and teenagers. Religious Education teachers who do not know which age group wears which shoes, which songs are leading in the charts, which magazines or books are in fashion, and which computer games are on the list for Santa cannot develop this ability to instill an integration of religion in life's blueprints (see chapter 6).

Plurality of Religion

A second aspect concerns the normality of plurality of religion. This can be divided into different levels. The *first* level concerns the plural of religion. For example, in German-speaking lands, it has become increasingly well-known that Islam is the second most popular religion, after Christianity. Some 5 million people in Germany are Muslim. In reaction to the large numbers of Muslim children and adolescents, Islamic Religious Education lessons have been introduced in some federal states. Judaism is substantially smaller numerically, but it is also a public presence. At the moment, it plays an important role because of the Germany's past. An appropriate degree of culpability is still fought for. The relation to Judaism presents perhaps the biggest challenge to Christian Religious Education. No other relation demands such a high level of sensitivity. The remaining major religions are only conspicuously visible in the large cities. It is not the statistics of religions that act as a challenge to Religious Education lessons, however, but rather the mere existence of different religions. Here again it is a case of asking ourselves how we ought to deal with the heterogeneity of the claims of ultimate truth which these religions embody (see chapter 7). The *second* level concerns pluralism within Christianity. Since the split of the eastern and western Church, there has been an increasing differentiation in a multitude of Christian churches. The Reformation must be mentioned as a very central event, but the process of differentiation continued in Protestantism with a comparable level of fervor as in Catholicism. This form of religious plurality demands that Religious Education lessons encompass the Christian ecumenical movement. The *third* level concerns plurality within a denomination. Culturally, Roman Catholicism has many different facets; consider the differences in Catholicism in Poland, the Netherlands, Italy, and Germany, and the differences among Europe, North America, and Latin America. Even within the context of a specific church, differences come to light. Plurality does not just denote the opposing roles of bishops and laymen but goes through all ranks. This means that today, even denominational identity can no longer be thought of as separate from religious plurality. The *fourth* level of religious plurality concerns the differentiation of *Kulturchristentum,* i.e. church-represented Christianity and the Christian-religiousness of the individual. *Kulturchristentum* refers to the fact that multiple traces of Christianity are contained in publicly represented beliefs and attitudes to life without being legitimized through any tie to a church. Church-represented Christianity influences our attitudes and the way we live our lives through direct reference to the Church. Finally, Christian-religiousness of the individual refers to the particular specific religious attitudes and practices of individual persons. There has probably never been a time during which an individual religiousness has been fully congruous with Church doctrine. Popular religiousness and mysticism, for example, have always appeared in various shapes and forms and, more often than not, have had a tense relationship with the "official" religion of the Church. Nowadays we speak of secular religiousness, a phenomenon that can appear in conjunction with sports events, music concerts, body cults, etc. There are, then, the many different religions, the various forms of Christianity, the plurality within a denomination, and the cultural differentiation of religion. These four levels of religious plurality form the backdrop against which religious education takes place today. This "religion in plural" does not make it impossible for learning processes that introduce certain religious traditions, but it does call for us to constructively examine and come to grips with this plurality.

Plurality as Pluralism

The third challenge for Religious Education learning processes arises from the discussion about postmodern society. It is a matter of developing plurality as pluralism. Plurality indicates the unordered juxtaposition of the many attitudes and forms of behavior; pluralism is the conscious approach of dealing with plurality. Plurality is an unavoidable basic fact of existence, but it is not necessarily a value in its own right. Plurality opens up varying options to an individual and grants an increased amount of individual freedom. On the other hand, plurality can be very fragile – in the absence of clear, reliable orientation patterns and securities, for example. Plurality can ask too much of people. Not just this aspect, but also the answers to the fundamental question "what matters in life?" given by an individual, society, and the world around us as a whole force a pluralistic way of dealing with plurality. Everything and everyone are not all the same and should not be all the same. In this respect, Jürgen Habermans and Wolfgang Welsch rightly stress the need to search for elements of unity and consensus in the midst of multiplicity. Concerning school education, the challenge lies in perceiving and appreciating plurality and not fading it out or pretending that it simply does not exist. Teachers cannot shield pupils from plurality. Education actually takes places at the point when the question of what is desirable is understood as a subject matter in its own right. Conflict over which position should claim validity is not unusual. Pupils must become familiar with methods by which persons with conflicting views can reach a settlement by non-violent means. In this situation, the following concepts are important:

- first, to be able to tolerate ambiguous positions;
- second, to learn about basic styles and techniques of reasoning;
- third, to have the ability to understand the perspectives of others, to address them, and to be willing to learn about the arguments of others;

- fourth, to be able to use experiences and social traditions which are culturally available; and

- fifth, to have not only the competence to reach agreements, but also to learn to live with those outcomes, even if they have rendered no consensus.

Religious Education lessons must help in teaching these skills if they are to contribute to general school education. It is also possible pluralistically to work through religious plurality with respect to religion as explained above. The lessons take part in an exercise that is permanently looking to Christianity: throughout history, the Church has continuously had to construe what Christian faith is, what Christianity wants to say to humankind under the terms of its current cultural context, and whether Christianity is ascertainable from past. Subject-orientated didactics of Religious Education do not just present the results but involve them in such hermeneutic processes. These stresses on hermeneutic and problem-oriented Religious Education lessons are still current.

Growing up in Plurality

Concepts of Religious Education easily succumb to the danger of pushing their own topics so far into the foreground that the impression arises that every thing revolves around religion and a belief in learning processes. For children and teenagers, Religious Education is merely another subject along with all the rest, and – from a general point of view – not a very central or pressing subject. Apart from this, the tasks and challenges of elementary development met in childhood and youth cannot be related to any particular school subject, but they can indeed quicken or complicate school studies at large. Certain aspects need to be mentioned here.

The Changing Childhood

One of the biggest inspirers of pedagogy, Jean Jacques Rousseau (1712-1778), promoted the idea of understanding childhood as not merely a transit stage on the way to becoming a *full* human being, but as its own area of life with its own set of laws. The same dignity should be accorded to children as to adults, and children should be treated with the same level of respect as adults. The 20th century has been proclaimed the *century of the child* – and childhood has, especially in the last third of the century, undergone a demonstrably rapid change. With the drive of modernization in the sixties and seventies, it became known that the general reform of society (e.g. democratization) would have consequences for the methods of educating children. The questions were asked, in what might the specifics of childhood lay, and how might they be fostered? It also became known that the children's future lives were becoming increasingly less foreseeable, or, at any rate, could not be predicted based on the present. During this period, many negative diagnoses of that period were made. The loss of social relations, the failure of the parents and the school as educational authorities, and a change in nutritional habits were noted. A change was observed in the way children played, and the reduction in the amount children played out in the open and the consequent lack of exercise were viewed with worry. Television consumption was critically judged, as was the new full agenda of the time. We cannot ignore the fact that some pessimistic diagnoses could actually be verified. Looking back with the benefit of hindsight, it does not appear to have been a matter of comprehensive trends. Parameters of judgment were often idealizations of the examiners' own childhoods, which, sure enough, proved inept in the changing times.

Until the nineties, pedagogy had regarded the childhood stage mainly from a theoretical perspective of socialization. Socialization is, in contrast to individualization, one of the concepts created by society, saying that childhood and youth are transition stages to becoming a full adult. Since the nineties, constructive approaches that call attention to the fact that childhood is also a construct have been increasing in importance alongside the perspectives of socialization. For some, society constructs an image of childhood; for others, it is the children who construct a picture of themselves and of the world around them. It appears to be the case that in the current intellectual models of childhood, the classic notion of "childhood happiness" has given way to a conception of "adult-similarity." Pedagogues speak of a process of removing the frontiers between what is considered an adult and what is considered a child. Whether alone or with children, adults go to adventure parks and take pleasure in doing so. Children, as their parents, use the mobile phone to communicate with playmates and to arrange meetings. Even if this depiction is somewhat exaggerated and does not take into account specific social and class differences, it still illustrates the change of childhood. Childhood is no longer just the preparation for the later fuller life, which until now has required abstinence and procrastination. Many adventure and fun park industries, as well many sports and outdoor pursuits centers of which grown-ups make use, are potentially accessible for children and vice versa.

Changes can be most easily identified in the family realm (cf. Anderson 1997). Children are invited to participate in decisions about their future at an ever-earlier age. They are not just allowed to, but they are expected to, encouraged to, and obliged to decide independently on a multitude of questions concerning themselves. Naturally, this also applies to the topic of religion. The enlarged space for maneuvering does have limits, however. Parents and children draw on current ideas and theories, and to all intents and purposes they allow for traditions (e.g. of the Christians) and the institutions which embody them (the churches). That happens even when their notion of their own position in life is seen as detached from a church. Nowadays, parents are generally tending to avoid regimented interventions into their children's lives in favor of encouraging the child to show more self-determination. Self-development values such as autonomy and independence are favored, but values of order and duty, such as discipline and subordination, are not.

Since the sixties and seventies, there has been an increasing tendency towards one-child families in the western European countries. On the one hand, social contact with the child's brothers and sisters is missing, but on the other hand, the parents compensate for this with a high level of emotional devotion. Most children are very happy in their families. The quality of the relationship between parent and child appears to be more significant than the quantity of other relationships in the child's life. The small size of the family leads to an absence of conflictive and non-conflictive experiences with brothers and sisters, and the school increasingly compensates for this deficit, which is with increasing regularity being diagnosed as a disciplinary problem. At school, children meet with groups, whereas in their spare time, one-on-one relationships are the predominating play relationships.

Lastly, childhood has become an object of commercialization. That which commercialization affects has stepped alongside the classical youth group event-clubs and contractors of arts and sports programs; even private tutoring, which takes place during the free time of the afternoon, has developed into a demanded market. Although the parents usually meet the costs, corporations and salespeople have also started to regard children and teenagers as consumers. The spending power of 6-17 year olds in Germany alone is estimated at 9 million euros, which corresponds to 900 euros per child/teenager per year. Leisure centers, the computers and mobile phone industries, and the music sector all try to attract young customers. It is not without reason that the private television channels popular among adolescents run product advertisement en masse. It is also true that the level of education of the family and its generally associated income are still guiding forces in terms of consumer interests.

Individual Development Tasks during Adolescence

If we look at older manuals, it would seem that we used to know exactly how to define the beginning and the end of adolescence. At present, it is difficult to establish a ny c lear b oundaries. G irls a nd b oys s tart puberty e arlier t han t heir parents' and grandparents' generations, for instance. Nowadays, adolescents who have finished their school education and/or vocational education are significantly older. On the one hand, the amount of time during which the child is dependent on his/her parents is increasing, while on the other hand, adolescents are mentally and physically so developed that they are able to stand on their own. The end of adolescence is being postponed. At the same time we are also witnessing another phenomenon, namely that *youth* as a general value is receiving social attention. It is no longer just business that tries to increase sales by alluding to *youthfulness*, but it would seem that all generations now succumb to the lure of youthfulness. Health spas, adventure sport companies, and fitness studios all offer promises of youthfulness and are loyally patronized by older people with enough money.

In this limited life period, teenagers undergo much change and development.

- They experience the way their body changes, and with those changes comes a certain bodily awareness. They must learn how to relate to their body and how to accept their corporeality. That is not always an easy task, particularly when their own appearance does not correspond to the prevailing ideals of beauty.

- During puberty, the task of finding and consolidating their own sex role arises. This feat is not identical to the acceptance of their corporeality. By the term *sex role*, we understand a cognitive concept that transcends the biological results (of being either a girl or a boy) and leaves us with mixed patterns of masculinity and femininity (cf. Riegel/Ziebertz 2001).

- A crucial problem during adolescence is the development of self-consciousness and a feeling of self-worth. Who we really are becomes indicated, among other ways, by the person for whom others take us, i.e. how we appear in the eyes of others. Self-worth, social skills, and social status are all interdependent. Being incorporated into network relations and receiving a secure allocation of social status inside and outside of school strengthen young people's feeling of self-worth. Social relations with people of the same age are especially relevant in this matter. Electronic or virtual relationships are of increasing importance today, but it is questionable, however, whether virtual peer groups are able to qualitatively substitute for tangible, flesh-and-blood relationships.

- During adolescence, teenagers explore their boundaries of action and development. They establish their place in society. This calls for certain questions, such as is my life aimed towards marriage and family, which career or which sort of vocational training should I choose, does a course of higher education come into the question, and which branch of study is the right one?

- The establishment of their own place in society demands that they become aware of their increasing personal responsibility. Public activities have consequences, and in problematic situations, society responds differently than the way a family would. Teenagers must learn to assume responsibility for their own actions and behavior.

- Finally, the personal system of values develops during adolescence. The influence of the family is fundamental during this development, but by primary school, children will often have already noticed that alternative beliefs exist and that they must form an opinion about these beliefs. Adolescents have to learn to stand by their points of view and to withstand opposing opinion. Concomitantly, they must also learn to confront other attitudes with tolerance and never in a rash manner. A personal system of values develops, and during childhood and adolescence, a heightened sensibility towards questions of values exists. The school can, should, and must escort and support this development (see chapter 8).

The aspects outlined here can be seen in individual pupils with varying intensity and can be more or less problematic. Besides their subject-specific interests, all teachers are required to consider the overall physical and mental development of their pupils. For teachers of Religious Education, these problems in themselves are problems of the quality of the subject matter. All of these questions deal with the evolution of the self. According to the Christian faith, God's special regard is held for the self, i.e. the ego, the individual human being whom God has called by his own name. Religious Education explains life and the world from this standpoint of God's love for the individual person. The more these lessons succeed in making these concerns discernible, the more plausible the idea of God's caring for humankind becomes.

Common Challenges during Adolescence

Teenagers at the beginning of the 21st century are growing up in a society that places high demands on the self-organization of the individual. The debate about post-modernity has shown both that and why "growing up today" cannot fall back on set traditions and cannot simply take "secure" social integration for granted. It is not the case, however, that children and teenagers inevitably wander around without direction in the currents of plurality. The present situation is much more ambivalent. It knows a more and a less of everything, a so and a not so. In regards to how we deal with teenagers, this will mean adequately assessing the degree of differentiation of life requirements and conclusively dismissing a one-dimensional view of "the youth." Differentiation is also offered where a plurality of teenage attitudes, fashions, forms of behavior etc. is depicted as a problem, whereby plurality is understood as an indication of decline. This view underestimates the fact that *differentiation* is a central activity of adolescence.

Teenagers break away from others – first from their parents and family, next from teachers and classmates, and later from certain fashions and group trends, etc., in order to establish themselves as individuals. Individualization takes place when we distinguish ourselves. What is interesting about this is that the result is in no way a fully heterogeneous youth culture. In fact, trends arise that demonstrate the way in which teenagers try to develop individuality within the plurality – which they do *in reference* to the societal institutions and traditions and not, for instance, against them.

It appears that in the current youth culture, attitudes and actions are integrated that are often seen as exclusive. In a large youth survey (Jugend 2000 I, 93ff), a range of such ambivalences is named. It is worth noting some examples:

- In society and among teenagers, virtues such as readiness to take risks, spontaneity, and mobility are valued. At the same time, loyalty a nd r eliability, a nd e ven a l ove o f o ur n ative l and, r ate highly, i.e., variables are not all equally variable or subject to instant decisions.

- Individual independence, along with wealth and power, is imperative in making our way socially in life. Nevertheless, it would be wrong to deduce from this that teenagers support ego-orientated values. In fact, trustworthiness, authenticity, and credibility are highly regarded, as is t he quest for equality and solidarity.

- Society supports values such as creativity and speediness, but we just as often come across a n approval of discipline a nd persistence.

- A central principle o f modern s ociety is flexibility. That which can be essential at school and in professional life does not necessarily have a negative counterpart in the private domain. Flexibility does not inevitably lead to isolated relationships; the case is rather that long-term relationships in narrower and wider fields of relations continue at the forefront. The task remains to integrate ourselves into existing relationships.

- In society, the significance of external control systems has diminished. This does not lead inescapably to raging egoism and an increase in deviant behavior. In fact, the control is internalized. The choices and decisions with which we are confronted are accompanied by an internal control. The significance of interdisciplinary problem-solving thinking is increasing. Today, this is all the more important since closed systems and clear interpretations do not apply. In this way, our entire life becomes a "project."

If we go along with the aforementioned youth survey, then we agree that in general, teenagers have a positive image of themselves, of the world around them, and of their personal future. On the other hand, this evaluation only gives us an average, and it implies that there is also a "less." On average, a positive view on life, aspiration, and a disposition towards performance and success prevail. A point dealt with in Ulrich Beck's analysis of the "risk society" (1992) is hardly disputable: Postmodernity provides an increase in freedom, but it offers no guarantee that this increase will personally be experienced as positive or that it will be possible to explain it productively. To name but a few examples: there is a close connection between school and career opportunities. The pressure of selection starts early on in primary school, where success or failure can predetermine a student's success in secondary school. Not all pupils can take the pressure. Studies and investigative literature list the psychosocial costs: headaches, nervousness, sleeping problems, stomach pains, etc. Clearly, it is understandable that not all children and teenagers are equally capable of reaching the top goals. Nonetheless, a failure is tragic for the individual and, at the end of the day, must be dealt with *on a personal level*. The more that high-grade educational achievements become the norm, the stronger the competition becomes. This ambivalence must be kept in view, even when the overall findings first appear in a positive light.

Contributions of Religious Education Lessons

The achievement of today's adolescents in finding their way in these areas of conflict and developing a survival strategy cannot be praised highly enough. School education, inclusive of Religious Education lessons, must continuously point out that in a broad sense, education does not solely apply to subject material. It includes universal age- and development-related cycles, which do not just have an individual side, but also a social and societal side. Religious Education lessons are required to contribute towards making the adequate resources available.

- Religious Education lessons must recognize the varying distribution of material resources and should be sensitive towards discriminations that arise from material inequality.
- Religious Education lessons should answer positively to "autonomy" but recognize its social consequences and flank a drifting off into isolation by actively constructing social networks (e.g. through group or project work, inclusion of youth groups, etc.).
- Religious Education lessons should not artificially gloss over and simplify today's differentiated society but create opportunities appropriate to the age and development of the pupils to practice decision-making and processes of negotiation.

- Religious Education lessons should show high regard of individuality and offer teenagers help in finding a balance between the colorful patchwork ego and the rigid personality.

- Religious Education lessons cannot escape a *lebensweltlich*-orientated approach. If it cannot provide any basic assurance to life, it ought to give the pupils the tools to enable them to answer positively to life, interact with one another, discuss principles for a successful life, detect sources of hope, and discover sense and meaning.

When people look back on their Religious Education lessons and remember them positively, they usually speak of good experiences in the areas mentioned above. This should encourage teachers to be open to such constructive qualities in Religious Education lessons, even if this stands in contrast to the overall school climate.

Religious Education in the Context of Religious Plurality

Let us return to the basic requirements of Religious Education – to plurality. Were it to be asked whether plurality is a goal in itself or whether plurality ought not to be restored to unity, the answer, in my opinion, can only be nei-ther/nor. In fact, the goal must be a quality development of plurality. This goal runs contrary to a compulsive striving for unity just as much as it does to a practice of acting arbitrarily or with indifference. It is not sufficient simply to affirm plurality as a matter of principle, as not everything that plurality brings out is desirable. Religious Education concerns itself with giving the skills of differentiation to young people. The diversity (the difference) that characterizes plurality must itself be made into a topic of study. Teenagers ought to perceive difference and learn to understand and judge it, and, through the process of discussion, they should also be able to consolidate or revise their own position. Just as all education occurs through the examination of the environment, modern teaching of Religious Education must also include the current plural religious-ideological environment. In this context, pupils and teachers are already an environment for one another. Religious Education in diversity must be seen as an education in freedom. It establishes a concept of communication that understands communication as an educative method – pupils learn through this process of sharing and discussing ideas.

Identity in Plurality

From a cultural point of view, history is bursting with attempts to produce unity in or harmony with everything. Particularly against the background of modernity, such attempts are no longer feasible without immense political, social, and psychological consequences. They inevitably lead to totalitarian compulsory measures and a loss of freedom. An upbringing that entertains such ideas runs the risk of degenerating into ideological indoctrination. In a cultural respect, German history, for example, provides us with compelling evidence of such attempts to formulate incontestable truths and salvations, religions up to the present day not excluded. In the Western press, Islam and to an extent Judaism are associated with such fundamentalism, although in reality fundamentalist currents are parts of every religion, culture, place, and country on Earth, Christianity included. For example, the Catholic Church attempted to resist plurality in its cultural and socio-psychological form by retreating to its small flock of faithful followers. Compared to the confused milieu of plurality, retreating is to step back to secure ground where the religion may not be questioned. We strategically endeavor to gain acceptance of a position against the plurality of Christian religious belief, but we do not look for the argumentative debate with differently minded people and people of different faith. To force unity can be seen as offensive and confrontational, but also as equally subtle.

If the theory of teaching Religious Education goes down this road, then its objective of Christian religious identity will only be determinable by means of exclusion. To some extent, those excluded draw upon this negatively circumscribed identity. Fundamentalism and sectarianism are no longer so very far apart. Both movements are little suited to aid constructively the foundation of plurality of faith and value convictions in churches and society. Undoubtedly, an important motive is a fear that within plurality, we might no longer be authorized to act, that we may not be able to endure the diversity, or that for all the plurality, we may not be able to see or establish things in common. Here the learning processes demanded are those that not only support autonomy and sing the praise of emancipation, but also those that endeavor to promote reintegration – and not just as a one-time effort, but as a repeated process (cf. Francis/Katz 2000). In relation to the teaching of Religious Education, this creation of identity entails learning about the foundation of unity in, with, and by means of multiplicity.

Anything Goes?

In the many-voiced song of post-modernity, some advocates see variety as a goal worth striving for in itself. Aware of the possibility that *unity in all* may be thought of as being culturally and religiously passé, the plural state of affairs is extolled as a normative ideal. *Anything goes* was the maxim introduced by Paul Feyerabend years ago as a new paradigm for the philosophy of academic theory. The essential question is, if everything is equal, is it really of equal value? These questions can hardly be unreservedly answered with a yes; a yes cannot be ethically upheld, nor is it even practically feasible. It cannot be upheld because, for example, we could then be indifferent towards the value of a human life, and it is not feasible because current conflicts of interest cannot be denied. Questions of religious practice come up against the notion that religious devotion always implies a connection to a truth that is not arbitrarily changeable. Empirically seen, religious relativism seems to correlate to the privatization of religion ("to each his own belief"). Regarding the teaching of Religious Education, the task remains to work out the consequences of this attitude and to motivate the assumption of responsibility. Here it is also called for to take a stand. The plural society is not as normatively abstemious as it may sometimes appear. A wealth of interest groups is incessantly active in trying to bring their ideas to life. Religious Education ought to contribute to helping young people to learn to become bearers of ideas of value themselves.

There is, therefore, a demand for teachers of Religious Education who are prepared to engage in argumentative debate and who do not shy away from factual conflict. Neither should they avoid conflicts, nor should they resolve them in a rash manner, but they should understand that working through competing and antagonistic views is a way towards forming a Christian identity. Above all else, this will require their willingness to present the representation of the plural pattern and to ask about its qualitative implications. *Anything goes* is an attitude of many people who would like not to disturb the diversity as it currently exists, as long as their own interests are not disturbed; but coexistence in a church and society calls for agreement. This challenges the approach to theories of Religious Education uncover the "laziness" of relativistic compromises. Teaching of Religious Education must not provide concrete instructions of how to act, but it can help in developing principles and criteria for a concrete form of judging.

Truth and Dialogue

If diversity of belief in faith and value cannot simply be repressed, but it is still important to us what prestige this diversity should claim, then a stance is called for that answers *yes* to diversity. In the West, we take freedom of worship for granted, and we must not forget that we owe this freedom to pluralism. Plurality is not a problem of the modern times, but rather an achievement that cannot be surrendered without losses. Plurality is the essential substance of freedom. To want socio-cultural pluralism but to refuse religious and ethical pluralism is not possible. What we say and what we actually feel about this question often diverge.

The German Cardinal Karl Lehmann emphasized that pluralism does not just call for Christendom and the Church to enter into dialogue with the plural culture, but that this dialogue in turn also draws upon an understanding of our faith and of the construction of Christian identity: "Under these conditions of extensive pluralization and individualization in society, conditions that also affect the Church, dialogue is the only appropriate method for dealing with this very concrete diversity and the unavoidable pluralities" (Lehman 1994, p14;). It is the historical nature of our understanding that allows Christians to join in this pluralism of social and religious provenance without even disclosing the truth of the revelation. It is not the revelation that is placed under reservation, but our historically and culturally conditioned interpretation of it. This insight allows us the room to see the multiplicity of beliefs in faith and values not as an evil to be eliminated, but as an undeniable fact (Schillebeeckx 1990, pp21 *et seq.*). In this way, heterogeneity is not raised to up to a principle. In fact, the richness of diversity favors an exhaustive establishment of the truth, albeit if the acknowledgement refers to an eschatological perspective.

A Christian upbringing must take plurality seriously, help to develop it constructively, *search* for contact between opposing claims, and promote plurality in the sense of a task and a challenge (cf. Schlüter 1994, 41). Divergent claims of ultimate truth cannot be avoided, nor can we try to resolve the difference through force. In the knowledge that due to human limitation an absolute solution is still to be found, people are left with no other choice but to search for the truth under the terms of plurality and to negotiate its value – not *on the other side* of the multiplicity, but in it. The truth cannot be established without discussion.

Differences as an Object of Education

The theory of Religious Education must ensure that plurality is not viewed with indifference, but rather is seen as *differentism* (Drehsen): as a situation of differing values, norms, and attitudes towards the world and faith! No one single opinion can claim ultimate definitiveness. This also stands for the contents of Religious Education in junior education: it must be open to supplement, amendment or even revocation. Religious Education that includes the plural aims for the reappraisal of religious pluralism as religious differentiation. Here a confrontation with substantial religion takes on a particular importance. *Substantial* refers to the content (i.e., the doctrine) of a religion, which, like Christianity, commands overly rich evidence of divine experiences and which deduces the secret of the faith by means of narrative. Paying attention to *lebensweltlich* requirements in the teaching of Religious Education does not mean treating religion merely as a *product* that, whatever its form and contents, simply needs to be endorsed. A critical analysis of *lebensweltlich* styles of religion is called for, especially in an educational context. Nevertheless, it seems worthwhile to develop an objective relationship towards the religious situation of our time. Assimilating the existing plurality into teaching methods will involve our providing direction pointers for individual search *processes* by means of differentiation.

An Education in Freedom

"The days of authoritarianism are over," write the authors of a study on values (Zulehner/Denz 1993, 261). This particularly applies to the area of practical orientation in life. An extraordinary high need for freedom exists, but the Church satisfies this need least of all. According to the people asked, the Church instead heavily invests in the representation of value convictions for which there is no demand. It is a matter, as some empirical studies have shown, of two levels: a material level concerning the concrete contents and a formal level that refers to the nature of the prevailing form of discourse.

The authors of a former European study of values leave no room for doubt: nowadays, what a person believes in, the way they do so, and which values receive attention are no longer enforceable by decree. "People attach importance to self-control, tolerance, freedom, communication, dialogue, and openness" (Zulehner/Denz 1993, 262). Participation is called for in forming a resolution over what should and should not be valued. From a church's perspective, these developments should not be seen as an attack on its authority. Modern pluralism and autonomy do not force churches to renounce their substance, but they do open that substance to discussion. As Zulehner and Denz explain, the Church of the future "will live off the tension between outlined identity and liberal openness. One of its most important characteristics will be diversity" (1993, 263). A change already seems to have taken place in families. Research shows that parents increasingly feel that they can no longer concretely anticipate what children and teenagers of today will need as adults of tomorrow. Children and teenagers are invited to participate in decisions about their own future at an ever-earlier age. They are not only allowed to, but they are expected to and obliged to make independent decisions about a multitude of questions concerning their own lives. Parents of today are tending to reduce the amount of regulated interventions in favor of encouraging the child to show more self-determination, and they particularly encourage this self-determination with questions relating to religion. Religious Education lessons must react to this change with a reform of its own concepts. Religious Education lessons can present the truth of the salvation of the Christian religion, as they can that of all the religions, but the students themselves decide whether they accept that message.

Religious Education as a Communicative Act

This form of working through plurality, which is given precedence in this chapter, sees the process of teaching Religious Education as a communicative exercise. In Religious Education lessons, shaping the belief and life experiences of the youth has no way of being effective other than by pursuing the path of communication. Because the models under debate are often considered to be connected to diverse roots, it is no longer just a matter of the correct concretion of what is at the core a common basic belief, but a matter of an analysis that reaches right to the roots. To search for unity within the diversity and not against it also means n ot a lways being able to count on t otal consensus, but learning to live and work with either partial or temporary agreements. If this possibility is not offered, we will end up colliding with the structure of the modern consciousness. In short, it is not committed participation in the quest for agreements that is under consideration here, but the question of how this might be brought about.

The crucial medium with which to find unity within the differentiation is communication. Communicative didactics of Religious Education emphasizes the fact that that communicative activity establishes identity because it deals with processes of understanding and interpreting that relate to the person in his or her relation to the topic. In a society where *learning* is a key concept, the process of education can have not only a functional meaning in which it is geared towards the prepared answer, but a ll answers can t hemselves be at t he mercy of this process. I t i s w orth a voiding t he t wo extremes: n either s hould l earning p rocesses be placed under obligation of striving for total consensus, nor should heterogeneity b e d eclared as the c entral p rinciple. The intermediate p osition answers positively to pluralism in culture and religion as well as on the level of subjective awareness, but it also sees communication as the medium with which to arrive at an agreement within the plurality (Schülter 1994, 41).

Communication is a term describing a process; it refers to the notion that beliefs are developed through interaction. Education adopts a spiral form in that it repeatedly brings us to convey our ideas, ask other people for their ideas, and allow our own ideas be enriched through knowledge in order to finally think these ideas over anew. It is not just an education in how to accumulate knowledge, but also an education in the process of how to think and to judge, in how to advance our insight into the message of religion in its relation to the self and to coexistence. In such searching and questioning, we establish an identity. It occurs as a stage-managed elucidation of the personal biographical requirements, as interpersonal exchange, and as a cross-generational, historical assurance (Van der Van 1996). The intrapersonal communication is about encouraging teenagers to ask themselves what they see as stable or fragile in their lives; it is about clarifying the topics that concern teenagers. These efforts are aimed at the biographical-life-historical aspect of Religious Education, at the reconstruction of a more socialized view on religion, values, and norms and their consistency and inconsistency in the light of today's experience. In interpersonal communication, questions of sense and meaning are taken out of a private sphere and reintegrated into a social sphere, whereby teenagers learn to talk freely about their own orientations and those of others, which, in turn, helps both parties to develop these orientations, i.e. they learn to adopt a position. In this way, the biographical *who we have become* is no longer based wholly on individuality, but its social embedding is stressed. Religious identity, as with identity in general, is also dependent upon the mutual establishment of meaning between the individual and the context. Here, the possibility of religious identity under these circumstances of modernity is put into question. The intergenerational communication transfers the individually undergone and reported experiences from the horizontal structure to a vertical. This involves confronting it just as much with the experience of other generations as well as with the promises targeted on the future, which Christianity conveys as substantial religion. Adolescents should bring traditions of the Christian churches and the messages of the faiths as a whole into a critical correspondence with their everyday encounters with the world, understand them as answers to their questions, and be able to determine their own conclusions. For the Christian tradition, this will involve recalling the story that exists between God and the people, a story that is told by the many stories of the Bible.

Conclusion

Plurality is a basic fact in our modern diverse and complex society that does not come to a halt outside the school gates. Religious Education lessons are, like other subjects, challenged to develop future ways of dealing with the different cultural and religious views. Religious practice is no longer just a case of mutual verification of a joint possession, but is also characteristic of the process of its acquisition. In the theory of teaching Religious Education, this problem is discussed under the catchwords *acquisition* and *conveyance*. It will increasingly become a matter of working in a way that is structure building, i.e. that establishes the sort of communication milieu in which practical questions about life and searches for sense and meaning can come together with substantial religion. Nowadays, an appeal to substantial religion alone is no longer enough. This demands a hermeneutic competence from theologians, enabling them to act as frontier-crossers. It is a matter of having the competence to oscillate between the internal and the external and among Christian traditions, individualized religious styles, and general models of cultural religiousness. It is also a matter of the competence to establish connections with the goal to perceive religiousness, to talk about religiousness, to judge religiousness, and – in these advantageous conditions – to reach a decision of faith.

2

Religious Education in a Multicultural Society

This chapter establishes a relation between multiculturalism and Religious Education. The underlying question here is that of which problems, challenges, and aims arise for concepts of Religious Education from a multicultural social context. It is a feature of the multicultural society that it has many facets. This chapter will focus on two facets that represent central characteristics of the multicultural society: plurality and the concomitant pluralism. Plurality can be understood as recognizably different values, norms, concepts of living, and ideas of faith. Pluralism is the legitimate form of heterogeneity in a society.

It is frequently taken for granted that the so-called multicultural society allows multicultural or even multi-religious Religious Education. For instance, an introduction to the Christian tradition is deemed to be made more difficult, if not quite impossible – or not advisable out of respect for other convictions. Pluralism is said to force neutrality and objective representation upon us and undermines Religious Education in any case in the sense of a particular religious tradition (cf. Ziebertz 1995).

Seen this way, pluralism seems to be a kind of independent variable. I would argue against this notion of pluralism. Given a positive twist, my hypothesis is that the so-called multicultural society, whose pluralist character interests us more than anything else, as we shall see, is a *discursive object*. The multicultural society is not simply objectively there (recordable, for example, from the numbers of fellow Muslim citizens), urging certain consequences upon us, but rather it is a multiform construct. When we concern ourselves with multiculturalism, we take part in a discursive universe that is all about analyses, definitions, and intended directions (cf. Wilkerson 1997; Kincheloe/Steinberg 1997; Torres 1998). I want to refer to three concepts of pluralism, compare them, and inquire what they have to do with Religious Education. In this chapter, I do not want to concern myself with didactic or practical teaching questions, but will primarily take an interest in the cultural and political context of Religious Education.

Concepts of Pluralism

The three concepts of pluralism I have chosen are represented by Jean-François Lyotard, Jürgen Habermas, and Charles Taylor, who have each stressed different aspects of the reality of pluralism.

Heterogeneity and Equality

In his emphatic confrontation with post-modernity Jean-François Lyotard (1984) raises the question whether unity is possible within modern or postmodern pluralism. According to Lyotard, unity of knowledge comes about through so-called meta-narratives. Meta-narratives involve the central ideas that legitimate everything and guide the pursuit of knowledge (see below; cf. Cahoone 1996, p481-513). According to Lyotard, the past of modernity had three great meta-narratives at its disposal: first, the Enlightenment, with its promise of the emancipation of mankind from political and religious oppression; second, idealism, with its notions of clear aims and reasoning, leading to the development of culture and society, even of the universe; and third, historicism, with its attempt to find meaning by means of an interpretation of history. According to Lyotard, these were three generalizations that could claim to offer a homogeneous interpretation of the world, which have all failed: Enlightenment had promised emancipation but disappointed the hopes placed in it; idealism has been seen as deceptive because of its overly optimistic view of the role of knowledge; and historicism has had to admit the ambivalence of the belief in progress (possibly even its destructive consequences). These three universal claims have failed, and with them, every attempt at uniformity has been superseded. Strictly speaking, we must interpret a term like *supersede* in two ways. First, there still are those people who support the wish for uniformity, but Lyotard means that this wish will empirically fail because of the postmodern structure of Western society. Uniformity does not help the development of the West, which is characterized by increasing differentiation. Put into other words, even if one desires uniformity, he cannot achieve or enforce it. Second, Lyotard says that uniformity is also not normatively desirable, i.e. when attempts at uniformity fail, that is a good thing. Let us look at the arguments.

Attempts at unification will fail because social developments are clearly moving in the opposite direction, towards a reversal of unifying tendencies – a process encouraged by new technologies. According to Lyotard, it is a characteristic of new technologies that they first split all information into its smallest components. Second, once split, the components are highly variable, being capable of integration into greatly varied systems. This process, first the splitting, then the possibility of the variable integration of the separate components into different systems, spells the death of all uniform thinking. According to Lyotard, culture mimics industry. Certain rituals and symbols plainly show what this means.

Though Christianity enjoyed a monopoly of certain liturgical elements, symbols, and rituals in Western countries for a long time, and though these had been embedded in a normative super-narrative structure supported by ecclesio-hierarchical authority and the claim to truth formulated by the Christian Church, these same rituals may be found again today not only in esoteric circles but also in advertising, sports, and popular music. As single elements, they are henceforth taken out of their original narratives and function in a new ambience. For Lyotard, this comprehensive process of the collapse of major systems of ideas results in all language games being allowed, all patterns of activity being accorded equal status, and all ways of life and value judgments escaping any test of truth. For these reasons, claims to uniformity would inevitably fail in the face of the postmodern constitution of Western societies.

Moreover, they ought to fail. For Lyotard, the fall of the uniform systems and the advent of pluralism is no negative indicator, but rather it is a development that must be seen as positive. There is no longer uniformity – nor need there be any longing for it any more. It is a plus that nowadays, no pattern of cognition or living can claim precedence over any other. In the end, we should welcome the fact that nowadays, no form of spiritual oppression can be legitimated. Those places in the world where an attempt is nevertheless made to create models of uniformity become embroiled in conflict. We have had to pay a high price for our desire for totality and unity, for the reconciliation of intellectual concepts and sensory perception, for transparent and communicable experience. In the background of our desire for reduced tension and greater stability, we can hear the sound of those who wish to start the terror again by clutching at the phantom theory of suppressing reality. The response to this should be to declare war on totality (cf. Lyotard in Welsch 1994, 272). Lyotard believes that totalitarian systems of left and right are evidence, now as before, for the correctness of his conclusions. Our knowledge and political understanding demand that totalitarianism be eliminated.

Heterogeneity and Consensus

More than almost anyone else, Jürgen Habermas (1981) opposed this position. He shares Lyotard's analysis of the social differentiation of modernity. Like Lyotard, he cannot see a way back to a unitary society or unitary culture. He also shares the view that diversity makes crossing borders and mediation difficult. Against this, Habermas posits the obligation to find agreement. He thinks that socio-cultural differentiation is ambivalent because a series of negative consequences are connected with this development (cf. Welsch 1994, especially 270-275). They go as far as attempts to impose unity by force, for example in fundamental movements of a political and religious character. In this context, Habermas considers the advocacy of total heterogeneity an act of historical, social, and political cynicism. It is a relapse before modernity, a relapse into irrationality. For Habermas, representatives of post-modernity and neoconservatives are therefore birds of a feather (Habermas 1985). Much as Habermas cannot see a way back to unity, he is just as disinclined to leave the issue unresolved. Habermas explains this by reference to the different rationality-types. For him,

- cognitive-instrumental rationality directed towards truth,
- moral-practical rationality directed towards the good, and
- aesthetic-expressionistic rationality directed towards the beautiful

have emerged as differentiated aspects arising from a unitary understanding. Communication is therefore the process of bringing and keeping together these separated aspects. This is to be brought about by feedback between the experts and the everyday practices.

Habermas's aim is not the neutralization of difference but the linking of the experience of difference with attempts to mediate. For him, diversity in modernity is only reasonable if it is communicatively mediated. Mediation is a communicative act whose aim is the comprehension, not the creation, of uniformity. Unlike Lyotard, he believes a meta-language to be practicable if it assimilates the meanings of the differentiated languages so that mediation can really occur.

Welsch reduces the controversy to the following position: "Basically, the dispute raises a single question – beyond multiplicity, do we still envisage a unitary form of types of reason, and, if so, which one? Is there salvation in pure multiplicity, or do the sundry types of reason require a unifying principle or bond to be considered as types of reason at all? How would a type of reason look that did not reintroduce, by the back door, the totalitarianism that one was just congratulating oneself on having got rid of by a decisive transition to pluralism? ... Philosophically speaking, it is clear that the thesis of pure multiplicity is not tenable" (Welsch 1994, 274ff).

Habermas can only speak of agreement when he first stipulates consensus as a fundamental possibility. On the other hand, this consensus cannot be found in a material (i.e. context-based) way but only through a formal value-free process. Its sole value-content is, if one likes, the practical autonomy of the communicatively active. Completely in accordance with Kant, the individual is allowed to develop an idea of the good life autonomously, but the recognition of this idea is meant to be tested not only as a mental process with reference to the ideas of others (as in Kant's categorical imperative) but also through discourse involving all those concerned.

Equality and/or Recognition

Another approach is tried by Charles Taylor (1992). He asks what each of the different positions in a society claims and what they demand of others. His answer is that each of these positions demands recognition by others and, as a rule, no one is satisfied with declarations of respect. The significance of the recognition factor is, for Taylor, bound up with the fact that dialogue is a constituent element of identity. The essential basis of identity is the experience of winning the recognition of others. Identity is particularly vulnerable if this recognition is withheld. Feudal societies were determined by inequality. It was expected that certain stations of life such as the clergy or the aristocracy were to be honored because of their status. In modern Western societies, the principle of equality counts for all human beings. Their identity can no longer be defined in terms of honor due to their status; rather it must be defined in terms of the concept of dignity accorded to all. There must be no first- or second-class citizens. For example, every person is to be equal before the law. The principle of equality is universal. It concentrates on what is equal for all and demands equal respect, ignoring all differences. Thus, it is fundamental to equality that it expresses the principle of liberalism and liberty.

In the discussion of the pluralist, multicultural society, Taylor identifies a second approach that he calls the politics of difference. This states that every human being should be respected because of his unmistakable identity – i.e. because of the particularity that distinguishes him from others. This position requires recognition for what is not universal. The particular is to be recognized and encouraged. Seen in the light of this second position, the first is blind liberalism, which ignores particular identities and forces them into a homogeneous straitjacket. Under the cover of this liberalism, hegemonic cultures would be able to secure their power-base. A further criticism arising from the position of difference is that the equality principle does not guarantee what a culturally "special group" is most fundamentally concerned with – namely, the assurance of its continuance.

For the practical shaping of life in a pluralistic, multicultural society, a material path and a procedural path offer themselves. Representatives of the material direction assume that a certain comprehension of the "good life" exists or can be developed. The idea of the good life functions like a signpost: it shows for what others and we have to strive. Representatives of the procedural direction (like Habermas) emphasize fair and equal dealings amongst people to find balance and establish understanding. There may be an idea of the good life at the end of the procedural way, but it cannot be its normative starting point. It is the respect we owe others that requires caution on the part of the material-normative school.

According to Taylor, the procedural way cannot keep a multi-culturally pluralistic society in existence. Proceduralism may guarantee equality of treatment, but it neglects the significance of the continuance of a culture – more exactly, the central meaning of material concepts of the good life. With regard to balance, he argues that attention to equal treatment must rank alongside attention to the integrity of a culture. He opts for an open approach to both positions. He believes that a society must be allowed to put forward a definition of the good life without condemning those groups that think differently. Nevertheless, it can still be a liberal society that does not violate the principle of equal esteem, provided it develops appropriate principles for dealing with minorities. It must, for instance, respect minorities and grant them basic rights like the right to life, freedom of religion, freedom of speech, etc.

For Taylor, equality of respect and the simultaneous taking into account of particular characteristics are both possible. This does not at the same time mean, however, that these groups enjoy recognition in the sense of having values ascribed to them. In Taylor's view, the question of whether all cultures are of equal value remains open. He sees no sense in demanding such recognition. To see something valuable in other cultures is more likely to be the result of a voyage of exploration involving encounters with other people. For this purpose, he uses the image of the fusion of the outlines of ideas, borrowed from Gadamer. We know that this kind of fusion means that all positions change from their original forms.

Taylor is not an egalitarian. This is why he distinguishes between equality of esteem and recognition. Our modern liberal society requires equality of esteem; recognition may be a possible outcome. Still, he does demand recognition as a suitable attitude for encounters with others. We have to assume that when people have lived for centuries in certain cultures, something significant has emerged and that it deserves respect, but the question of whether and what kind of respect it deserves cannot be decided apodictically. Thus, Taylor sees his concept as a third way between the extremes of a return to ethnocentric attitudes and the appeal to homogenize and make everything equal.

Comparison of the Concepts of Pluralism

Following these considerations, is it possible to decide which of the concepts describes reality appropriately? There is only one answer: all of them and none! First, all of them, as they present an analysis of modern society and use an empirical approach to interpret the facts of a situation; but equally, none, as not one of these concepts reflects only the empirical facts of a situation. With all three authors, descriptive, evaluative, and prescriptive elements overlap. They all try to seize reality and give it meaning. The inter-relatedness of these three elements can be demonstrated by all the theories of pluralism (Schwöbel 1996, 724ff).

- Descriptively, they refer to the multiplicity of powers that are exercised independently of each other in modern societies.

- Evaluatively, the line-up of the separate powers with each other is examined – e.g. the identity of individuals expressing certain opinions is examined.

- Finally, there are prescriptive considerations recommending a particular shape to pluralism in present and future.

Theories of this kind, like every other act of cognition, are to be understood as attempts to construct reality. They are not merely speculative because they seize on reality. They do not reflect reality objectively, but they rather reach out to it from different points of view. In what follows, I will venture to make a comparison of the three concepts and evaluate them with regard to their implications for Religious Education. I will differentiate between the empirical, evaluative, and prescriptive levels and the level of action.

Empirically, the authors quoted have both common features and differences. They describe the societies of Western modernity as heterogeneous. For Lyotard, this heterogeneity is a matter of principle. Habermas's starting point is social differentiation, but in the process of modernity, he detects an understanding that wills a certain civilizing progress (expressed negatively: we do not want another Auschwitz). Taylor, too, is aware of heterogeneity, but interprets it less in the sense of single detached parts than as grown cultures that present a heterogeneous picture in comparison with each other.

In an evaluative sense, the differences are more serious. For Lyotard, there are no bridges linking the heterogeneous positions. Society survives when the different groups demonstrate mutual respect in the face of their otherness. Habermas acknowledges that the individual enjoys greater liberty in the pluralist society. Negatively, he finds that pluralist societies favor fundamentalist and neoliberal attitudes. Fundamentalists entertain totalitarian claims, and neoliberals favor an anything goes arrangement; historically both are, therefore, cynical groups, according to Habermas. Nor does Taylor want to turn plurality back into uniformity; plurality is basically good. He distinguishes, however, between the right of existence of individual cultural traditions and the recognition of their values. If, as Taylor assumes, modern societies were to become more plural and multicultural, the different strands could certainly ask to be respected, as long as they were based on a democratic constitution; as a rule, they could demand equality before the law but not yet equal recognition in the sense of appreciation of their values.

On the prescriptive level, we may interpret Lyotard's position as an appeal to abandon the desire for unity and to guarantee equality in principle, i.e. not to give precedence to a particular group over another. For Habermas, this seems to contain too much neoliberalism. He insists on his project of modernity, which is meant to civilize societies. If one supports this project, then not everything goes. Taylor does not call upon the emotional appeal of modernity, but he would share Habermas's view that the principle of equal value ought to be rejected. This principle may well lay claim to neutrality, but it reveals itself as neoliberal ideology. Taylor's argument does not stem from a consensus-orientated will but from the legitimacy of an *I*-position, which for him is, nevertheless, the position of the majority-culture. This culture is also justified in seeking its own continuance. The aim is legitimate, although relationships with minorities have to be regulated in a humane way.

As for the means of living together in a heterogeneous society, the three concepts make different proposals. Lyotard does not develop a differentiated course of action. He expects that, within a society that is heterogeneous on principle, local areas of agreement restricted as to time and place will emerge. Their permanency will be rather uncertain, and they will be subject to change in terms of composition and aims.

Empirical, Evaluative, Normative, and Modal Aspects of the Theories of Pluralism			
	Lyotard	Habermas	Taylor
Empirical	Heterogeneity in principle	Heterogeneity meta-rationality exists	Heterogeneity existence of grown cultures
Evaluative	good (avoids totalitarianism)	good with reservations (negative: fundamentalism, neoliberalism; positive: growth of freedom)	good with reservations (negative: ideology of equality and duty of recognition of particularities; positive: growth of freedom)
Prescriptive	giving up desire for unity, equality in principle; no rules of precedence	project of modernity – heterogeneity reasonable only through mediation	from an *I*-position respect for other cultures, recognition need to be able to grow
Modal	local agreements	formal procedural discourse	orientation through cultural tradition (material), recognition by way of encounter

Habermas's project of modernity is implicitly bound up with the duty and necessity of consensus-orientated communication. Consensus-orientation ought to precede communication: first, because without the hope that understanding is possible communication is pointless; and second, because consensus is the aim of communication, as people cannot survive in a complex society without unifying activity. The technique of understanding, according to Habermas, consists of change of perspective, i.e. the mutual ability of both sides to reconstruct one another's position and to derive a common position in the general world of life common to both. Here we note a sharp contrast with Lyotard, for whom consensus-orientated attempts at discourse spell the doom of pluralism. Such attempts aim at taking others over and at totalitarianism. What matters for Taylor is to show respect for all cultural movements. For a deep mutual appreciation of values and recognition to be achieved, encounters and familiarization would be necessary. This would possibly lead to a fusion of the outlines of ideas, and all participants could then emerge as changed people. It would not, however, make sense to demand this fusion. As the content is so very important, formal procedural communication is not an adequate means of reaching this objective.

Concepts of Pluralism and Religious Education

The next step I want to take is to evaluate the three concepts and look at their consequences for Religious Education. An evaluation is always based on one's own point of view and is related to a certain context. Reflections in general about Religious Education in multicultural societies do not make much sense in my opinion. On the one hand, decisions about educational questions are, in the last resort, taken in the different countries. On the other, in relation to questions of religious upbringing, the different historical developments, the role of church and state, the existence of religious communities (in terms of numbers and support), etc. are of central significance. The term *multi-religious education*, for example, thus has different connotations in England compared with Austria or Germany, where such backgrounds still function, and the talk of globalization should not blind us to this fact. The road between the non-globalized and the possibly future-globalized world is a long one, and it is not certain that the development will be a linear one in the sense of neutralizing local cultural features and affecting all sectors to the same degree. Processes of differentiation are always accompanied by differentiation-reversal (cf. Helaas 1998). The latter occurs in the many micro-narratives that replace the function of the earlier meta-narratives in local contexts. Now let us ask what criticism we can bring to bear on the above positions.

Equality and Equality of Status

The first thing to be acknowledged positively about Lyotard's concept is that he clearly rejects fundamentalism and the possible consequences of totalitarianism. Leotard wishes to prevent the scenario that Huntington has dramatically depicted as a clash of civilizations (1996). Heterogeneity is a matter of principle, and human beings should not try to claim superiority over others. Every individual and every group should be able to live according to their own value criteria. They ought not to put pressure on others; nor should others put pressure on them. As long as this is so, peace reigns, but we have to admit that the world's religions, including Christianity, have often in the past and present been identified as sources of conflict.

Let us now go beyond Lyotard. We find there is a problem if the concept of equality of status is seen as a pedagogically normative appeal to make only value-free Religious Education possible, when equality of status is interpreted to mean that it is impossible to make judgments about equality of values. The consequence could be that all values and professions of faith might be chosen at will. Now one could go one step further and argue that I or the group to which I belong need not be affected if others represent false values, make religious neuroses acceptable, cultivate an inhumane morality, etc. The principle of heterogeneity is to be accepted as long as one's own circle is not disturbed. It is not an empirical question but an ethical one, whether all ideas are actually equal: more precisely, whether they should all be treated equally. There is something cynical about the question, "why should I worry about loutish behavior next door?" This is pointed out by Habermas, and rightly, in my opinion. What forms should education and upbringing take against this background? To put it more pointedly: ought adolescents to be equipped to have no scruples or simply to shrug them off? Against the background of the modern credo that divergent positions rank equally and that every form of a claim to truth is obsolete, can we draw any other conclusion about the possibility and legitimacy of Religious Education than that Religious Education is impossible because its object, religion, embodies a universal claim to truth? If at all, is it only possible to think of a distanced representation of the various religions that is neutral as to values?

The equal status of all positions poses an ethical as well as a pedagogical problem (cf. Ziebertz 1998a), and it is by no means empirically divided. On the *ethical* plane, it cannot be a matter of indifference how the concepts dignity of man and human rights can be invested with any meaning, what the objections to racism are, whether peace and justice can come about, or how we can achieve harmony with the creation. From a pragmatic point of view, there is a duality about humankind's practices on this planet. In their lives, human beings have to live with each other, but the consequences of their decisions will have to be borne by future generations. On the *theological* plane, Schillebeeckx points out that the religions, in their view of man, humanity, etc. diverge – despite all they have in common, the differences cannot be completely eliminated. As a Christian theologian, one would deny the essential experience of Jesus Christ if, for instance, one shared with certain forms of Eastern thinking the relative passivity of the animal world in the face of injustice, suffering, or the infringement of human rights. If Religious Education is conceived as arising from Christianity, one cannot ignore a Christian theological perspective on heterogeneity. On the *religio-pedagogical* plane, an approach that fudges questions of claims to truth is dubious. Pupils are on a road that develops their view of the world. How else are they to be helped pedagogically if not by a critical examination of the content of worldviews and their claims to truth? It is all a matter of arguing, comparing, and judging values. If a sect that used brainwashing and a religion that prized humans' freedom above all else are compared to each other, the value of both would not first be established through dialogue. There is a prejudice in the form of a conviction that the freedom of the individual is of higher value. The communication in religious lessons already has this motive of content as a normative prerequisite. On the *empirical* plane, the idea of the religions' equal status in no way meets with unanimous agreement. Religious instruction does not disregard the attitude of the students if it does not start from the equal status of religions. Empirical research shows that the students' opinions are rather distributed (cf. Ziebertz 2001/Imagining). A comparison of countries demonstrates that it would be foolish to ignore contextual cultural differences. The principle of the equal status of religions would, at least in western Germany, have to be asserted against a considerable part of the pupils.

Formal-Procedural Approach

What was stated critically by Lyotard seems to correspond positively with Habermas's concept. For the latter, it would after all be a step backwards for civilization if one wished to dispense with the quest for unity. There seems to be an irreconcilable contrast here between Lyotard and Habermas, but because Habermas also makes heterogeneity a basic social condition without wishing to constrain it by a totalitarian idea of unity, only the formal way of procedural communication is left to him. There is no doubt that Habermas's choice of the procedural w ay i s n ot v alue-free. O n t he c ontrary, by f ocusing o n the p rocedural, he wishes to make the subject the center of interest and reveal the basic structure of communication in which freedom can be won and dominance over others avoided. One can, however, criticize the neglect of the material basis, the essential nature of the values themselves. One could put the question to Habermas, to what extent is the consensus-orientated approach viable if it is to be understood as a formal-practical approach that is neutral in context? What is the intrinsic value of the themes that are to be communicated? Here we need to ask, what value in itself does the worldview of a particular religious tradition in the classroom have? Furthermore, is the change of perspectives as a way of finding truth adequate as part of Religious Education? Does this approach perhaps suggest that a kind of unitary religion is possible and that we can move towards it systematically through communication? In view of the way the revealed religions understand themselves, is such thinking at all to the point, i.e. does one do them justice like this? Seen in context, neither today's Christianity, nor today's Judaism, nor today's Islam, despite all the religious differentiation within each, would agree to be pinned down to such an aim.

To favor a discursive-formal procedure as a means of cultural integration on the ethical plane is an advantage as applied to the equality principle; in religio-pedagogic and empirical terms, there is criticism. In ethical terms, the procedural a pproach u ndoubtedly r epresents p rogress b ecause i t d raws a ttention t o the problem of power-hungry human activity. It strips this activity down to the basic structures of communication. In the communicative process, the autonomy of the actors ought to be safeguarded by a commitment to appropriate procedures. Theological criticism is concerned with the void within this approach. As indicated above, the question of how the search for truth ought to be conveyed theologically still remains an open one (cf. Habermas 1997, 98-111). Against the background of Religious Education, we could have a religio-pedagogic problem, given that teachers are asked for their points of view in the classroom. Pupils would not understand their teachers if they refused to say anything about their own points of view in order to be neutral about values. If, in the classroom, we are concerned to discuss the views held of religious sects, then, as a rule, pupils opt very clearly for freedom and against religious indoctrination. They expect that what they are taught will reinforce the arguments to be adduced for religious freedom. A teacher does not indoctrinate if he expresses himself in this spirit because freedom is one of the basic values of modern democratic societies. If a teacher maintained neutrality towards the content of what was taught, pushed on to elucidate a sect's particular way of looking at things, and finally tried to find a third, common perspective, it would be a very dubious educational venture. Teachers as pedagogues are not merely guardians of the rules of changing perspectives. Criticism notwithstanding, there is a weighty and positive reason for the formal principle. In practice, the classroom situation does not produce the clear a lternatives formal and material. B oth act r ather as critical correctives towards each other. If Religious Education wants to make a contribution whose content refers to values, knowledge of the formal perspective can function as an important corrective and allow people to remain aware where the bounds of indoctrinating teaching lie. Teaching apart, what counts for a school as a whole is that it made a fundamental choice of values when it adopted the label Catholic, Protestant, or Christian. Is it to withdraw from this in practice? What reason is there for it not to show its religious affiliation to advantage in the classroom? If parents send their children to these schools because of their affiliation, is this fact not also a call on the parents to strive for running of the schools in the spirit of their affiliation?

Equality and the Process of Recognition

If I now review the theories of pluralism that have been reported on, I do so from a certain point of view. I believe that Taylor's theory gets particularly close to the problems of contemporary cultural upheavals. At any rate, I see many parallels to the cultural situation in the German-speaking countries to which I wish to refer – not because it is exemplary, but because I am familiar with it. In cultural terms, there is no generally shared and accepted view of the equal status of heterogeneous positions. Equally, there is no agreement that social integration could be best assured by formal procedures. The common view is rather that a Christianized culture is still the normal state of affairs. In Bavaria (and not only there), education in the spirit of Christianity has even been declared an educational aim by the state.

In my opinion, Taylor's position is close to reality in Germany because the difference he refers to between equality of esteem and recognition is very clearly demonstrable here. Similarly, we find that recognition follows from familiarization and encounter. This means that time is a factor playing an essential part. The process of time does not neutralize cultural or religious traditions seeking to come closer, but these traditions are rather concerned to raise their profile. Christianity is the dominant religion in Germany (Roman Catholic and Protestant in roughly equal numbers). According to the constitution, Catholic and Protestant religious instruction is an ordinary school-subject – in state schools as well as private religious schools. It must be carried out in accordance with the principles of the two Christian denominations. In view of the special situation in eastern Germany, a number of individual decisions have been made there in favor of multi-religious teaching. The city of Berlin is no less multi-religious but has nevertheless adopted a different course. Here, the Islamic community will in the future be allowed to carry out Islamic religious instruction in the schools just as Christian churches carry out Christian teaching. The Berlin decision is a good example of how the road of respect for other cultural and religious movements can lead to equality of recognition. The Islamic community has now reached a goal it has been aiming at for years. It had to fight for it. The non-Muslims for their part had to give up their old reservations and establish a new relationship with the Islamic religion. This example shows that such situations are always about interests, i.e. about content. Moreover, as interests are of great importance because of the content they represent, it does not make sense to demand "equality" from some distant vantage point; nor is some obligatory formal discourse any more use. If one really wishes to encourage the balancing of interests, settling of conflicts, guiding of desires, making of decisions, etc., a material dialogue must be carried on. The result may also be failure, as is currently shown by the Church of Scientology's lack of any prospect of gaining the same kind of standing as the established churches. In Germany, Scientology continues to be seen as a sect and often even as a cult. Its views of humanity and its practices do not correspond to the cultural values that are generally accepted as shared basic values. The link with and commitment to content is therefore a significant element in the shaping of pluralism.

Against this background, the status of the majority religion does not remain unchallenged. Majority religions can also lose their place. The further secularization in the sense of a flight from the churches proceeds, the more difficult it will be for the Christian churches to maintain their socio-cultural position, e.g. the right to religious instruction in all state schools in accordance with their principles. These rights derive from times when the Christian churches represented the general view of the world. Should the empirical situation change drastically, these rights would be undermined. They would be more open to attack than now. The churches are conscious of this fact. They are taking great pains to maintain their position. They are scarcely interested in an open discussion concerning the equality of religious traditions.

Does Taylor offer a theoretical legitimization for this practice? In a way he does. If I have correctly understood Taylor's interpretation of the pluralist multicultural society, he would not recommend neutrality in terms of a worldview. He is more inclined to take the coexistence and co-operation of cultural (and religious) traditions as his starting point. In this, he does not ignore the actual distribution of power, but he obliges the majority culture to embark on an adequate relationship with the minorities. If we claimed, "as we have a diversity of worldviews, schools should not embark on worldview-based teaching" (independent schools with religious affiliations excepted), then this would not make sense within the framework of Taylor's concept. Anyone arguing like this would add a further worldview – neutralism – to the current ones. Following Taylor's approach and looking at the religious landscape, we could demand that

- religious traditions should be assured that they can develop and can integrate new members,
- the grown cultural "power-relationships" are to be recognized but not established as final,
- dealings with minorities are to be qualitatively regulated,
- religious traditions are to be treated with equal respect, and
- equal recognition, however, only follow from encounter, i.e. fusion of the outlines of ideas (Gadamer).

Challenges

Reflections about Religious Education in a multicultural society cannot ignore the fact that any Western society has historical and cultural roots characterized by great diversity. This is all the more important for questions of Religious

Education because where different religions are to be found, the level of each religious profile varies, the churches do not have the same social role, and the legal requirements governing religious instruction are scarcely comparable. Concepts of Religious Education that take no account of these differences are idealistic. That is why at the end of my reflections, I would like to remain within the context of the German-speaking area, where conditions of Religious Education in schools are to some extent comparable. In this cultural context, Taylor's position seen empirically seems to me to be the most adequate. It best addresses the conditions that arise in Germany in connection with questions of the further development of Religious Education.

We have to proceed on the assumption that the Christian churches in Germany, as the dominant religious tradition, will try to defend denominational teaching for as long as possible. Currently, in cultural terms, there is agreement that Christianity can bring about Christian social integration through religious instruction without this policy being directed against others, but to commit oneself to religious instruction on a Christian basis means much more: it also means giving other religious traditions the right and the possibility of such instruction. We are, therefore, not concerned with exclusivity, but rather, for instance, with granting Islam the right to its own teaching program in regions where there are large Islamic communities. The churches are also open to restricted interdenominational and inter-religious encounters but not yet in the sense of integrating this principle into the curriculum. Where such teaching is proposed, the Catholic Church, for instance, opposes it with its demand for the teaching of ethics or philosophy organized parallel to the religious instruction to serve as a substitute subject for pupils without church affiliation. As far as the Catholic Church is concerned, there is currently no prospect of acceptance for a multi-religious concept based on equality or the equal status of the religions. This is no less true for an inter-religious concept based on the procedural approach.

As it was indicated earlier, these considerations are part of a discursive universe – and the universe is in motion. Consequently, one cannot simply proceed from what was true until yesterday. One must also ask whither tomorrow's road is meant to lead. We must expect the unchallenged dominance of the Christian religion, to which Religious Education owes its place in state schools in Germany, to decline. Change, however, does not happen overnight. How is Religious Education to change in view of future developments? Our current understanding is that it is to enable students to encounter Christianity as it presents itself. A major campaign by the churches will be to keep this aim valid for the future. At the same time, teaching will have to become more open to a dialogue with the other ideological and religious movements present in society. The transformation of today's Catholic or Protestant Religious Education into multi-religious education is not high on any agenda. Religious Education will continue to provide a (primarily cognitive) acquaintance with the Christian religion and, at the same time, make an opening towards other traditions. The opening is most likely to occur in the way Taylor has described, as a process of encounter. Anything else would be a drastic cultural break, a development that I consider unlikely.

Religious Education can prepare for this situation: it ought of its own accord to assume a dialogue form – on principle. I must restrict myself here and wish to point out only three aspects. Religious Education should

- first, adopt new theologies of dialogue much more widely than hitherto and also conceive of the treatment of the Christian tradition as a questioning process;
- second, adopt a position of dialogue towards pupils and, by an appropriate presentation of the subject, ultimately raise its degree of acceptance; and
- third, include a self-relativization in the treatment of the Christian religion.

With regard to the theologies of dialogue, Vatican II has already emphasized the common element of the religions – that they are all concerned to answer the fundamental human question of the unsolved mystery of existence (cf. *Nostra Aetate*, N o.1). Within C hristian theology, t he n umber o f theological c oncepts constituting a suitable basis for a dialogic approach has increased immensely in the last few years. For example, the theology of religions has deduced that an attachment to one's own claim to truth is not identical with an attitude of superiority (Schillebeeckx 1990). Religious Education has to treat this claim as an *open* theme because human beings can name truth always only fragmentarily. This includes openness towards complementing, correcting, or even withdrawal. This does not mean that Christian theology treats God's revelation of himself as relative, but only the interpretation and the historically changing perception of this self-revelation. Formulated truth must necessarily take second place to the whole truth of the self-revelatory God. It is not the Gospel that is a subject of discussion, "but the multiple possibilities of access to its vitally significant meaning, which continues to be linked to the diversity and variety of the relevant socio-cultural conditions" (Drehsen 1994, 262; Ziebertz 1998b). Dialogue-based Religious Education can profit hermeneutically from such theologies.

Second: subject orientation. Religious Education also has to prove its dialogue character by turning productively to the world of the pupils (cf. Schweitzer 1996). Teaching m ust not constrict itself to the subject matter and misunderstand the dialogue as a dialogue which confines itself to the specific topics being discussed. We must also consider how pupils approach the subject. The appropriate didactic theory is offered by constructivism. Constructivist didactics focuses on how pupils, starting from their own world, arrive at religious meaning. It does not propose patterns of information transfer or mediation but patterns such as acquisition. It represents the opposite pole to the much-practiced subject-materialism. To the careful preparation of answers, it opposes the necessity of the hermeneutics of asking. Whereas traditional didactics focused on content and interpreted knowledge as a reflection of the presence of this content in pupils' minds, constructivist didactics attaches particular value to the many lenses through which the content may be viewed. It demands that learners deal with and identify religion. It shows that learning is not merely the other side of the teaching coin (i.e. not only reaction, reception, and processing of information) but is also an independent activity of the pupils. Teachers create conditions for learners' self-organization. Their task is to animate rather than to instruct. Teachers develop methods of interpretation, which they offer to the students. Whether their offers are meaningful depends on their relevance to the pupils' experience of life.

Third, as regards self-relativization, Religious Education in a plural, multicultural society has to take account of a decisive principle, namely the difference between a claim to truth and a claim to validity. This differentiation allows every group within pluralism to adhere to its own claim to truth; however, no group has the right to formulate its claim to truth as a claim to validity for all (cf. Huntington 1996). This distinction is intended to bring about a tolerant discourse, which neither posits heterogeneity absolutely nor seeks to achieve unity at any price. The discourse is tolerant because it assumes that people can live and work together without agreeing about content (Schlüter 1994). Though Religious Education gives pupils some knowledge of the Christian religion, it must not (even at a Christian school) link this with any claim to validity that necessarily produces a reflection of content in the minds and hearts of the pupils. The object of Religious Education is the empowerment to make a personal decision in the course of grappling with denominations and religions, with worldviews and ideologies.

In countries with situations similar to Germany's, we will be heading for a form of Religious Education that will be conceived much more strongly than hitherto on a dialogue basis in its theological, hermeneutic, and didactic orientation. This teaching will not give up the aims of its religious roots, but it will also not put forward such aims as valid for all. More strongly than before, it will enter into honest deliberations with other religious traditions. It will open up to the possibility that humans and religions can change through comparison and deliberation with others. Nevertheless, it will also plead that, analogous to Taylor's culture study, we do not yet have the Archimedean Principle at our disposal that would allow us to see the religions relatively.

Part II

Reflecting on the Goals
of Religious Education

.

3

Religious Didactics as a Reflection of the Process of Religious Learning

Religious didactics, as an academic discipline, concerns itself with the factors that are important to both the theory of religious learning and religious learning itself. This chapter describes some of the aspects of how religious didactics approaches its field and describes what this field is. Special attention is paid to the extensive conceptual premise that religious learning varies in importance at different stages in life. School, therefore, is only present in certain periods of personal development.

Comenius entitled his large textbook from 1657 *Didacta magna*. Didactics was considered as *ars docendi* ("the art of teaching"). The etymological origin stems from the Greek *didaktikè technè*, or respectively, *didaskein* ("learning"). In today's understanding of didactics, the description as "the art of teaching" is no longer satisfactory. Didactics, as it is taught in universities, is a reflective scientific discipline that seeks to explain all factors relevant to the teaching and learning process, including the responsibility of the learning processes. It attempts to understand and explain the dynamics of instruction and learning as the purpose of theory formation, ultimately to achieve the competence to plan and execute specific goals of person, thing, and situation in teaching and learning. The following is a set of aspects assembling a preliminary map of the field.

Religion and Didactics

It is first necessary to clarify the connected term *Religious Didactics*. The focus here is obviously on didactics, but concentration is placed within the determined context of religion.

Religion in Religious Learning Process

The central meaning of religion in the context of Christian education is based on Christian tradition as it is represented by the churches and reflected by theology. The overall meaning of religion is not, however, therein exhausted (see chapter 4). If one looks at the phenomenon of religion, one immediately notices the many non-Christian religions. Apart from the large religions (world religions),

Christianity is itself plural in structure. Variety is easily detected within the Christian tradition, and even within a specific Christian denomination. One must also consider the many independent religions, which are some more, some less like the standard traditional forms.

Religious Education in schools does not concern itself with the diversified forms of religion. Children who undergo religious instruction are, as others, citizens of the same society. Therefore, the functions of Religious Education must include making pupils aware of religious plurality and giving them the ability to communicate in such a system. This does not occur in a tradition-free and context-free space (Ziebertz 2001e). The focal point of the teaching is determined by the religion or denomination in which it takes place. This, however, should not prevent exposure to the plurality of religion. As citizens in a civil society, students must be taught of the important roles that church and religion play in economic, political, cultural, and social life. Thus, religious didactics, under the present conditions of Religious Education, has the function of making future teachers competent in dealing with the complex appearance of religion. This goes beyond providing religious information and includes the anthropological meaning and dialog surrounding religion. This goes beyond general and requires the full description of religion, which has developed historically and has been shaped socio-culturally. Just as Christian religious instruction will stress the importance of Christian tradition, teachings, and life, so will Islamic religious instruction stress the importance of the Koran and Islamic tradition. Nonetheless, regardless of where religious instruction takes place, the political and cultural expectation is that the location will not cause ignorance of other religions, but rather that instruction will take an ecumenical, inter-religious approach. The goal must be to reach a neighborly relationship of religions, between which many differences exist and will continue to exist in the future. Within this community, the differing religions can continue to grow individually, and they can help create a hospitable international community and positive future for humanity.

Religious instruction is not unaffected by the many conflict areas present between religion and the churches or between the churches and society, such as that between children, youth, and the churches. In view of the conflict, neither the Christian churches nor Christianity in general can sufficiently define what religion is. Religion is always more and also something else. The conflict between church and society is apparent, among other things, in the fact that society as a whole and, more exactly, certain subgroups of society no longer accept Christianity as the naturally determining religion (at least not consciously) from which values and norms are derived. The conflict between youth and the churches becomes most significant when the concerns and authority of the Christian churches and the ways of life that the churches endorse are no longer freely accepted. These examples show that today's religious instruction must, at the core, focus on dialog. It is no longer enough to use religious didactics simply as a means of passing on the content of a particular religion.

Didactics of the Religious Learning Process

The subject of the field of religious didactics is not sufficiently covered by the term *religion*. The compilation of the words *religious didactics* refers to the fact that religious didactics goes beyond the contents of religion to a special allowance. This special allowance can be defined as the following:

> *Religious Didactics is the scientifically grounded reflection of religious learning and the reflection of the teaching of religious learning.*

Religious didactics, therefore, considers how religion can be taught and learned. This definition should not be simplistically understood. Learning processes are complex procedures, i.e. reflection must consider all aspects involved in learning and teaching. Included in this are

- the reflection of conditions and contexts of learning (anthropological and socio-cultural suppositions),
- the reflection of the possibilities and boundaries of religious learning in school (science orientation vs. spirituality and the introduction of faith),
- the reflection of rationale and responsibility of the religious learning process (normativity),
- the reflection of the interaction between teachers and students (as well as among themselves), and
- the reflection of the methods and media.

This list is by no means exhaustive of the many aspects involved. With respect to school learning, these are some potential aspects with which the discipline of religious didactics is concerned. It is not however necessary or possible to take all aspects equally into consideration.

Furthermore, the definition suggests that the reflection of religious learning processes should be scientifically founded. What is meant by this statement is that today, teachers can no longer simply determine how their occupation can and should be practiced. Individual reality undoubtedly remains an important personal feature, one that lends a special note to Religious Education. On the other hand, it cannot replace the planning, execution, and evaluation of the religious learning p rocesses, w hich a re b ased o n s ystematic e xperience a s t hey a re r eflected in theory.

As a scientific discipline, religious didactics first has the responsibilities of increasing knowledge in the topic area and deepening insight. This occurs with the help of fundamental and applied research. It has, however, a further function relating to practice. Religious learning occurs in many different places: family, kindergarten, community, school, colleges, adult education institutions, etc. Religious didactics includes these institutions in its subject area, as long as learning takes place there. Each practice has specific conditions that must be considered on a didactic basis. Due to the established academic atmosphere at universities, the position of learning has an emphasized significance at these institutions. This justifies the concentration of this group on school learning. Students of religious didactics participate in the scientific discourse that was just referred to. With the help of theories and concepts, they gain a reflexive knowledge that helps them become familiar with the multiform aspects of learning processes and helps them gain insight into the complexity of learning processes. In the view of its formation, the following definition concretely describes the field:

> *Religious didactics helps to create a scientifically responsible reflexive authority for the planning, execution, and evaluation of religious learning processes, as well as its educational responsibility.*

The concept *reflexive authority* contains two aspects. First: the abilities to oversee the teaching and learning processes and to analyze their components. This authority is an important characteristic of the teacher's professionalism because it is only on this basis that intentional interventions are possible. A second component of this reflexive authority is self-reflection. The teacher is thus capable of keeping a critical eye on his/her own behavior. Professionals must be able to reconstruct and evaluate their acts because it is this objective distance with self reflection that allows the space required for changes to come into view.

Theory and Practice

Religious didactics, like other practical disciplines, experiences stress and conflict between theory and practice. Teaching and learning occur in specific practice; however, the practice concept is unclear and uncertain, and, therefore, requires some clarification – but it does still fit within the theory concept and is clear in the connection between theory and practice.

University Practice and Instruction Practice

The reflection of religious didactics on instruction and learning pursues two related goals. The first deals with theory formation and the other with practice relevance.

- Theory formation is necessary in order to achieve generally accepted precedents of connections, which are important in the practice of teaching and learning (the theory of practice). Not every generation of teachers must invent new methods and means, but can rather refer to existing systematically won knowledge and "abstract experience."

- Practice relevance is inevitable because didactics is closely connected to the reality of learning, which seeks to shape and help improve it. It operates not exclusively for "science and the sake of science," but is rather in the service of the practice of teaching and learning.

The demand for practice relevance is rarely understood as though the work of religious didactics on universities had a direct effect on how a lecture is prepared for, but it can, to a limited extent, anticipate how a lecture will run. This desire is not only rarely fulfilled – but it would even be a disappointment. University practice and practice at schools are far too different. One could say that in fact, religious didactics does not represent a practice of religious instruction and learning, but rather reflects an appropriate practice (perhaps for religious instruction). The practice of the university is a practice theory and experience guided reflection, but the university does not simulate instruction. Nevertheless, religious instruction and learning do occur at the university, i.e., there is a practice, into which lecturers and students are merged, but this practice is different from the practice of instruction, for which purpose university instruction occurs. The university is its own practice site, where instruction and learning take place, and where, through university-typical means, practice reflection is achieved. On the one hand, this practice serves a valuable purpose in that it contributes to the universal formation of education. There is a direct goal; yet on the other hand, the reflexive activity is indicated by a unique vocational field reference with which the university practice furthers itself. The indirect target is the transformation of religious learning in the school. Indirect means that this transformation of instruction at the university is not tackled directly; rather, the university will allow future teachers to build the necessary foundation.

Education students acquire a reflexive competence that will help them (later on) to accomplish an effective practice. The pretence with which university religious didactics operates hopes to achieve, through the reflection and abstraction that occur in everyday school life, theoretical answers for influencing control with the goal of making change possible. Students should acquire the competence to learn how to reflect on the practice of instruction scientifically. Work experience during the period of study is not equivalent to the everyday occupational experience, but is rather a reflection of the vocational field. In this first (primarily) theoretical phase of formation, religious didactics makes its specific contribution in the reflection of the factors that are crucial for successful teaching and learning.

The Difference between Theory and Practice

The question remains of how the relation between theory and practice can be better understood. There are three different positions.

The first position assumes that the theory of practice precedes the practice, and that practice is simply the use of theory. This conception is deductively conceived. It assumes that theoretical concepts are more or less able to be directly transferred into practice. The theory defines how the practice is to be. The critics of this model become inflamed first by the suggestion that practice has no value on its own and is only an application field of theory. So one can rightly ask, is it possible or meaningful to develop universal theoretical solutions to individual problems? The focus of religious teachings in a large city may not necessarily apply to instruction in rural communities, just as that which applies in a characteristically confessional region may not apply in a diverse region, etc. The second criticism focuses on the appreciation of those concerned. Are the teachers simply users and recipients of an assumed theory? What about their own insights and subjective theories? It is clear that professionals do not adequately characterize practice. Third, the assumed identity of theory and practice is rejected. Instead, it is asserted that there is a fundamental division between the two. Therefore, (theoretical) reflection of practice is based on a practice reference, and practical concerns always imply a theoretical reflection – however, the two remain separate. Only under the premise of the difference can one positively speak about the practice-correcting function of theory. If both are identical, this possibility cannot exist.

The second position reverses the thinking of the first model and explains practice as paramount. Theory should inductively take up the rules and convictions that train those who are acting. For example, in liberal theology practice is with critical-emancipated intention allocated a critical function opposite theory. Daily religious practice, its values, its norms, and its convictions are to lead to theory (theology) instead of controlling it from above. In educational circles, the appreciation of practice is not uncommon. Educational concerns attach much importance to practice within different areas. It is common that the learning process should be set to the actual status of the student. The proven practice has, in this perspective, an unusual value. The question is, however, whether theory should and can develop directly from practice. Some critical questions are, is each practice equally good? How do we determine bad practice? Does theory not also have the function of critically challenging practice?

The third position proceeds from a basic separation of theory and practice and, and it places both in dialectical relation. Practice is not dominated by theory, and theory is not dominated by practice. Both function on their own respective rules, and each leads an independent existence. The placement exists only dialectically. New developments occur when theory and practice are mutually and critically referred to one another, without one absorbing the other. In this presentation, teachers are practical people who first base their practice on their subjective theoretical reflections, plans, and designs, who second, as professionals, are likewise able to read research results and participate in theoretical discourse, and who third, in the context of their practical experience, can independently produce applicable theoretical insights and concepts. Teachers are not, as practical people, active only practically. In fact, it is often emphasized that practice accompanies theory. In the opinion of scientists, they are theoretically active as theorists, and open to outside influences. Even the formulation as "vocational field-referred theory" makes clear that the driving force behind theory is practice.

In light of the third position, the following can be said about the scientific practice o f r eligious d idactics: r eligious d idactics s tudies t he p ractice o f r eligious instruction and learning from a theoretical view, i.e., it observes the practice, tries to understand it, and sketches active models and scenarios. Religious didactics breaks practice open in order to be able to write new and better theories of practice. Students thus acquire a cognitive map with which they can survey the domain of school and Religious Education. This map helps to clarify the field, highlights the conditions and consequences of particular actions, and allows for critical observation of routine and habit. This reflexive power is a prerequisite for the future occupation, but is itself not identical to the future practice of teaching at school.

Religious Learning Processes: Reflections, Plans, and Answers

Religious learning processes, in the context of the planning of schools, are no longer concerned with the institution but rather the profession. The ability to reflect and the competence to plan, as well as the development of principles for the educational and theological responsibility of teaching and learning, rank among the natural building blocks that religious didactics is concerned with.

Teaching and Learning

Teaching and learning are related to each other. With teaching, the concern is with all of the factors of a teacher or group of teachers from whom students are to learn, i.e. didactics concerns itself with the way teachers plan instruction, perform it, and evaluate it. Learning, however, defines the modifications in the area of the knowledge, insight, abilities, talents, and attitudes on the part of the students. Learning processes are characterized by the fact that they cannot be attributed solely to maturing processes or natural development, but rather are the result of an interaction with extraneous causes (e.g. on the part of the teacher) and active world adoption (on the part of the learner). Learning is not to be understood as identical to models of conditioning (Pavlov) or operational learning (Skinner), but belongs within a more educational-theoretical context. Thus, learning was for a long time understood, for example, in the sense of a funnel model. With this picture, the aspect of placement comes above all into view. Today, didactics is interested just as intensely in the aspect of appropriation. This designates certain specific processes, such as how the child accepts information, processes the information, and adopts the information as his/her own. Today, we know that life orientations and conceptions of the world cannot be sufficiently explained by transfer processes but that they result substantially from the co-operation of students. One should not forget that teachers can also learn from the students. The manner in which students give acknowledgements to the teacher and the contents contained therein should be used as feedback for clarifying the teacher's own role.

Reflection of Intentional Learning Process

Religious didactics concerns itself with a special form of learning. One differentiates between incidental (coincidental, unplanned) and intentional (consciously planned) learning. Incidental learning constantly occurs throughout one's life, from birth to old age. Presumably, the largest proportion of familial learning is a result of incidental learning processes. Intentional learning is aimed for, planned, and foreseen. In curricula and teaching materials for school, intentional learning is brought up in discussion. Teachers are expected to give attention to this form of learning. Intentional learning must become familiar, as it is the subject of exams. Nevertheless, both forms of learning take place in school. Religious didactics reflects primarily on intentional learning, the learning that is pursued and planned for consciously and directly, but remains conscious of the fact that incidental learning does take place and can thwart and/or support teaching goals. If, for example, during a period when ecclesiastical issues are being discussed, the church, because of a scandal, appears frequently in the media, questions about the tension between sanctity and sinfulness will have to be addressed. In this case, instruction does not address the effects of incidental learning. If what is incidentally learned is not visible, it cannot be included.

Conceiving and Accounting for Learning Processes

Religious didactics reflects on the questions of how religious learning *can* and *should* be conceived using scientific accounts. It concerns itself with the *can* by, for instance, sketching theoretical and practical learning models and reviewing empirical effects by which they can take account of suppositions of age and development of the students and by which the institutional and social context can be included, as well as learning and teaching materials that are consciously selected, etc. Yet it also concerns itself with the *should* – the responsibility of the
60

educational-didactical influence. It must itself explicitly deal with the *should* because each educational effect intended for the students is an external influencing force whose normative core requires this special attention. Indoctrination is forbidden in schools – and should not be used as a resource in educational work elsewhere. Therefore, the questions of what, when, and why teaching and learning are taking place are particularly important to justify. Religious didactics must deal with these normative questions.

A Record of Religious Learning

Religious learning is lifelong learning. As humans spend only a select period of life in school, the formation of a Christian-religious worldview is not solely dependent on the school. On the other hand, children and young people are particularly adaptive and disposed to learning. Therefore, the chances of the school's ability to lay a strong foundation for a religious attitude can be estimated as being quite high.

Who Writes the History of Life?

Not very far back in history, learning was considered a function reserved for children and youth. A well-known German proverb says, *"Die Schule bildet für das Leben"* ("school prepares one for life"). Thus, the corresponding view arose that children enter the first class as a blank page and leave filled out. In school, they should receive everything they need to lead a successful life. Since then, the sentiment has developed, especially from the religious point of view, that upon entering their first class, children are by no means a "blank page," even though they know very little about church-represented Christianity. It is likewise evident that upon leaving school, the "page" is not completely filled out. The page is in a continuous process of being filled out, as learning is a lifelong process. A further detail reveals a problem with the view of our learning as a page that is written on. This picture arouses the impression that the writing comes from a third person and one is simply a passive participant in the learning process or that someone outside dictates what is learned. We know today that this simply is not true. Ultimately, each individual is the author of his/her life story. Each individual will write in the book of his/her life who and what he/she is – and what he/she has and has not learned. The integration of life experiences in a way that one can say "I" can be motivated and accompanied by learning processes, but not manufactured.

Religious learning, thus the acquisition of the competence to reflect and interpret life in the dimension of final questions, particularly of a specific faith, does not come to an end (Schweitzer 1987). In the process of life, experiences and contexts change, and these changes result in new reflections and interpretations.

61

Adjustments to earlier conceptions have been necessary throughout the history of learning. This is true for all aspects of life – the religious dimension of reality is not excluded. For example, starting from a certain point in time, the conception of a magical God lost relevance and plausibility. It is new interaction models that ask, should the relationship with God not be put principally in doubt? New models, however, are not naturally innate, but are, in the best scenario, learned. This is why students need incentives that not only affirm but also challenge. They must learn that when God does not intervene in the world on behalf of a prayer, a victim, or a promise as was requested, one should not place the existence of God into question altogether, but that perhaps the problem is the individual picture of God.

If one concedes to young people that ultimately they themselves make the entries into their life book, the question arises over appropriate company. Three relevant aspects will be briefly indicated in the following: Offers of Religious Education should be explicitly checked for their contextual conformity, their appreciation of age, and their developmental orientation.

Contextual Conformity

First to the contextual conformity. We limit the religious-didactical attention in this section to the area of the school. As it concerns religious learning, Religious Education is the focal point. This is particularly due to necessity in the context of teacher training (religious instruction as a proper discipline), and so it is understandable that the actual learning place has special value for religious didactics. In school, we encounter specific institutional requirements that make their intensive work necessary. As with other subjects, religious instruction is structured on a curriculum. The curriculum is designed to foster consistent learning throughout the school period. There is comprehensive theme distribution, giving each topic its place amongst the others. Aside from form and contents, religious study is like any other school subject. It is based on certain standards, which shape today's everyday life in schools. Teachers in this discipline usually teach other subjects as well, in order to better integrate religious studies into the collective curriculum. Naturally, in-school learning has boundaries. Religious studies, as other subjects, must be arranged to operate in the allotted time slot (usually a period between 45 and 90 minutes) and to fit within the primarily cognitively oriented learning processes, and it must more frequently consider the very different conceptual makeup of its students. Next to instruction models that focus their attention on knowledge transfer, considerable emphasis is placed on learning through experience (that is, learning with head, heart, and hand), which integrates cognition, emotion, and pragmatics. Despite the dominance of knowledge orientation in school practice, this new approach offers many possibilities. With a realistic view on the institutional requirements, it attempts to offer new possibilities for the school and additionally recognizes many of the boundaries that are inevitably connected to the institution. The achievements of Religious Education are clearly connected to extracurricular spheres of learning, particularly the family, the community, and other institutions such as the comprehensive community youth-work programs (such as those in church-supported youth federations).

Age-specific Orientation

The concentration on the teaching and learning in schools is accompanied by an age-specific containment on learning processes with children, youth, and, to some extent, young adults, meaning a span of ages ranging from approximately 6 to 20 years. Questions of familial and pre-school religious learning, community, work, and later schooling, which normally are included in the realm of Religious Education and didactics, are factored out in this section. The age spectrum of 6-20 years covers several stages: the phase of childhood, the transition through adolescence, and finally the ascent to young adulthood.

- In the first four to six school years, we are dealing with children. Even if children conceptualize the world as rich in meaning and prefer to view it as a playful place, the rational responsibility and motivation of religious learning will not allow itself to be played away. As early as primary school, children discuss the question of whether or not there is a God. One cannot answer these and similar questions with relation-type games. A good integration of differing inlets is important at this stage of schooling.

- In the next phase, the process of adolescence has special meaning. Adolescents experience particular problems with respect to their surrounding environment (family and school). Old securities break away and new ones are only formed through long and sometimes painful processes. Religious development during this period is extremely fragile: conventional truths are challenged, and "nothing seems to make sense"; refering to the authority of tradition has no effect. Sometimes the deconstruction of religious convictions can reach, in the eyes of teachers, "brutal" extents. During this time, there are also radical inquiry and denial as challenges to instruction, which attempts to offer satisfactory models for further discussion and experience.

- In the end, during the last phase, the concern is trying to help future-oriented young people develop a religious dimension of reality in a way that keeps pace with the experience of individual possibilities. Perhaps the religious-didactical challenge is, above all, focused on showing the possibility of achieving all one's desires in a modern world while at the same time being Christian.

This integration can have a paradigmatic character for the coming adulthood.

In all phases, religious-educational and religious-didactical perspectives should not be deficient, overly simplistic, or condescending. Children and youth are not simply premature incomplete adults. Each age group has its own questions and challenges that carry equal importance if viewed from the perspective of a child or a sophisticated adult.

Developmental Orientation

Religious learning, while considering the school period, must also consider the reflections of developmental characteristics. Age and development correlate with each other, but they are not identical. The concept of *development* refers to a r ange o f a spects, e .g. c ognitive o perations (Piaget), m oral j udgment (Kohlberg, Gilligan), levels of identity (Erikson, Marcia, Mead, Ricoeur), the self (Kegan), r eligious judgment (Oser), a nd r eligiousness/faith (Fowler). E ach o f these theories recognizes tendencies of development. They describe development processes t hat extend from relatively simple to rather complex insights and thinking operations. Empirically, some questions remain open, but its heuristic value is undisputed. Development and age are connected inasmuch as certain development stages take place in specific age groups. There is, however, some dispersion, which can span over several years. The age category of "10 years" does not thus directly indicate a universal level of development for fourth grade students. For example, it is a well-known fact that girls reach puberty before boys. This psychobiological difference has much more to do with sex than age. On an individual student basis, it is also important to note that not all students develop equally along the same timeline. Piaget called this unequal pace of development *decalage*. Examples are the child, a young human who is capable of formal operational thinking but believes in a magical relationship with God (*Do ut des*); and the adult, an older human who holds a sophisticated occupation but retains his/her childhood religious beliefs. This shows the importance of paying attention to the effect of both age and development in religious learning. The perspective of development allows for an adequate diagnostic estimate of the starting point, the direction, and the pace of advancement.

Learning for Life

The explanation of the subject of religious didactics is first related to the term *religion*. On the one hand, the phenomenon of the multiple forms of religion comes into view, and on the other, the plurality of the Christian perspective is brought up in discussion. The subject of religious didactics includes the "notion" of didactics. Whether one defines didactic broadly as the school of all forms and levels of teaching and learning or narrowly as the school of instruction, the focus in both cases is on always teaching and leaning – this book focuses on the schools. Religion does not come up exclusively as an historical, biblical, or systematic interest, but rather in the perspective of teaching and learning. Religious didactics does not provide a final authority on instruction, but rather provides a scientifically justified means by which one can reflect upon practice on a descriptive-analytical basis and develop starting points for direct intervention. The difference between theory and practice is firmly established. It is the indeterminate influence of theory on practice, and vice versa, that opens the possibility for criticism and innovation. The direct goal of university religious didactics in Religious Education is to achieve a reflective authority on students. The indirect goal is the improvement of the practice of religious learning. The goal of religious learning in schools is the development of an attitude within the students that encourages them to learn to see the world in light of religious traditions and to explore the possibility of trusting faith in God. The dispute over religion, and more specifically over the question of God, is not limited to school time. The school is relieved of this duty – it is not solely responsible for how people deal with religious questions. Instead, the school welcomes young people who have incredible potential for learning. This potential offers many possibilities for religious learning in school. It should also be noted here that religious learning takes place not for the school, but for personal life. Therefore, the students, as authors of their religious biographies, are rightfully the focus of religious-didactical attention.

4

Religious Education as an Opening of the Religious Dimension of Reality

Our experiences at school are open to two interpretations. On the one hand, there is still a need on the part of the students to discuss life's deeper questions, such as faith, hope, and meaning. On the other hand, we cannot ignore the gap between the students and traditional religious institutions. The classical criticism of religion that dismissed religion as merely an illusion has gone away. Religion is still very much present in modern society. Religion is a dimension of modern reality and an important part of many modern people's lives. Nonetheless, let there be no mistake – religion cannot simply be interpreted as the Christianity represented by the churches. The following analysis shows that Religious Education in the postmodern context has to work with a very broad understanding of the concept of religion. This means acquiring a sophisticated understanding of the religious dimensions of reality. Christian Religious Education integrates real and present religious dimensions with the Christian faith.

The Religious Dimension in the Modern Context

Religious Education in schools takes place within a social and cultural reality. Questions dealing with Religious Education can no longer be answered within an internalized theological field. Religious Education is carried out in a social setting where the plausibility of the religion as a whole is up for discussion. The Christian churches of northwestern Europe are experiencing profound changes. Up until a few decades ago, it was possible to interpret these changes as a process of secularization (cf. Berger 1999; Swatos/Olson 2000; Woodhead/Helaas 2000). The presumption was that increasing modernization would inevitably lead to a loss of importance, maybe even to the end, of religion. More recently, there has been more and more doubt associated with this version of the secularization theory; there are still many instances when it does not do justice to the complex, multilayered nature of the actual process. It is only today that we can really tie religion to concepts like plural and religiousness. Religion in the Western world is still often, but not always, identified as Christianity. Christian religion is, itself, no longer limited to the traditional Christian churches. There are individual religious styles that may or may not associate themselves with traditional Christian systems of faith. For this reason, the secularization theory is increasingly criticized for being a linear theory of decay. The criticism here does *not* say that there never was a process of secularization or that there is not one in progress now. The process of de-churching is, however, only *one* facet of a highly differentiated religious field. There are plenty of reasons for Christian theology in general, and religious educators in particular, not to get hung up on the decreasing affiliation with the churches, but to concentrate on the religious field as a whole. Modern people do not live in two worlds, one religious and churchly, and the other profane. They live in *one* world, where worldliness and religion has to be integrated. From a theological and religious educational point of view, the most productive question to ask is, what is the relationship between religion and faith as transmitted by the Christian churches, and how can we use educational processes to optimize the benefits and conditions created by this relationship (cf. Ziebertz 1999; 2001)?

We can safely assume that no person can have a spiritual life without also carrying an interpretation of his or her world around, no matter how primitive or unimaginative that person is. In those instances where the person does not use a religion to interpret the world, he or she makes use of other visions that fill the same function. Concepts of Religious Education, therefore, always have to relate everyday life and anthropological insights to understandings of faith as passed on by the Christian churches. Religious Education should assume a very dynamic interaction between culture and religion, in which not just differences but also common factors are recognized. There are many areas where Religious Education can tie into religious presence in our society and modern people's personal involvement with religion. Both serve to legitimize Religious Education; i.e. religion as a recognizable dimension of reality deserves to be brought up, reflected on, and taught in a school context. In this way, a class in religion will balance a general interest in religion with religion as passed on and experienced in traditional Christianity. In other words, young people's search for a footing, a meaning, and a hope is always focused on an issue or aspect that is also important to the Christian faith. Religious Education can demonstrate this connection to its students. It can show that and how the message of Christian faith deals with every one of those questions that are anthropologically defined as mysteries of our existence. In this model, a broad understanding of religion on the one hand and the concretizing of Christian tradition on the other would work as two focuses of one ellipse. The religious instruction, then, would help to initiate an orientation within the religious dimension of reality and would open a platform for a personal choice of faith.

What is Religion?

The importance of a broad understanding of Religious Education becomes much clearer when one analyses the very concept of religion. We are used to speaking of *religion* – the concept is a familiar one. In the nomenclature, it is a natural part of the concepts of religion teacher, religion class, and didactics of religion. If Religious Education wants to open up the religious dimension of reality, then we have to be clear about what reality we are referring to.

Etymologically and Cultural-historically

Etymologically, *religion* has three roots: first, the use of *religio* by Cicero (106-43 B.C.), who derived it from *relegere* ("constantly check" or "conscientiously regard"); second, the term *religari* ("tying oneself back...to God") used by Caelius Firmanius Lactantius (ca. 250-325); and third, the use of *reeligere* ("re-choose" or "reelect") by St. Thomas Aquinas (1225-1274). All three meanings refer to humankind specifically turning to something very special. This etymological history is, however, not enough for an understanding of *religion* because even though we know that the word has roots that go back two millennia, the term as such was not commonly used until the 16th century.

To discover the meaning of the term *religion*, we must also fall back on cultural-historical research. The latter demonstrates a close connection between the concept of religion and European history of civilization. The term *religio* did not denote a category for the old Greeks; it simply expressed the respect felt for the gods. It became a categorical word during the later Roman Empire, when Christians used it to describe *their* religion as the *religio vera*. Yet in the context of the Catholic Church, the word *faith* dominated up until the Reformation. On the cultural-historical level, the term mirrored the way people dealt with the breakup of the previously singular Christian faith.

Hohmann (1994) describes three phases within the cultural-historical development of the concept of religion:

- First, the concept of religion served the *purification* or "the keeping clean" of religion: During the Reformation, the Christian system of religion was replaced by magic, astrology, superstition, etc. From a certain point of view, its sense of *religio vera* returns.

- Second, the concept of religion served the *universalization* of religion: during the 16th century, Latin America was being conquered, and the Europeans searched for colonies all over the world. The question arose of how to describe the Christian religion and the religious conceptions found among native people within a universal construct. In order to reconcile the various myths and cults with the well-known content and form of the Christian faith, the concept of religion served to universalize the two. It allowed the definition of various dimensions of religion that could be used all over the world.

- A third aspect is the *differentiation*: the concept of religion, the way that the Enlightenment and later philosophies and religious sciences used it, allows for a distinction between Christian faith of revelation and deism. It also allows for the appreciation of various wordplays within religious critique and the comparison of various streams, such as pietism, French Jansenism, English Methodism, etc., with one's own beliefs.

The general meaning among all the distinctions is the transcendental aspect, i.e. the connection and orientation of people or groups of people to one last, super-worldly reality. This could be the numinous force of final values, an ultimatum, final meaning, gods, demons, etc. (cf. Kehrer 1998 as well as the definitions below).

Concepts of Religion

Emilé Durkheim: Religion is a solidary system of perceptions of faith and attitudes, tied to sacral things. These perceptions and actions unite all those who adhere to them in a moral society called "church."

Rudolf Otto: Religion is the meeting between Man and Holiness.

Gustav Mensching: Religion is the experienced meeting with Holiness and the responsive action of Man chosen by Holiness.

Max Weber: Religion is the collected meaning of the world.

Paul Tillich: Religion is the emotion of that which absolutely concerns Man.

Niklas Luhmann: Religion is the social ciphering of crises and the undefined.

Bronislaw Malinowski: Religion is a modus of compensation for the fear of death and experienced injustice.

Peter L.Berger/Thomas Luckmann: Anthropologically and socially, religion is a process of individualization.

Arnold Toynbee: Religion is the overcoming of egocentrism through the unity with the spiritual reality behind the universe, with which we harmonize our desires.

J. Milton Yinger: Religion is a system of convictions and actions through which people wrestle with the final problems of their existence. Religion expresses the refusal to give in to death. The quality of religious existence is not only the belief that evil, pain, confusion, and injustice are fundamental facts of life, but also the belief that through a system of practice and religious conviction, Man can be freed from these facts of life.

Wilhelm Gräb: Religion is the culture of symbolizing the last horizons of meaning in the everyday orientation of life.

The following study of the various scientific disciplines dealing with religion will add a whole series of specifications to these general definitions.

Sociology of Religion

Religious sociology focuses its study of religion on the *function* that religion fills in society and for the individual. For Emilé Durkheim (1858-1917), a classic author within this discipline, religion serves an integrative role in society. Religion is the concrete holding society together; it embodies values and norms used to integrate the individual into the community as a whole. Religion is the collective consciousness in a society that stands apart from the individual, yet of which he or she is also a member. For Durkheim, the collective consciousness has a sacral character (1995).

As a sociologist, Durkheim is not interested in a theological understanding of religion (as a message of revelation, for instance); he instead asks how religion *works*. For Durkheim, religion is first cult and second obligation. The term *religion* as "cult" means symbolically compressing the binding cult norms. In this way, the cult integrates society in a more stable and lasting way than purely contractual agreements ever could. The question being asked now is whether Durkheim's concept of religion is still topically relevant. Critical voices point to the absence, at least in northwestern Europe, of such an integrative religion. Others still see Christianity as being active in the form of memory, which touches the individual and social lives in a variety of ways (Davie 2000; Hervieu-Léger 2000; Rémond 1999). Durkheim's theory, however, goes beyond religion as a concrete religious community.

Durkheim's view of communal symbols and convictions comes very close to that which we today call civil religion. This means convictions and patterns of values that have a lasting effect on people's thoughts, feelings, and judgments, such as the belief in a higher power, moral benchmarks, the family, the nation, etc. In our case, a Christian cultural pattern is a fact in Europe that cannot be denied. It is pervasive in everything from models of life and morality to the justice system and architecture. We speak of a civil religion when these patterns have gained a life of their own and exist without reference to the Christian religion. Opening up the religious dimension of reality is, then, a cultural-historical task. Students are familiarized with the roots of Western culture, which was essentially shaped by Christianity.

May Weber (1864-1920), another must-read within religious sociology, sees the main function of religion as bringing meaning to social action. Social action and decision-making cannot find their meanings within themselves. Using Western history as an example, which Weber describes as a process of rationalization, he shows how the Protestant Ethic has served to legitimate entrepreneurial action and decision-making. On the other hand, Weber also believes that religion's function as a source of meaning is slowly wearing out. The higher a society evolves, the more the economy and industry will be able to justify itself. Economic principles of rationality rather than a Holy Cosmos will hold society together. In case of a conflict, the former will take precedence over the Christian religion. What follows is the demystification of the world, i.e. the process of secularization outlined before. Nevertheless, a society ever more often guided by principles of rationality will still not be able to ignore its irrational experiences. The contingent experiences will remain, i.e. the experiences of the finite; the fact that everything could be different; the fact that there are alternatives to every decision, but a decision still has to be made, etc. Weber arrives at the conclusion that the ever more rational society will eliminate religion on a certain level, but will always need an other-worldly binding in order to master these situations. Religion, then, becomes a sector-specific event. It is pushed back into the private realm and loses its function as a social means of integration and control.

Christian theology can follow this functional description up to a certain point. Christian religion wants to provide meaning and help people get a grip on their lives. In those instances, however, when society functionalizes religion in order to get a grip on the remaining irrationality that society cannot master itself (as suggested by Lübbe 1986), theological resistance is called for. Christian religion does not see itself as a function of society or the state.

More recently, Niklas Luhmann (1927-1998) analyzed religion from the point of view of system theory. He begins by distancing himself from Durkheim and Weber. Durkheim assumes an integrative function of religion and overlooks that religion, from society's point of view, can also be dysfunctional (e.g. as a potential for protest, resistance, etc.). He also criticizes Weber's focus on the interpretational function of religion. According to Luhmann, the need for interpretation could be changed or even disappear because of the process of evolution. Luhmann concentrates instead on religion as the *practice of mastering contingency* (cf. Luhmann 1977, 10-30).

Luhmann's concept is based on the differentiation between system and environment. *System* is a formal term. The individual person can be a system, and so can an institution. *Environment* means everything that excludes a system. Human existence, from the point of view of system theory, is action and decision-making in a system-environment relation. The environment is *faszinosum et tremendum*; it asks questions and creates queries that humanity must answer or solve. Furthermore, the environment always offers more alternatives of action than could practically be chosen. In this way, the problem of contingency is not an evil to eradicate, but rather a continual challenge. It cannot explain itself, nor does it get used up. The latter point in particular means that the experience of contingency is a permanent motor for the development of religion.

Using religion, the undefined complexity being experienced can be transformed into defined complexity. Religion provides security and orientation in this situation. With a view to Luhmann's ideas, it is undeniable that the Christian religion wants to help with the mastery of contingency. Spiritual guiding in the face of a finite life, embodied by the drama of death, has always been a central concern of Christianity – but it does not want to end there.

Finally, we will examine Thomas Luckmann's influential studies. In a very decisive way, Luckmann (1967) has replaced a substantial conception of religion with a functional one. Luckmann's radical novelty lies in the fact that he unhinges religion from the familiar church connections, viewing it in a purely anthropological way. As differing and heterogeneous as those subjects that activate religion are, that is how different the forms of religiousness are. For Luckmann, religion is an essentially individualized and privatized event. What we understand to be religious thematic is a dramatization of the subjective autonomous self in his or her search for self-realization and self-confirmation. Religion is the question of how a human person becomes a human person.

According to Luckmann, a person becomes a person thanks to the community in which he or she lives. This community offers the means to achieve individualization through systems of meanings. These systems of meaning help the individual to exceed him- or herself as a purely biological existence (self-transcendentalization). Through self-transcendentalization, the individual experiences him- or herself within the continuity of past, present and future. Systems of meaning help to see life as an ordered "whole." Individualization is, through its very being, a religious process. The means used is neither the religion nor religious, but rather the process of individualization as a whole. With this concept, Luckmann has introduced one of the widest concepts of religion that there is – but it does not conflict with the Christianity of the churches.

The advantage of Luckmann's concept is that it includes a broad spectrum of faith content and forms that fill a religious function. The disadvantage is that everything that consists of ideologies and worldviews can also be identified as religious content and form. Christian theology can learn from Luckmann – learn to expand its horizons of analysis and define religion in a more inclusive fashion. Overall, Luckmann's theories are quite helpful in seeing religion as something natural in modern life, recognizing its importance for the process of individualization and justifying its need to be taught in class. Christian theology cannot stop at this point and simply see Religious Education as a process of self-transcendentalization. Quite apart from the anthropological need for religion, there is also the self-revelation of God.

Psychology of Religion

Those studying the history of religious psychology look back at a very critical relationship between psychology and religion. Religion appears in a particularly negative light when considering the ideas of Sigmund Freud (1856-1939) (cf. Freud 1962). For Freud, religion is an infantile and irrational matter, distancing humanity from the reality around it. Religion provides humans with an infantile safe-area, where he can seek refuge from unpredictable Nature. In the kingdom of religion, everything is exactly the way humans desire it to be. This security, however, is gained at the price of a fundamental loss of reality. Religion is not the result of thinking, but rather it is an illusion designed to realize humanity's deepest desires. Freud arrives at a drastic conclusion: he sees religion as a danger to scientific progress and evolution. He sees his goal in the transparency, uncovering, and eventual redundancy of religion. People, according to Freud, cannot always stay children. A mature person has to deal with the reality that surrounds him or her. Education cannot be allowed to remove the "hard stuff" from life and compensate for it with religion. Education should enable people to deal with the reality that surrounds them.

Concepts of Religious Education have to take Freud's criticism seriously and must take control of the effects of Religious Education through self-criticism (Mette 1983, 128 et seq.). Religious Education can be oppressive. From a psychotherapeutic point of view, there is a long list of factors that could make a person sick, factors that can then be traced back to religion.

Günther Hole (1994), for instance, refers to Paul's cosmic and anthropological dualism when he speaks of the polarity of body and mind. This splits people into soul and flesh, where the soul is a positive force and the flesh is a negative force. Christianity, as a whole, has a very dark picture of humanity attached to it, especially with a view to the Fall, the original sin. Christianity fosters symptoms of neurotic diseases: a stern *Über-Ich*, the internalization of stern authority figures (parents, educators, God), as well as sadistic attacks against one's own ego. Rigorous religious content could suppress the need for expression and growth within the ego. Some of the consequences include the development of guilt complexes that exist independent of actual guilt, feelings of low self-esteem, inhibited response to aggression, addiction to harmony in interpersonal relationships, the inability to say "no," a tendency to retreat in critical social situations, etc. (cf. Hole 1994, 216). These negative findings do not say that religion always has these effects; but the danger is certainly there.

Yet religious psychology has changed as well, and it has expanded its horizons. Other concepts have been developed after Freud, concepts that see religion in a different light. Seen empirically, religion can even be identified as a source of happiness in life (Francis et al. 2002). This is also the direction taken by the psychologist Wolfram Kurz (1994). For him, the "promotion of a person becoming himself" and the "promotion of his psychic development and maturity" are central issues of psychology. The main point is taking care of oneself, tending to one's self-preservation. This issue is one that Kurz closely links to religion. Religious Education can clarify that God's promise of redemption to people takes the existential burden off their shoulders – that of taking care of themselves. Not having any existential worries allows a new kind of happiness and calmness, a benevolent acceptance of one's light and dark side and their coexistence. A person does not have to fight for fulfillment in his or her life, but simply be aware of it. He can work with and in the world, developing his talents and refining the development of him- or herself. He can also offer his talents for someone else's benefit and rejoice in seeing other life grow. Work is also a central issue within the therapeutical theories of Viktor Frankl. Kurz sees both themes, growth and dedication, as strongly anchored in biblical tradition: people should make the best of themselves *and* participate in the preservation of the world around them.

This is where we find the real task of Religious Education: making a positive contribution to the strengthening of the ego. Religious Education can reiterate that life is worth living, strengthen the conviction that young people are valuable to adults, remind those with problems that they have already solved problems competently in the past and thereby help their self-confidence, transmit a feeling of security, and pass on the hope that life will turn out just fine. Expressed in the negative sense, the central goal is to avoid feelings of fear (threats), feelings of guilt ("I can't do anything right"), feelings of inferiority ("I am worthless"), and feelings of meaninglessness ("life is a big nothing"). Christian Religious Education is a guide to dealing with these feelings and mastering one's experiences with death, emptiness, and guilt. Biblical stories are helpful at this point. Where there is fear, the Christian God is a power stronger than death; where there is guilt, God unconditionally accepts people (cf. Kurz 1994). Religious Education imparts the composure to have trust in and hope for a life that has already been accepted by God and that has always stood and continues to stand under God's favor – even before a person has "earned" it through good behavior and performance.

Theology of Revelation

Even within Christian theology, the understanding of religion is under debate. There is no universal definition, and, according to Waldenfels (1991); there will never be one in the strictest sense either, since the point in question (God, the

Holy, etc.) escapes human comprehension. Theology itself is part of a discourse universe where we try to say something meaningful about religion. It is interesting to note, however, that many facets of the above attempts at defining religion have been adopted by theologically motivated religious philosophy. Waldenfels (1991, 418) sees a general agreement in the fact that religion is visible in those places where people relate themselves to an all-encompassing authority. Within everyday searches for meaning, within experienced sympathy and faithfulness, within experienced solidarity, love, and justice, within experienced forgiveness and hate for an enemy – in all of these we see the basic experience of a benevolent law and order. Christian theology cannot depreciate this experience, let alone deny it, when arriving at its own concept of religion, but it cannot simply accept it as it is. The "necessary order" has both a concrete face and a concrete name to it within the Judeo-Christian tradition. Christian theology is widening the concept of religion considerably, or possibly rendering it extremely concrete, beyond the scope of anthropological and social phenomena when it speaks of a permanent challenge posed by God to humankind. This challenge is the extensive promise of salvation made by the self-revealing God who shows people the way to freedom and bliss. Christian religion can be reduced neither to inwardness nor to an abstract, socially produced meta-philosophy. In the self-impartation of the Judeo-Christian God, we find a call to a special form of existence within a plural of suggested meanings that may be opened through turning to God and our neighbor. It is all about making a decision to have faith in God. Without the concept of "faith," the concept of religion in Christianity cannot be properly determined. According to Seckler and Berchthold (1991), the content of faith is centered on the God who looks ahead and takes our welfare into account (Matthew 6:25 et seq.). This faith describes accepting God's salvation through Jesus Christ (*fides quae*) as a decisive act through the individual (*fides qua*). Above all else, it has – and this is the difference from other religions – a Christological orientation. The carrier of God's message (Jesus Christ) is himself part of the content of this faith. In Jesus Christ is the path to salvation, which is understood as an open invitation to all humankind (Gal 2:15ff; Rom 3:21-31). There is another facet that is important considering religious criticism: the Judeo-Christian faith does not look to cover up any particular social conditions, whether good or bad, rich or poor, etc. It does not sell an illusion or work like an opium but rather calls a critical consciousness to life, developing the habit of seeing the real misery (Marx) for what it is. It is about comforting, but it also includes resistance against injustice and suffering. In this sense, religion can indeed, as Luhmann states, be dysfunctional (e.g. a theology of liberation in a totalitarian state). The critical perspective here is not just a consequence of self-transcendentalization, but also an opposite thereof. In this way, the Christian understanding of religion supersedes a concept like that of Invisible Religion developed by Luckmann.

Religion and Faith as a Fertile Tension

Theories of Religious Education need concepts of religion for both its comprehensive and narrow forms. A broad view of religiousness creates the base we need for exploring the search for meaning, hope, and salvation of humankind without staking a claim to an independence of Christian education from the churches. Christian Religious Education is based on "religion" because religion allows faith to be formulated in words without letting faith become the same as religion. Paul Tillich is a much-quoted source when it comes to this particular understanding of religion:

> To be religious means to question the meaning of our lives passionately.... Such a view forms religion into something universally human.... Religion in its truest sense is being human, provided that it is a matter of the meaning of life and existence to those examining their existence. Many people are seized by something that concerns them, but they feel distanced from every religion because they take the question of the meaning of their lives seriously. They believe that their deepest interests, concerns, and requests would not be expressed by existing religions, and so they reject religion "out of religion." This experience teaches us to decide between religion as life in the dimension of depth and the concrete religions, which have won the religious interest of humanity through their symbols, institutions, and furnishings. If we want to understand the situation of modern people, we must begin with the concept of the essence of religion and not with one specific religion, not even Christianity (cf. Tillich 1969, 9).

This does not mean that Tillich advocates a religious didactic cut off from tradition; such an interpretation would be misunderstanding his message. Tillich, rather, maintains that a tension exists between an existentially based openness for religion on the one hand and the concretizing of content for this openness through a historically concrete tradition (such as Christianity represented by the churches) on the other hand. Tillich himself later wrote, "Without a final content, every religion collapses," and "God" is the name for "that whose content absolutely concerns us" (Tillich 1969, 26). For this reason, it is difficult, maybe even impossible, to carry out Religious Education without bringing up the sort of concrete historical religious tradition that has been shaped by questions like these.

When falling back on religion, we assume that all people have an existential openness (at the very least potentially) for the religious dimension of reality. On the other hand, a concretizing in the sense of the Christian faith requires a decision. If such a decision has been made, then the existential background will still be there. In view of the *concretizing of content* through faith, this background may become less important. It can also remain a constant source of question and searches – a challenge (Ziebertz a.o. 2001). This tension has often been touched on by no less than the Catholic dogmatic theologian Karl Rahner:

> Whenever Man lives as a person, wherever he gets daringly involved with another person and devotes himself as a person, whenever he forgives without being pushed by external forces, whenever he feels lonely or isolated, whenever he feels free and like he is the master of his destiny, there lies a piece of Eternity, a piece of transcendence in his life, and when Man thinks things over and opens himself completely up to these experiences, in the end he explains this Eternity as an absolute. During such life experiences, we have had an experience of the spirit. ... The experience of Eternity, the experience that Man is more than a piece of this temporal world, the experience that the meaning of Man is not contained in the meaning, happiness, and fortunes of this world, ... and when we have this experience of the spirit, then we (we, at least in the sense of Christians who believe) have also already had the real experience of the supernatural (Rahner 1957, 107f).

These classical theological outlines demonstrate, in a quite topical way, that religiousness and faith have a very tense relationship with each another. We are dealing with the very multifaceted concepts of religion and religiousness (and, finally, faith). This multifaceted characteristic can be approached as a source of wealth, but also as a danger. Depending on how the danger is approached, religion is, in the end, played out against faith. If faith is reduced to the "I-hold-this-to-be-true" of theorems, then even theological criticism is justified. Seckler and Berchthold (1991) point to the fact that, for example, the Catholic Church has fixed, defined, and dogmatized faith for two thousand years, but that, in the end, it is not theorems and formulas (Ja 2:14-26) that should be the focus, but rather "the deed itself." The real object of faith is God. The recognition of God is an *inter*relation between the existential experiences, maybe the acceptance of a comprehensive power or authority *and* the Christian tradition of God's self-revelation, available to everyone and passed on by the churches as communities of believers.

One goal of religious didactics is certainly the opening up of the rich wealth associated with religion, i.e. bringing up the issue of being human in this world in its most radical light, and making religious communication available. The Christian faith in God does not stand in opposition to this, but rather concretizes the content. Religious didactics, then, is not based exclusively on anthropological deliberations or exclusively on dogmatic ones. It has to assume that the differentiation between subjective and church religion is irrevocable. It is up to religious didactics to pick up the tension, making it fertile and useful for the purpose of educational communication. For Christian religious didactics, this means "demonstrating the fundamentally religious that is present in humankind as well as its conformation and shape within that which is Christian" (Fink 1987, 27).

Opening up the Religious Dimension of Reality

After having analyzed the concept of religion, there are several answers to the question as to why the religious dimension of reality should be opened up. Two central dimensions, the social and the individual-anthropological, will now be discussed with a view to their roles within teaching objectives.

The Importance of Religion in Shaping Culture

Fortunately, a society is not just a technically operated giant system. Societies have culture, and the central roots of the Western culture are clearly to be found in Christianity. Even if the culture has pluralistic characteristics, there are still plenty of norms and values that appear self-evident and that we no longer need to justify. This is where we see the socially integrative face of religion. It binds people to agreement and promotes the cohesion in a society. Obviously, there are many things being questioned, and some rules that were once agreed upon are up for discussion. Whatever the preference may be in personal cases, education m eans m aking o neself f amiliar w ith t he c ultural h eritage – to w hich the Christian tradition obviously belongs. This does not mean simply making young people into vessels filled with a "culture of the past." Rather, they should be made to understand the roots of their own culture and given the capacity to develop or transform them for the future. Dealing with the roots of Christianity also means bringing up the dark sides as well as the plethora of positive impulses to be found there. The dark sides of Christian history include those times when religion has been made to fit or justify outside interests. Christian history classes could be made to show the negative aspects of Christian churches carrying the State on their shoulders. The class could then also show the important contributions that the churches have made to the common good, e.g. in the educational and architectural fields. There is great topical relevance within the influence that the Christian religion has had on our image of humankind, human dignity, and the Western u nderstanding of individual freedom, lawmaking in democratic states (e.g. labor, family, and social laws), and even economics (e.g. co-management). Similarly, we also should not forget our sense of time – the way we divide our lives in weeks, Sundays off, Christian holidays, etc. Today, some of these influences are in danger of disappearing. For example:

- The Judeo-Christian image of human dignity has influenced asylum-seeking legislation – the latter is now being changed to fit demographic and political considerations.

- The Judeo-Christian image of work and respite is the basis for having Sundays off – this image now has to compete with economic interests for prioritization.
- The Judeo-Christian image of the uniqueness of each person has patterned the constitutional law of many Western countries – today we foresee the technical possibility of copying a human being through cloning.

Opening up the religious dimension of reality has an explicit social and political worth, especially considering the social conflicts listed above. Students, as citizens of their respective states, must have the capacity to make responsible decisions and judgments. This means having a knowledge of the Judeo-Christian roots of our society. If this is highlighted as the educational task, then the central issue is no longer the influence and power of the Christian churches in our society, but rather the introduction of a certain view of humankind and coexistence as such. The modern image of *humanum* has partly been pushed through in opposition to Christianity, but it has also been helped by the Christian biblical image of humanity. Opening up the religious dimension of reality means acquiring knowledge and insight into the achievements of the Christian religion in the cultural, social, economic, and political fields and being able to make a decision as to their viability and desirability for the future in comparison to the alternatives offered in public discussion. Christianity's contribution to the social integration of the individual into the community and society's stability as a whole does not consist of simply defending the status quo but rather of getting involved in the discourse over values in the future life and starting the discourse in those places where indifference seems to reign.

The Importance of Religion for People's Life Orientation

The person, the human being, is a companion to the religious dimension of reality, particularly on the social and political level. It is an open question if religion is an anthropological attachment of the person or not. "Open" means both sides present good arguments without one or the other being able to offer proof to put an end to the debate. This also means that it is possible to agree with one side because good arguments speak *for* it. Apparently, religious didactics has predominantly joined the "yes" side and conceptually tied itself to this side of the question, but what kind of religiousness are we talking about here, which then supposedly makes up an anthropological annex to humanity? The answer to that can only be gained based on a broad understanding of religion. Four dimensions that play a role in childhood and youth (but not exclusively during these times) come into consideration.

Basic personal situations: open to interpretation and need to be interpreted

During puberty, young people experience a rebuilding of their personality. They are more aware of the way they dress because they want to be popular. Suddenly, d issatisfaction a rises b ecause o ne's o wn body i s p erceived t o b e u gly. The first great love opens floodgates of emotion, and the despair is correspondingly deep when the relationship ends. Experiences of injustice or war shake the trust held in politics or the civilized world culture. The questions "who am I," "what do I want to be," "why is this happening," etc. are perceived as existential problems. Religious educators will be ready for these questions, since they will have asked them as well. Religious Education assumes that human experience needs interpretation. The Old and New Testaments testify to the fact that people have had existential experiences during the thousands of years of Judeo-Christian tradition, and they go on to show how these experiences have been interpreted in a dialogue with God. The spectrum of possible themes is almost infinite. It includes erotic love (The Song of Songs) as well as questions of social injustice (the Prophets), suffering (Job), mercy (the story of the Good Samaritan), and the future (the Kingdom of God). In view of the openness of human experience, Religious Education opens up the interpretational reservoir of the Christian tradition.

People Practicing Self-transcendentalization

Analyses of human behavior reveal that transcendentalizations are not limited to people with a connection to a church. Thomas Luckmann (1967) has suggested a differentiation between small, medium, and large transcendentalizations. Small transcendentalizations are directed at a transcendentalization of the personal body. We are seeing this in a booming fitness and wellness culture or in the expression and performance of self-production. Medium transcendentalizations are directed at others. We see this in times when the need for a relationship is great or when the family is appreciated to a very high degree. The large transcendentalizations, finally, describe every movement towards the ultimate concern, which Christianity calls God. The possibility should not be dismissed that in certain esoteric wisdoms, God has been replaced by something else. Luckmann explains the "normality" of transcendentalizations with the wish of superseding oneself, the wish to be more than just biological. People do not just want to be a random product of evolution. For religious didactics, this means not assuming a crisis of transcendentalization neediness. It should simply build on the fact that the transcendentalizations in and of themselves indicate people's basic desire to be more. Religious Education can make it clear that transcendentalizations have their roots deep within human existence. This is a religious dimension of reality, ready for the taking. Religious Education has a critical role to play in finding out which "new gods" appear in the transcendentalizations and what their connections to superstition and magic are. It also has the constructive task of justifying, in a reasonable way, the Christian motivated transcendentalization towards the God of Abraham, Isaac, and Jacob.

People experience the temporal and finite dimension

Mastering fear and death in one's personal life is one of the central themes within the Christian religion. As an existential experience, no one can escape the questions that arise out of our finite existence. It is not, however, only the personal fear, which makes temporalness and finiteness important topics. There is also the general fear of the world as a threat: the fragility of our existence; our hopeful search for happiness, and the experience of never quite attaining it; the discrepancy between progress and destruction of (e.g. ecological) basics of life; the discrepancy between growing wealth and growing poverty; the ever-present divide b etween the n orthern a nd s outhern h emispheres, e tc. The r eligious d i-mension of reality lies is the fact that world itself does not provide any answers to these issues. Opening up this dimension means taking the need for integration seriously, being able to experience the world as a meaningful whole, and giving the individual a sense of belonging in this world (cf. Berger 1988, 3-28). Here, Christian tradition offers the image of an inclusive history of salvation. On the other hand, we must once again be careful not to see Christian tradition as a practice of consolation, but rather as a legitimization of resistance in those places where change is possible.

People being confronted with the question of meaning

Youth is usually considered the stage of life in which the questions of meaning are asked. Today we know that asking for the "meaning of it all" is a basic part of modern existence. The ambivalence of the process of modernization (more freedom and risks) is the basis for new quests for security. Even when the search for meaning is not identical to the Christian religion, the latter still guides the asker through the "front gate" of religious questions and experiences. *Meaning* has many faces. In religious didactics, the goal is to develop meaning as a n o rientation m atrix f or l ife, o ne that c ombines p ast, p resent, a nd f uture. Life has an intentional origin, and it is lived today through hope and confidence in the future. Biblical tradition is available to us as an event that is 2000 years old. The core of this "old" tradition is, however, the present, when seen from the future. The temporal structure of the biblical message, then, corresponds to the structure of the human search f or meaning. This connection cannot be suffi-ciently processed with the brief objectivity of a teaching statement, but only through a process of experience, much like the Exodus out of Egypt or the Em-maus experience, which demonstrate a growing *experience of God through en-counter.*

5

Functions and Objectives of Religious Learning

Without objectives, planned learning does not exist. Objectives describe the results that a learning process should provide for students. They make the learning processes transparent, controllable, and criticizable. Religious Education is not a special area in the collective field of education. There are specific goals for each s chool s ubject, but a ll o f t hese g oals correspond to o ne o verarching perspective – that humans, due to their personality and dignity, are themselves the goal and not the means to achieve something else.

In the literature of Religious Education, the proposition that religious instruction is a special subject is found as often as that which says, religious instruction is a subject like any other. On the one hand, what general education and Religious Education have in common and why it is important to accentuate these similarities are established. On the other hand, based on these similarities, it is shown where t he differences i n R eligious Education l ie. An important catchword i n this context is *Transcendence* (cf. Groome 1980). Transcendence evaluates all education efforts based on their orientation to past, present, and future and identifies the uniqueness of Religious Education. With the help of this analysis, a distinction between education, Religious Education, Christian Religious Education, and catechesis is possible. Goals and functions of these forms of development of a transcendental reference are shown. In a third step, it considers the dimensions of religious learning: of instruction and spiritual and community development, as well as transformative treatment. Finally, through connection, it i s s hown w hich g oals R eligious E ducation f ollows w hen s pecific f orms o f Religious Education and specific learning dimensions are set up in a relationship.

The Transcendence–Reference in Education

The meaning of *education* goes back to *educare*, within which we find *ducare* and *ducere*, which basically mean "forth" or "lead up to." The verb to lead entails a dimension of time. "Forth" refers to present and past times, and "up to" indicates a period of time that lies ahead. Education is thus an activity of the present that is equally connected to both the past and the future. Thomas

Groome (1980, 5-19) shows that and why *Transcendence* is a central theme in this time reference.

Education wants to lead forth. For education, the importance of the *past* is only in the experiences of earlier generations. The past saves up a collection from which it can grow. First, this means that learning processes do not always have to start from point zero, but instead can build on the positive experiences of the past. The negative past experiences also offer examples from which to learn. The result of this ambivalence is that education exists in necessary reference to the past. This relation to the past is deductive, and deduction is inevitable. Deduction can become dangerous if it is understood as an exclusive principle; i.e. when education is nothing other than the passing on of that which was thought of before us or when the past becomes the standard for the present and future. Education must be more than just the passing on of information, and young persons are more than simple consumers of past experiences.

With respect to education, the *present* is the time that plays the deciding role, as education takes place in the present. The knowledge obtained is for use here and now. Therein lies something very important because in light of a past orientation, it becomes clear that students should not only take on tradition, but must also be able to discover a truth-for-themselves in what they learn. It is in this sense that Jean Piaget described learning as a process in which critical reflection made in the past is viewed with the eyes of today. The creative dimension of learning is thus situated in the fact that occupation with the past should not be seen as leading to deadlock, but should rather be understood as a challenge. The didactical benchmark is the present. The present comes into discussion when one speaks of the interests of students or when we shine present light on past meaning. The reference to the present in education is inductive. Induction is inevitable. It becomes dangerous if it is understood as an exclusive principle and the past is either displaced or forgotten.

Education wants to lead forth or move forward – it refers to the *future*. In education, the focus is on the not-yet dimension – that which is still to be discovered. Nevertheless, this future is open for students, teachers, the church, faith, and society. Young people should be prepared for this open future. Therefore, we often fall back on a *closed* concept of the future. Education should execute itself by the example of proven models. What is to come is more or less certain. Yet is education not misused in this way? Is this not a false concept of the future, one that deals with the positioning of self in the present, but not actually in the future? For the sake of the future, we cannot use positioning of self in the present as the benchmark for the future. If so, there is the threat of stagnation instead of a promotion of progress. Alternatively, we should open up the positive power in reference to the future: everyone wants a future, whether young or old, rich or poor, Christian or non-Christian. This future is what the field of education is concentrated on, not only the survival of here and now. The future must have an open character, including vision and utopia, without which we are missing the idea of a better world. Through reference to the future, the dimension of utopia in education develops a more important meaning; it concerns the ability to achieve a better world. This reference to the future is *transformative*. It does not simply add together the past and the present and from that decide what will be. Organizing education by transformation is much more a creative activity.

Therefore, according to Groome (1980), education is the *transformation of the present into the future with the knowledge of the past*. It deals with the contentious holding together of all three dimensions. This function, which applies to all areas of education, is not specifically religious in nature, nor is it only educational. What is critical here is that the aspect of transformation refers to something transcendental. Therein lies the opportunity for the discussion of human existence. Education does not only provide knowledge, attitude, ability, and skill; it is also a way to bring adolescents to an understanding of the art of life and to help them realize their potential. All school education should be focused on this function. Physics instruction, just like geography instruction, must find a way to achieve this goal. They too are interested in a future for humankind, in ensuring ample resources for future generations, and in a way of thinking that knows that the future cannot simply be put under the control of technology, but is rather obligated to explore new possibilities and strive for a higher quality of life. This dimension of transformation applies to every area of education, not only religious instruction. In light of this, one can speak of the fact that education includes an instance of transcendence without having to say that all education is religious. For religious instruction, this consideration provides the advantage that a basic connection to all education efforts is thereby created. Metaphorically speaking, it concerns the following (cf. Groome 1980, 20-21): teachers are partners with their students, and they take them along on a journey, to help them discover their origin, give this meaning in today's light, and develop a vision of the future together. The goal of an education focused in such a manner is the ability to arrange one's own life and one's action in the world: in the present, for the future, and with the knowledge of one's origin.

Nevertheless, the question arises of how we can be sure that there is hope for the future. In the context of the educational division of labor (in the sense of the different subjects), every subject must contribute in its own way by discussing the possibility for hope. This duty does not solely fall on the shoulders of Religious Education, but it has an equal part. Religious Education focuses, as every other subject, on a common goal in a specific way. This system has the advantage of not separating the function of Religious Education from all other subjects in school, but rather stresses that its place in the school is an equal and important part of the collective structure of school education. It is thus important for teachers that they place Religious Education on the same professional level as the other subjects. If school is able to integrate the goals of Religious Education in the overall goals of learning, students will also appreciate Religious Education as an equally important subject. The cohesion of all education lies at the forefront. We next examine the individual subjects of instruction. The examination shows differences; the intension is not separation.

Goals of Different Concepts of Religious Education

If the general conception of education entails a transcendental trend, what then is the special situation of Religious Education? Religious learning can be broken up into three specific areas, none more or less important than another. All three are considered when talking about religious instruction, not only one or another. More accurately, we are concerned with three perspectives, which can reciprocally permeate each other. They can enter discussion as an independent perspective or as a complementary viewpoint. What we are talking about is the difference between Religious, Christian Religious, and catechetical-Religious Education. Once again, following the religious-educational work of Groome (1980, 20-28), we can see what is connected to the collective goal of education and the special features of religious instruction.

First, to *Religious Education*. As *religious* education, the religious instruction focuses the discussion of the question of humankind on transcendental aspects, on the final and ultimate reason for our existence. Religious instruction encourages the consideration of this question, and with good reason. It can point out how this question is also the focus of many different contemporary forms – in music, film, and literature, but also in philosophy, medicine, and physics – and equally s o i n w orldviews and s pecific r eligious traditions. The adjective r eligious in Religious Education signifies the specific, while the noun "education" shows what Religious Education has in common with education in general. This means that Religious Education does not only concentrate itself on work that is connected to the tradition of faith, but also on the relationship between itself and the community at large (e.g. society or humankind). Religious Education shares the concern over the quality of education with the other educational institutions. It does, however, concentrate explicitly on the existential dimension of life. An extension of the above-mentioned journey metaphor could be formulated thusly: on this journey, Religious Education uncovers the ultimate reason of existence through reference to religion and worldviews. The goal of religious learning is the development of the ability to organize one's own life and the world in the present, for the future, and in conscious reference to an ultimate reason of being.

In the title of *Christian Religious Education*, an additional adjective, namely *Christian*, is found. This reminds us that the search for the ultimate reason of existence cannot be thought of as simply historically based. We meet religion in the context of certain religious traditions. Even the modern religious styles in the West are nothing without reference to Christian semantics. During instruction, Christian Religious Education focuses on a certain tradition in which a special reference to the Ultimate appears, thereby using a specific system of symbols in the context of a particular community. The adjective Christian placed before religious education is a reminder to Christian (both Protestant and Catholic) Religious Education that its practitioners do not have a monopoly on religious education, but rather that this is a particular type of Religious Education. The term *Christian*, from the ecumenical perspective, keeps alive the picture of a universal church. Looking at it another way, the term religious education coming after Christian is a reminder that the question of transcendence is much broader than can be adequately covered by one religious community. By referring the Christian religious relationship back to Religious Education and education as a whole, we can see its special character. It is not something completely different from other education models; rather it shares with them a basis of educational responsibility. It does, nevertheless, stress something specific and thereby makes an offer to students to consider this special relationship with the ultimate reason for our existence. The journey-metaphor is therefore more precisely stated thusly: On this journey, Christian Religious Education uncovers the embracing of the presence of God, speaks of the message of the kingdom of God (tradition), and shows the way to a prosperous life (i.e., hope). The objective can be described as this: Christian Religious Education seeks the development of the ability to organize one's own life and the world in the present, for the future, and in a conscious relationship with the liberating message of the kingdom of God, his presentation of life and the world, and his promise of fulfillment.

There remains only the *catechesis* to differentiate. *To catechize* means "to answer" – answer by the concrete Word of the Jewish-Christian God, as the churches acknowledge him and as theology accounts for him. *Catechesis* is a church-based term. It receives its contents and principles primarily from dogmatic theology, moral theology, and liturgics. Catechesis is in this narrow understanding *one* aspect within the broader concept of Christian Religious Education. Catechesis sees the journey as initiation of a Christian church-based community within the greater society. The intention of catechesis is the direct preparation of "agreement in faith." This can no longer be presupposed in today's Religious Education in school. To follow a catechesis model, religious instruction would really be pushed to its boundaries. On the other hand, this special feature serves as the reference point linking it to Christian Religious Education. The idea is to immerse oneself more deeply in the Christian tradition of faith, in an established faith, and in an established religious community. In order to continue with the above-mentioned metaphor (cf. Groome 1980, 26-27): catechesis sees this journey as initiation and socialization in the broad world of a Christian-church-based community. Accordingly, we can formulate the objective here: catechesis seeks the development of the ability to organize one's own life and the world in the present and for the future by introduction into the practice of the Christian faith, by increasing faith in God, and by participation in the rituals of an established church community.

Forms of Religious Education: Functions and Objectives				
	Education	**Religious Education**	**Christian Religious Education**	**Catechesis**
Function	Education takes humankind on a journey to learn boundaries, to shift boundaries, and to cross boundaries into a new world.	Religious Education sees this journey as discovering the ultimate reason for our existence within the context of a religion or, more specifically, of a worldview.	Christian Religious Education sees this journey as the embracement of the presence of God, from which the message of the kingdom of God gives an inheritance to and a promise of a prosperous life.	Catechesis sees this journey as an initiation and socialization into the practice of a Christian church-based community.
Objective	The ability to organize life and the world in the present and for the future with a knowledge of one's own origin.	The ability to organize one's own life and the world in the present and for the future in conscious reference to the ultimate reason for our existence.	The ability to organize one's own life and the world in the present and for the future in a conscious relationship with the liberating message of the kingdom of God, his model of life and the world, and his promise of fulfillment.	The ability to organize one's own life and the world in the present and for the future through an introduction into the practice of the Christian faith, through increasing faith in God, and through participation in the rituals of an established church community.

What form does Religious Education take when it seeks to appeal to both the cognitive and existential sides of students? The answers: every, and none. *Every* because the average religious instruction model always has an educationally building function; because it addresses religion in discussion as a social and anthropological phenomenon; because it, being tied to Christianity, focuses during instruction specifically on the development of the Christian tradition; and finally, because it keeps open the option to explore links to the broader establishment of a church. Religious Education in school equally corresponds to *none* of these forms because it does not only focus on either education or religion (the specific would be lost); because it likely does not fit the strict description of the typical model of Christian Religious Education in the sense it is described here, if, for example, it is shown as religious alphabetization – one thinks either of areas with few religiously affiliated people or of multi-religious areas (see chapter 2); and because it is unable to perform the catechesis. The importance of these distinctions lies in the fact that it is useful in the self-review of each practice, regarding the balance between generality and distinctiveness.

Dimensions of Objectives

The objectives of Religious Education range over several dimensions, four of which earn the special attention of the school of Religious Education. According to Seymour and Crain (1997), they are described as instruction, spiritual development, faith community, and transformation. There are overlaps between these dimensions, however, and to better identify the individual facets of religious learning, it is important to analyze the differences. In the practice of religious learning, the dimensions should complete each other. For example, spirituality has value for itself, but it likewise applies to others. At the same time, understanding mysticism and politics as complementary activities is an undisputed Christian conviction.

First, we discuss *instruction*. Arranged learning and systematic learning are particularly concise features of school learning. Religious instruction includes structured and formalized learning processes in which knowledge of religion in general and the Christian religion in particular is arranged. In order for students to open up the religious dimension of reality (see chapter 4), they need appropriate points of reference. They become familiarized with the phenomena that characterize religion and Christianity. Above all, instruction occurs cognitively as the relaying of knowledge, development of meanings, discussion of consequences, etc. Knowledge means the ability to arrange and assign meaning to experiences. Religious knowledge is an essential base for self-orientation and personal judgment. Christian life requires the knowledge of the biblical tradition, of the assertions of the Christian church to which one belongs, of the history of God's people, and of the symbols and rituals that are used in Christian-religious practice. Furthermore, knowledge transfer serves the cognitive familiarity. Even students dissociated from a Christian church do at least acquire the religious-cultural background of the Western world, which is substantially influenced by Christianity. They can be sure that throughout every year (at

Christmas, Easter, etc.), they will encounter vestiges of Christianity. Religiously educated students use the acquisition of knowledge to deepen their understanding of personal orientation. In the modern, rationally structured world, religious instruction has the goal of cognitively equipping future adults for the realm of religion so that their personal religiousness develops similarly to their general development (and does not persist at a child's level) and so that they can perceive and judge the religious dimension of reality appropriately.

The second dimension is *spiritual development*. With spiritual development, the person, or rather the inner self, is the focal point. Spirituality is life from the spirit. In religious learning, this spirit has a special meaning, but *spirituality* is no longer a term restricted to Christian religion. It is thus easier today to talk about spirituality because most people are now conscious that they are searching for defined turning points in their lives, that they want to find their inner self, that they want to explain life, and that they want to bring orientation and order into their lives. It is the field of religion that takes on this search process, escorts it, and gives it direction. Spirituality is the finding of spirit, which sets the force of integration and orientation free. To find oneself can mean to achieve meaning – through silence exercises, meditation, abstinence, or fasting. To become calm or at peace can mean to accept something new in oneself, to hear something new from outside oneself, or to sense the call of God. In this way, spiritual development in religious instruction is not left to the general, but rather is concentrated in the discovery in the light of faith.

A third dimension of religious learning is the development of a relationship between the individual and a *faith community*. This dimension gains special meaning in front of the background of modern life because with the increase in liberty that has released the modern individual, a shadow is cast, which manifests itself in social orientation and affiliation problems, isolation, a loss of bonds, ties, etc. The fragmentation of life clearly corresponds with the desire for togetherness. In Religious Education, the reference to group and community has a fixed place. On the one hand, identity (also religious identity) is not just simply the result of looking into oneself, but is the result of interaction. Interaction presupposes a group. On the other hand, religion is always in reference to community, in the formation of a life and belief view, of values and norms, etc. The dimension of community reminds Religious Education of the power that community provides through unity. It shows how the religious communities in general and a certain church in particular are understood as places of assemblage and agreement, how integration in communities occurs through participation, and how bonds are celebrated in community rituals. Humans need the support of and a connection to a community that belongs to both the immediate vicinity and the *oikos*, the world community. In religious learning, the community has still greater significance. The term *religio* means "to connect back" (see chapter

4). This reminds one that a community always includes community with God. Religious instruction should not only talk about community but also talk about the possibilities of community formation, either discussing the topic themselves or deferring the task to special groups in school or youth clubs in church congregations.

Finally, the fourth dimension is *transformation*. Not all religions stress this aspect equally; however, it cannot be excluded from the Christian tradition. The Jewish-Christian roots attest a strong reference to the world: the world has been blessed by the Creator, and Abraham is a symbol of this blessing (Genesis 17:3-8); and as Jesus spoke of the salt of the earth and the light of the world, he did not distinguish himself from his listeners, but rather gave them a mission (Matthew 5:13-16). The reference to the world in Christian tradition is a direct progeny of faith (John 17:18). The terms *citizen* and *Christian* do not exclude each other. The incorporation of the transformative dimension into religious learning processes focuses on making the individual conscious of the fact that in every case, the Christian religion encourages that humans awake and develop their potential for organizing the world and accept responsibility for themselves and for others. Religious learning can activate and accompany transformation by using the three-step see-judge-act process. The practical can be addressed in schools through action and project-oriented learning. In religious learning, these four dimensions are discussed – they are not equally weighted, but still discussed in a complementary sense (cf. Seymour/Crain 1997). In the following outline, a brief summary of the respective learning objectives is given.

Goal Orientation in Education Dimensions			
Instruction	**Spiritual Development**	**Faith Community**	**Transformation**
Recognition and insight into the meaning of culture (of inheritance), as well as an understanding of the states of the self and the world worth preserving and those requiring change.	Recognition and insight into the meaning of the convictions and attitudes that are capable of long-lasting support and helping with life orientation.	Recognition and insight into the meaning of dependency and reference to others, namely the development of the ability to cultivate and evolve one's own life in connection with the community.	Recognition and insight into the necessity for individual and collective action in the anticipation of a new and better world.

Objectives of Religious Education

The concepts presented thus far will now be brought together. The following overview presents a matrix that offers a horizontal arrangement of the various forms of Religious Education and a vertical arrangement of the previously mentioned dimensions. The value of such a synopsis is to enable each practice to better understand its relative placement and allow superior reflection and explanation. We must be reminded of the key concept: the focus on the attempt to account for integrative objectives of religious learning with respect to education as a whole and to present thereby a relationship between the anthropological, societal, theological, and ecclesiastical dimensions of religious learning.

Goals: Forms and Dimensions				
	Education	**Religious Education**	**Christian Religious Education**	**Catechesis**
Instruction	Understanding of the positioning of existence in the past, present, and future.	Understanding of the anthropological-transcendental composition of humankind.	Understanding of the faith of Christians in the dimensions of mysticism and politics.	Understanding of the meaning and spectrum of the churches' teachings about the incarnation of God in Jesus Christ.
Spiritual Development	Development of the question of the reason and meaning of our existence.	Development of the question of the Ultimate and opportunities for transcendence.	Mystical development of the question of spiritual living in the context of models that are a part of Christian tradition.	Mystical development of the question of a life in God's spirit, following the rituals of the Christian church to which one is related.
Faith Community	Relation between one's own life and the world.	Relation between one's own life and the world, which exceeds empirical explanation.	Relation between one's own life and the world as an organic connection within the history of Christian salvation.	Relation between one's own life and the world within the practice of the church to which one is related.
Transformation	Transformation of the known world into a new world.	Transformation of the world in light of the reason for our existence.	Transformation of the world according to the message of God's kingdom as one of love and justice.	Transformation of church practice for itself and for the world in anticipation of the kingdom of God.

This matrix can be read either vertically or horizontally. From the vertical view, one can ask which objectives the general educational concepts (those which, as shown, are transcendentally oriented) can identify for the dimensions of instruction, spirituality, community, and transformation, and, as long as the dimensions are not specified as religious elements, whether such further study is possible. In the next vertical column (Religious Education), the objectives are orientated towards the ultimate concern, which results in the students' approaching it with anthropological questions. About the interpretation of the Ultimate, one could say that the Ultimate is connected to the question of spirituality (from which spirit...) in order to reflect on its role in the development of community and its meaning in our actions. In the third and fourth vertical columns, the Christian concept of the Ultimate is presented. The Ultimate is given a name and a history. Here, the established Judeo-Christian God addresses each human personally and calls upon each to join his following. The horizontal view presents the four dimensions and asks how they can be interpreted socially, anthropologically, and in light of the Christian faith.

If one makes oneself conscious of the fact that religious learning in school can decreasingly rely on being church-based religious socialization, one will come to realize that religion should not be regarded as an "oddity of a past world," but rather as an element of continuing relative importance in and with the modern world (Ziebertz 1999). Religion does not open up a separate world next to the existing one, but instead offers a perspective from which to understand and explain the world in a different or new way. In order to address the heterogeneity of any given denomination fairly and adequately, it becomes ever more important to find in the future the appropriate balance between the objectives of general education and those of Religious Education. Religious educators must be able to show that the objectives of Religious Education have much in common with those of general education in school. This will contribute greatly to the acceptance of Religious Education by students, other teachers, and parents.

The starting point in addressing the question of the objectives of Religious Education is the undeniable freedom of individual human beings to realize the religious dimension of reality and be able to interpret this from the Christian perspective. In this chapter, the goals of religious learning were viewed in relation to those of education as a whole. With reference to transcendence, a common connecting factor is found, on which Religious Education concentrates in very specific ways (i.e., Religious Education, Christian Religious Education, catechesis), and which develops within different dimensions (instruction, spiritual development, faith community, and transformation). By making connections between these two perceptions, the perspectives of goals come into view, with which one can make the work of professional religious educators clearer and easier to explain.

6

Identity as Narrative and Process

The concept of identity has become a central tenet of educational sciences. This concept has lead to an educational and didactic focus on what the subject of education is. Students are no longer mere vessels to be filled with content, but rather they are the very center of all educational strategy and effort. The content of basic suppositions has lost its directive character and unassailability. These suppositions are becoming an offering to be tested, overtaken, rejected, or transformed. In this sense, identity is no longer described as the identity of roles. Identity is more than the internal integration of external expectations. Alternative concepts stress the interactive and narrative facets of identity. This chapter presents the various dimensions of these concepts and considers how they relate to concepts of Religious Education.

In raising and educating the young, we are also looking to guide their development of identity. Identity is the concept that best describes the subject that has come home to itself. The question for religious educators is, "do concepts of identity best suit my needs?" If yes, the concomitant question is, "which one?" Educational furthering of identity, according to my thesis, is not a question of the content or the role models being offered from outside, but rather a question of coaching the young as producers of identity. Older endogenous theories of identity have completely lost track of this aspect. In the alternative theses by Erik E rikson, the s ubject's o wn a ccomplishment l ies i n the m astery o f c rises that arise through the cycle of life and then in the formation of the identity through this mastery. Symbolic interactionism and later theories of communication based on it have finally shown how much identity is connected to people's interaction and linguistic and communicative decision-making. Today, we can speak on a much more multifaceted level about the production of identity, even without losing sight of the theories of interactionism. Such models of narrative identity assume that identity arises primarily through the stories that people tell about themselves and others. For religious educators, this means understanding and developing students as authors of their own life stories and teaching them to tell their story with the inclusion of religious dimensions.

Endogenous Identity?

One classical conception of identity assumes that everything that makes up the personal identity is already present in each of us. Identity is endogenously settled. Just like a flower bulb, which goes through the stages of a small green sprout, bud, and colorful flower, each person has a construction scheme inside which predetermines his or her identity. People have to recognize this construction scheme and make it into reality. Identity, in this sense, arises out of itself and works for itself. This model holds a certain fascination for many observers, as it highlights the perfection and autonomy of every human. It is, however, not realistic. Purely endogenous theories are too shortsighted, and overlook the fact that identity does not actually bloom by itself the way a flower does, which needs both sunshine and water to bloom anyway.

The endogenous concept of identity has been imported into the religious field and integrated into Religious Education (cf. Englert 1985, 219-224). The assumption was that each of us has a religious, or even a Christian religious, aptitude within us, which Christian education is supposed to bring to bloom. To put it another way: since religion, or more precisely all of Christianity, already slumbers in each of us, a systematic education based on the Christian tradition is nothing more than the midwifery to bring forth the Christian personality. Upbringing and education does not add anything to the person that is not already there, but it simply brings out that which is already predestined to emerge. First, there are serious doubts as to the verity of these assumptions; second, even Religious Education in this form has to take responsibility for its own educational intervention and consequences.

Identity cannot be interpreted endogenously by ignoring environmental factors (Keupp/ Höfer 1997). Identity sometimes has to be worked out and fought for in extremely conflict-filled circumstances. This is where Erikson's famous theory enters the scene. Endogenous theories are also considered shortsighted because they ignore the fact that humans are social animals. Social means interacting with other people in particular contexts of society and culture. Identity, then, is something that is worked out inside and through (never without) interaction. Both alternatives will be outlined here.

Erik Erikson's Concept of Identity

Erik Erikson's theory of identity (1959) was widely adopted in the field of religious education. For Erikson, identity is integrated into human development as a whole. It follows an epigenetic principle, i.e. all parts are a consequence of an original basic scheme that comes to fruition through various life cycles. The concept of a basic scheme should not be misunderstood as endogenous, but means, rather, that the development of identity is spurred on by crises that arise through and during the life cycles. Every crisis contains a specific development function. The individual exists within a field of tension, which Erikson renders concrete through two polar dimensions. This is where the development function to be filled is located. The crisis, once mastered, means progression on the maturity front.

The brilliance of this model is unquestionably its clarity and simple application in practice. This model not only allows an easy diagnosis of identity crises, but also demonstrates how to intervene in learning processes to reach a certain development goal. It does this by polarizing the positive field and the danger field. Erikson's concept is based on the idea that identity is a constantly crystallizing self, always stepping onto a higher level. The core is settled and develops in a socio-cultural fashion, i.e. through the mastering of crises that arise through the individual environmental constellation. Erikson concentrates mostly on the adolescence. It is in this phase that the master plan for life is brought to light. The creation of identity is, in any case, an integral part of childhood and youth. What happens there guides a lifetime. The model characteristic of this theory is, however, also a problem; several questions arise. Are youth, according to this model, being made to work out their identity in a standardized fashion? Does identity work like a railway system? Are developmental crises really only to be found in particular time periods? Can identity ever be a closed chapter? Does the principle of levels of higher development hold water? This last question could also be directed at the structural genetic theories of Lawrence Kohlberg and James Fowler among others, whose theories consider the final destination of development to be predetermined.

Identity from Interaction

A second alternative to endogenous ideas of identity is offered by interactionist concepts (John Dewey, William James, and George Herbert Mead). They demonstrate that identity is based on a balance between one's self-image and one's other-image and that this balance has to be permanently created *in* and *through* interaction (cf. Ziebertz 1990, 48-74; 1999, 70-87).

Interactionist thinking often falls back on the role model, but it does not see the development of identity as a monological assumption of a certain role. In the most extreme case, assuming a role means shutting down the active sense of personal initiative in the subject. In this case, identity would be a role identity, i.e. an identity that mirrors external expectations. Mead shows us that the individual not only internalizes external expectations, making them his or her own, but also takes up an interpretive position towards these expectations. These interpretations and positions have an affect on other interactive participants and vice versa. In other words, people mutually open up the significance of their verbal and non-verbal communications. Interactive participants are actively reconstructing the statements of the other, thus creating a relationship to him or her.

This is where the interactionists see the key to understanding the creation of identity: the inner, symbolic reconstruction of the behavior, experiences, and expectations of those interacting with the real or imaginary subject takes place within the interactions themselves. The internal reconstruction of the social structure of interaction enables the mutual anticipation of expectations, making it the center of dialogical action. Self-image and other-image are made to balance. There really is an assumption of roles, but not in a monological sense. The decisive insight provided by interactionist theories into the assumption of roles is that an individual *actively* reconstructs the attitudes of others within him- or herself. This reconstruction does not necessarily take place on an interpersonal level, i.e. in a dialogue between two or more people. It can also take place on the intrapersonal level, i.e. within the consciousness of a single person.

In order to understand this process, the levels *I* and *Me* are brought into play. The *I* refers to the unmistakable self-representation of the subject (self as knower), and the *Me* refers to the object of knowledge (self as known). To a certain extent, people can observe their own actions. Not only can they think about themselves and interpret their own experiences on a subjective level, they can also understand how they interact with others and how others, with their particular statements, desires, and commands, become a part of one's own thinking and feeling, and, in the end, how to react to this experience. In all of these movements of interaction, information, and meaning are exchanged, which the partners must interpret. In this sense, identity is the result of interaction, because *a person knows that, which he knows that he is, also because others hold him to be just that*. When the statements made by others no longer confirm the image I have of myself, there arises a problem of identity, which can only be solved through interaction.

In the continued study of interactionist thinking, one tried to make the *I*-identity into a landmark through which one could separate the interactionist concept of identity from role-identity. The concept of *I*-identity sees the most important condition for a person to express individuality as lying within the independent and creative energy of the *I*. The *I*-identity is understood to be a process and not a product. It is formed *in* interaction, and becomes the *I*-identity *out of* interaction. The process aspect means that a person does not just ask who he or she has become, but also who he or she wants to become. The communicative roles

Ego-Alter-Neuter have an important function in the creation of an *I*-identity (Mead 1934). In putting him- or herself in the shoes of someone else (Alter), the subject fulfils the first condition for creating a certain distance to one's own expectations. Taking the next step, recognizing the captivity of the dual interaction (Ego ↔ Alter), makes it possible to take on a third perspective (Neuter). From this perspective, a critical distance to the Ego and Alter positions is set up. The capacity for a mutual assumption of different perspectives is tied to the possibility of human communication, the most important symbol of which is language. Language is *the* action for creating and retaining meaning and enabling people to communicate the norms, rules, and goals of their common interaction. The point of communication is to be found in the subject himself.

The strength of interactionist theory lies in the connection made between the creation of identity and the process of *individualization*. The goal is *I*-identity, not role-identity. Furthermore, *I*-identity does not only arise through the mastering of crises, but it can also be recognized within interaction itself. When interacting, people relate mutually to each other, primarily using the symbolic system of language. The attention devoted to linguistic and communicative action has opened up our eyes to a learning dimension that goes beyond the question of learning content. Linguistic communication is not just an instrument but also a practice that actively constitutes identity. The communication becomes the content. How religious educators communicate is, in itself, a part of the religious message.

Narrative Pluralistic Identity

The question of identity is an issue that, at the start of the 21st century, must be defined with the conditions imposed by a postmodern Western society. This society is marked, among other things, by a very pluralistic base structure affecting all areas of life – including religion and worldviews (Ziebertz 2001a; 2001b). The plurality of modern life also affects the possibilities for making an identity. The question has even been asked whether an identity is even possible under the current conditions. The theoretical and empirical evidence of models that assume a core identity or claim to see the final stage of identity or the way to it is fading. The social and cultural changes in the so-called postmodern age are directly affecting the micro-field of personal orientation in life and lifestyle (see chapter 1). The personal freedom has been expanded, but so has the obligation to be independent and fall back on the ego as a center of activity and decision-making. The individual has become an entrepreneur who has to build his identity himself. He learns that the making of an identity is an endless task. The fragmentation of social points of reference, the dissolution of safe contexts (Giddens: *disembedding*), and the necessity of reintegration are ever-cyclical processes. This means that Erikson's concept of identity diffusion is not limited to a certain length of time but is, rather, a challenge for a lifetime. It seems to be a landmark of postmodern identity that one seeks a balance between the experience of being torn on the one hand and the need for identity on the other. With this in mind, identity is becoming less and less a concept with a positive content. Identity is becoming a metaphor for the process of people seeking self-assurance, consistency, and coherence in the face of all the potential options within plurality. This is where we find the concept of narrative identity, which says that people experience identity when retelling the events of their lives. In this retelling, life becomes structured, connections are made, contradictions are reconciled, and opportunities taken and passed by are evaluated.

Three-dimensional Structure of Identity

The concept of narrative structure has a three-dimensional structure.

- First, identity has a *temporal structure* (cf. Krauss 2000, 96 et seq.). The time that has been set is a central characteristic of each identity because every person asks the question "Who am I?" in the time stream of his or her own life. The point of origin is the present time. Expectations and goals for the future are set in the present time. Simultaneously, the past has a cause and effect relationship to both the present and the future. What there is *now* and what there *could* be in the future are partly determined by what has happened in the past. Hopes for the future that are not tied to the present and past are mere illusions. At the very least, a good prognosis for the middle-term future is necessary for a stable identity. This requires a balance between a pessimistic and optimistic view of the future, between an active and passive attitude, and between a wealth of ideas and no concrete plans. Leaning too much towards optimism means overshadowing the realistic chances; having too little faith in oneself means missing opportunities. As far as the time factor is concerned, ideals do have their place here, but they are of lesser importance.

- When considering the timeline of one's life, there is a second set of factors that comes into play: *reality and possibility* (cf. Greve 2000). Everything could have gone differently in the past; the present time contains an "is" and a "could have been"; and the future is completely open. Conjectures are especially of the essence here: "If I had only...then..."; "Should I or should I not?"; "Will this help or hurt me in the future?" etc. No matter how these questions are answered, every answer is finite (i.e., contingent). Even people who shape their lives materialistically and one-dimensionally and then search for self-assurance come upon this tension between what is and what could be.

- The third structural level of identity contains a *cognitive descriptive* pole and an *affective evaluative* pole. The indicative and conjectural representation of experiences within the flow of time can be "establishing" and "judging." One can simply recount experiences or one can take up a certain position and judge them. This judgment can be even more positive, the more coherence (connections) and consistency (absence of contradictions) the life story has.

These structural characteristics fill a three-dimensional space (see the following figure). Whether a life is seen as coherent and consistent depends on how remembered experiences *in* these fields (but also projections *on* these fields) are connected. In this space, one asks the question "Who am I?" and tries to answer it in a *story*.

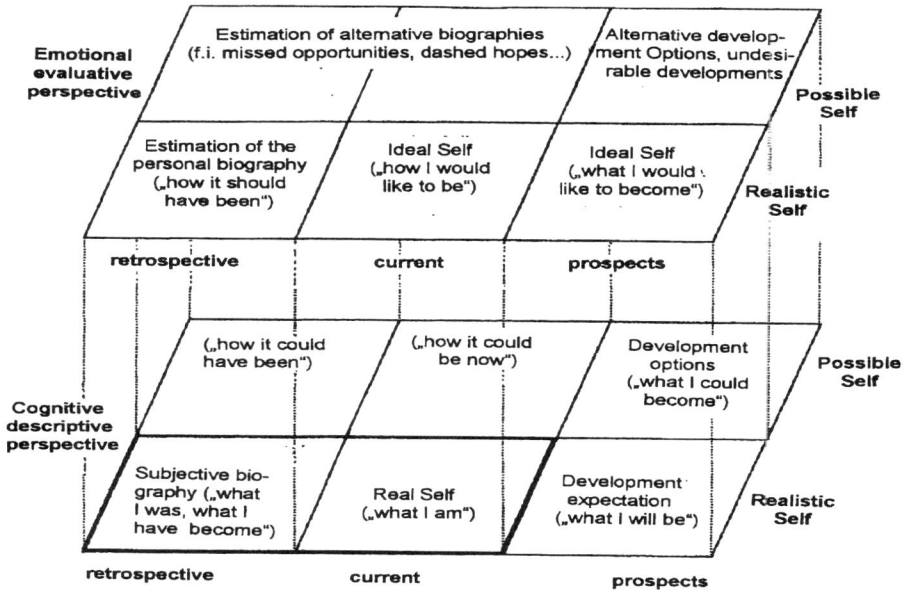

Grafics: Three-dimensional topography of the Self (Greve 2000)

Pluralistic Identity

In the retelling process, the subject makes itself the object of its study (the *I* becomes the *Me*). It can sometimes happen that the subject does not see itself as singular, but as a unit of several (cf. Hermans/Kempen 1993; Hermanns/ Hermanns-Jansen 1995). This arises from the recognition that in certain situations, one acted in a way that one normally would not, that one felt what one normally would not, that one thought what one normally would not, etc. The experience can also be significantly less dramatic. One might simply recognize the fact that one is not the same person in front of the church altar as in the riding club, in school as at home, playing chess as in the disco, etc. This does not lead to a fear of oneself, but rather to the recognition that there is a multitude of self-images that are activated at different times.

The multitude of self-images is not necessarily equal to identity. In order to speak of identity, there first has to be coherence (connection) between these selves. Second, the individual must actively invest in this coherence, whereby he or she expresses the fact that this self is something good and worthy. Third, this self must also be recognized by the environment because otherwise a very important *reaction* is missing, leaving a contradiction between the evaluation made by oneself and the one made by others (Krauss 2000, 124). The central recognition leading to the concept of narrative identity is the fact that these selves are connected and integrated through self-narration. Whatever was, is, could have been, or will be there in the past, present, and future and who I am in this or that context are not simply coherent and consistent, but rather have to be interpreted as coherence and consistency. People do this through stories. In a story told by and about ourselves, we try to make connections and to create "a whole." Both sad and happy moments must be made to fit into this story; retrospectively, they are both assigned a larger scope or meaning, given to them by the narrator. The single elements are being *made sense of.* People relate to the world in a narrative way; the narration makes the story appear as a single unit. Within the scope of a story, the multitude and contradictions of the experiences appear in a greater connection: there is a beginning, climax, low point, and an end. The self and others are incorporated into this narrative connection. The *I* or a set of *I*'s are permanently in the process of telling the life story with the *Me* as the main character. The point is not objective truths but a construction that is plausible and can be lived with. Since the circumstances of life constantly change, the life story never ends. New experiences must constantly be interpreted and integrated – and a new story begins. The stories are not about real interaction with physically present interactive partners. The imagination and fictitious interaction are equally important. In this way, a spatial horizon is constructed in which real and fictitious elements with chronological relevance are incorporated in an indicative and conjectural fashion.

Learning processes intended for building identity have to move away from the idea that identity may be gained in the same way as property. They should take the narrative process structure as a starting point for encouraging and supporting and students to take over the *authorship* and management of their life story. Concretely, Religious Education can

- shape the ability and willingness to question oneself and the world,
- help to find a "religious self" within the multitude of other "selves,"
- develop the capacity to encourage interaction between the "selves,"
- show ways to place one's own life within the scope of a story, and
- deliver "input" for the process of questioning – for instance, by taking advantage of the analogy between the time structure of the biblical tradition (i.e., future guidance delivered from the past) and the anthropological tie to the world (i.e., past, present, and future).

Identity in Religious Education

The connection between identity and Religious Education will now be dealt with again in greater detail. Is identity a useful guide in the planning and execution of religious learning processes throughout life? The German religious educator Henning Luther has answered this question with a categorical yes. For him, identity is not a fixable state, but rather a movement: "We do not have to find ourselves in order to live; we live in order to find ourselves" (Luther 1992, 151). In the emancipatory tradition of enlightenment, Luther interprets this movement as a process of leaving the age of minority.

Identity as a Liberating Concept

The liberating claim of the identity concept for guiding educational processes is derived from the issue of having to subjugate individuals to the rules of their environment, dominant traditions, and authorities. This concept of identity implies criticizing that which hinders people from attaining the level of dignity that they desire for their lives. From a theological perspective, it is humanity's image, molded after that of God's, which brings us to an understanding of our identity – an understanding whose goal is the liberation of subjectivity.

The subject-perspective means that teachers, including teachers of Christianity, have to put the individual person first. Only then, and only from the subject perspective, will the view be expanded to include society and its institutions. It is clear that without society, there is no identity. I will always only be *I* in a particular context. There is, however, a tension between the two dimensions of socialization a nd individuation, w hich, i n t he h istory of e ducation, o ften m eant putting socialization before individualization. The assumption is that when integrating the young people into the established, preexisting traditions and culture, the "becoming *I*" is automatically given. Today, we can no longer pit subject and society against each other. The question is how to conceive identity in such a way so as to combine the *autonomy of the individual* with the *integration in society* without making the integration have to rely on force.

Differentiation instead of security

For goal setting in education, this means not just defining identity through concepts such as unity, wholeness, and firmness, but also including the tears, fragmentation, and inconsistency of real life and using these experiences as a guide towards finding oneself. The point is that youth can feel betrayed when educators make them feel safe and supply the exact content for their search for an identity (Luther 1992, 158). Instead of a false (in his opinion) focus on security and positivism, Luther wants to keep an awareness of difference of opinion alive: it is especially in the negativity of existence, in the inconsistencies (aporiae), in the experience of finality (contingency), and in the mortality of all things living that a person's whole existence is turned to God. God is the critical level of judgment that questions all positive ideals and puts out the challenge to view the world in a different light. From an educational theory point of view, this means not speaking about God as the contents of learning, someone who legitimizes, stabilizes, confirms, or inflates life, but as someone who brings existence into question. In the first case, identity would be considered potentially finite and defined in its content; in the second case, identity would be *eo ipso* infinite with an open content. This does not mean opening the door to an educational irresponsibility. The form is the content. The goal is to develop the capacity

- to see the world as something "questionable,"
- to understand this question itself as the decisive *religious* question, and
- to interpret this question using the contents and symbols of a religious tradition.

Multiple Perspectiveness and Existential Depth

Compared to a one-dimensional self- and world-understanding, such a concept of religious learning aims for intellectual multiple perspectiveness and existential depth. Uncertainty points to uncertainty; it arouses religious questions. It is obvious that identity in this context cannot be positively defined as dedicated content; rather, it must be largely understood as a process and orientation for development, and it remains decidedly bound to the individual himself. A clear rejection of endogenous and material concepts is connected with such an under-
104

standing of identity, after which the identity of every person is already fully established so that education and cultivation completely and uniquely bring this construction to growth and fulfillment. Identity is mediated socio-culturally; it must be worked out in debate with the environment. In the end, the individual himself comes to terms with this argument over identity. This occurs in the writing of his story: at its root, identity has a narrative structure.

Questioning as a Religious Dimension

When one recognizes the questioning of the world and human existence as a problem, one is reflecting *religiously*. There are various strategies for smoothing over these questions (cf. Krauss 2000, 143-158). One could deny all inconsistencies, clutch onto a rigid worldview, suppress heterogeneity, call on ideologies of unity, reject opposition, and avoid plurality. What appears to be strength of character on the outside could be a desperate internal attempt to defend oneself against the threat of dissolution in a modern plural world. In Religious Education, we must not remain uncritical when attending to this need. The religious criticism by Marx and Freud is still a great challenge to this point. Religious Education can show in a positive way that it is *in line with* the Christian religion to strengthen the *I* through a questioning clash with the real world. Religious Education c an t each t he i ndividual h ow to d eal w ith d ifferent o ptions. I t c an show the paths of learning, get involved with real life, focus on the tension between desire and reality, and consider the options for bringing the desired world closer. Limits must be recognized in order to stretch and overcome them. Religious Education can show how people with faith have wrestled with such problems in the past. In the Christian tradition, this leads us to Abraham, but also to Esther and Jonah – and to Jesus. The Bible does, however, not just give us straight-forward models. Peter and Paul, Judas and Thomas – they all show us the role played by changes or doubts in life. Their experiences are available to us through stories. They may be used to inspire the telling of one's own story. Encouraging students to become the authors of their own religious biography is an important step on the way to religious adulthood and autonomy.

Conclusion

For the postmodern existence, there are no identities simply handed out for the taking. The possibility of identity diffusion is real, and it continues throughout life. The provocative question always comes back: "Who am I?" Identity becomes an infinite process. Later identity theories show that the search for a set and defined identity is a trap. Identity has a process structure to it and arises through the telling of one's own life. The fragments of life are placed in a framework: successful and unsuccessful decision-making and action, satisfying and unsatisfying social contacts, success and failure. Religious Education cannot offer solutions for the individual cases, but it is capable of passing on perspectives for viewing life. It can clarify that these are ancient questions, which have always faced humankind. It can show that the Bible has a wealth of stories about how people throughout history have connected these ancient questions with God. The narrative identity model opens up a new perspective for religious learning: seeing the openness of life as an adventure – the adventure of believing in one's own acceptance and then accepting others. The New Heaven and New Earth are no prevarication, but rather an invitation to walk down a path that even Religious Education can only show the mere outlines of.

Part III

Religious Education and the Plurality of Religions and Values

7

Religion, Religiousness, and Inter-religious Learning

Anyone who looks into religious educational technical literature regarding *inter-religious learning* gets the impression that it is a very popular term. Technical periodicals present catalogues of themes, corresponding anthologies, and monographs. How can the rapid ascent of the concept of inter-religious learning be explained? Is it simply a topic that is currently of heightened interest? What led to the increased attention in inter-religious learning?

Undoubtedly, in past decades the experience of pluralism became more intensive within the ranges of churches, theology, and Religious Education. Where pluralism occurs, the questions about the relationship between the plural appearances arise, and thus the question of the *inter*. The insight developed that pluralism is not only a cultural social development but also extends to sector religion. On the level of society (macro), one becomes conscious of the plurality of religion. On the level of religious institutions (meso), pluralism is assumed to be *ad extra* and *ad intra*. On the level the individual (micro), it is clearly evident that individual religiousness is no longer the mirror image of the religion of the churches but rather that there are many different personal religious styles. Certainly, pluralism on these three levels has not developed solely during the last few years. Nevertheless, within Religious Education increasing consciousness arose to take up pluralism as a constitutive concept in the formation of religious educational theory.

Inter-religious learning concentrates on the question of an educationally responsible association with diversity – the pluralism of religion and religiousness. Inter-religious learning is, above all, dialogical learning. *Inter* refers first to the encounter with large religions such as Islam, Judaism, Hinduism, and Buddhism. Pupils always approach other religions on the basis of their own personal religiousness. Many students are themselves, however, only partial members of their religion. If we speak of inter-religious learning, the *Inter* must include the diversity of their subjective religiousness. We want to understand inter-religious learning as an educational principle that provides insight into religion through dialogue (cf. Griffith 2001).

The argument in this chapter runs as follows: we first turn to the increasing awareness of pluralism in the worldview. This pluralism places pressure on religious teaching in general and results in portions of public opinion favoring multi-religious instruction. We explore the potential for reform of inter-religious learning and the future of religious instruction. Second, it is shown with respect to systematic-theological considerations and from a denominational point of view that not only is an inter-religious dialogical model of theology possible, it is necessary. The third part goes on to discuss principles of inter-religious learning. The focal point of the discussion is the *inter*. In order to understand the differences between religious instructions, one must be able to see the issue from differing perspectives. Inter-religious learning is, therefore, the process of learning to view issues from the perspective of other religions and forms of religiousness. The fourth part consists of some open questions that require further research.

Pluralism in Worldviews and Inter-religious Learning

It is undisputed that at present, we are once again in a period during which religious teaching at schools is under review. Social, political, and cultural changes place Religious Education under pressure. Rarely, however, does the question focus on whether or not there should be religious teaching in schools. Religion is much less often disputed than it may appear. Rather, the discussion centers on the question of whether Religious Education is to only inform about religion, or whether it may bring students into a close relationship with a certain religion. First, let us explore the starting point.

Religious Individualization: Which Belief, Which Religion?

Pluralism in worldviews is not only a social macro-phenomenon. In Germany, as well as in many other Western countries, there is an increased awareness of the difference between what church religion is on the one side and what religion can be on the other. Even if one focuses strictly on the difference between religion and church-established Christianity in western countries, the churches alone are rarely regarded as responsible for religion. Empirical findings show that the agreement with church-led forms of religion is decreasing, but to a different extent than the overall interest in religion.

This trend is significant for the future of Religious Education. Religious Education in Germany was, until 1968, the result of a situation that saw the two major churches maintain an unchallenged religious monopoly from the time of the Reformation. Even for religious sociologists of the time, religion outside the churches was not an issue. Everything that appeared to be "living religion" was mediated by the churches. In the past two decades, one could notice the emergence of a different view of religion, Christianity, and faith (see chapter 4). Today, findings make clear the level to which the differentiation between institutional Christianity and personal religiousness has reached. This complicates (with regional differences) the conventional task of religious educators of continuing the spread of the Christian faith. The conception of a Religious Education as "church in the school" can no longer be used as a guide. Any attempt to attach catechistic expectations to religious teaching is hopeless. This is how Religious Education, even from its clientele, is under developmental compulsion.

Multi-religious Instruction?

In view of this background, strong voices have spoken out calling for a structural reform of Religious Education: it may make one long overdue adjustment, free itself from a single religion, establish itself multi-religiously, and devote equal attention to all religious traditions, having no desire to pursue any one religion. Supporters of guided religious instruction could then use the decrease of individual religiousness for their arguments. A purely more informative (multi-religious) Religious Education for all students would solve some problems.

In public discourse, the question is not *if* religion should be taught in schools, but rather *how*. Answers are often provided by the experiences of other countries. England in particular is often referred to as an example of multi-religious instruction. Nipkow (1998, 448-494) and Meyer (1999, 97-263) show in their detailed analyses of the British situation that after years of strong endorsement of a religious beginning ("multi-faith-approach"), the current situation is more differentiated. The focus of Religious Education on the assuming, familiarizing, describing, and arranging of structures, contents, rituals, and social forms of religion, i.e. an instruction *about religion*, is what makes it subject to criticism. It is first asked whether the secular worldview, which appoints itself an ideologically free identity, is not itself an ideology. Their ideological character consists of the following:

- first, showing that religion provides only a relative claim of truth;
- second, attributing to the religion, with regard to education, only the instrumental character while dismissing the experiences of students; and
- third, erroneously assuming that the preoccupation with religion will have no consequences on the individual view of life.

In view of this criticism, an alternative is formulated, which conceives Religious Education as being *from within religion*. Thus, what is meant by instruction is effectively a similar structural approach to vitally important questions by religion on an anthropological basis. It is enlightening that even after many years of experience with multi-religious instruction in a fellow Western country, the question of whether the existential dimension of Religious Education should be reviewed remains.

Reform Potential of Inter-religious Learning

In light of the findings of religious studies that show a crisis, reforms appear both necessary and correct. The goal of reforms is for a more dialogically oriented religious instruction model – dialogue with an inter-religious learning accent. Who and what are the partners in this dialogue? My interpretation is the following:

- church represented Christianity,
- non-Christian religions, and
- the pupils themselves.

The dialogue is first focused on the students in order to give them the experience to spot an anthropological reference of transcendence so that they will not find these questions redundant. This dialogical attitude focuses second on church-represented Christianity because it is no longer the case that students are religiously socialized. Therefore, the Christian religion must be further explored. W hile e xploring a religion a ims t o r eveal w hat p urpose i t s erves a nd how it helps, special meaning is attached to the illumination of the anthropological depth of Christianity. The dialogue is directed finally to the non-Christian religions because they coincide with inter-cultural comparison and explain how non-Christians give their life depth and direction, how they create a realm of spirituality, how they worship, and what the personal consequences of their acts and beliefs are. It thus concerns the many meanings of religion. The question of being, as the council decree formulates in *Nostra Aetate* (Vatican II), is explained in the religions of the world – a world full of meaning, which is to be opened up to the students. Empirical findings show that students are undeniably interested in religion and that their interest focuses on religion in the plural.

Religion in the plural requires some clarification. Religions represent potentially competing offers of s alvation; therefore, information must be given on how the competing requirements for truth are handled and weighted. If inter-religious learning is understood as a contribution to the advancement of existing Religious Education, then questions should be clarified theologically, as it is the primary reference discipline.

Dialogical Theology

With respect to the relationship between Christianity and non-Christian religions, theological discussion has experienced substantial modifications since the

1970s. Even if it concerns only systematic-theological contributions, the beginning of dialogical theology concerning the conceptualization and legitimization of inter-religious learning is very important.

From Exclusiveness to Inclusiveness

One crucial modification was the acknowledgement by the Catholic Church that the Catholic Church was not the only way to salvation and that salvation might be possible *in* other religions but not *through* them. Whether the newest Roman assertion, *Dominus Iesus*, actually goes a step in the other direction is not discussed here in detail. Until the Second Vatican Council, the view of the Catholic Church was that the only salvation was in Christ. The harshness of this attitude against other religions was what actually broke up the council, so the inclusive position of the Council actually made them exclusive in stance, but efforts were made to adopt rules of tolerance. Karl Rahner (1983) expanded on the inclusive understanding by arguing that authentic experiences with God are possible not *through* other religions, but *within* them. A person who looks for God in other religions will find him. The other religions, however, do not offer a path to salvation. As far as Rahner was concerned, the fact that Jesus was sent to us by God to save humankind reveals that there is no other way to salvation. His approach is reflected in particular in the Council decrees *Nostra aetate*, *Dignitatis humanae*, and *Ad gentes*.

Theology of the Religions

In the 1980s, the question was increasingly asked whether the inclusive position represents a terminal point in theological thinking or whether it offers a perspective that not only legitimizes the removal of borders but also makes this the desirable position. Paul Knitter makes religious pluralism the focal point of his considerations and stresses the need for theology to shift away from a Christocentric position to one emphasizing a theocentric position. Only in this way can the view become free for a new (theological) determination of religious pluralism (cf. Knitter 1985). For Knitter, the theological legitimization, without being able to explain it in detail here, is the core message of the realm of God (Luke 11:20; 17:21). Jesus, in both his mission and his person, is deeply aligned with God; but Jesus also plays a special role, an emphasized eschatological function in the realm of God. The turn towards Christ first arose during the development of the texts of the New Testament. The New Testament makes the preacher into the one being preached to, and even the Christocentric Paul differentiates clearly between Christocentrism and theocentrism (1 Cor. 3:23). With this new view, in Knitter's opinion, Christianity would have the chance to abandon some of the attributes impeding dialog, such as exclusive, final, absolute, and plan, without becoming relativist. Christ and Christianity would not lose their uniqueness, but may, however, lose their claim to absoluteness. Christians may admit and testify that Christ is unique, but they do not need to assume that this uniqueness must be understood as exclusiveness.

Relational Understanding of Truth

Knitter's position, like that of some remaining theologians supporting pluralism, caused both agreement and contradiction. One effect is undeniable: these new theological directions introduced a new dynamic to theology. With regard to epistemological thinking, they introduced a modification to absolutist understanding of truth, which had thus far operated under concepts of "either/or." That which was once determined as "true" must always remain true. Theologians such as Swidler (1992) think truth to be more relational and conform collectively to the theoretical awareness of scientific development. Truth cannot be achieved through the exclusion of other perspectives; rather we are in pursuit of truth, which can only be achieved through a connection of all perspectives. Each view represents only a fragment. Each truth has its place in life, which applies to a specific time. The historical understanding can be only limitedly transferred to other times as our knowledge and understanding increase with the passage of time. Second, truths target practice and action, such that they are always oriented to the speaker. Third, they are bound to a location, with and/or from which they must be interpreted. Fourth, they are fragmented, which results from the limitation of language, a tool incapable of speaking of absoluteness. Fifth, the truth contains only interpreted knowledge and cannot be an absolute understanding of true meaning. Finally, they have a dimension of dialogue, as truth is not simply received; it is produced. Applying relational theory to truth does not qualify truth; rather, it considers the constitutional conditions, providing us with a standard to which we set human truth.

Religious Learning as Dialogical Learning

The summarized topics discussed here offer a relevant theological legitimization for a religious educational approach to inter-religious learning. Since theologians replaced ideas of superiority with ideas of pluralism, Religious Education can focus on developing communication between religions, thereby increasing mutual understanding and development of mutual tolerance in order to overcome the old apology. An understanding based on dynamic relational truth promotes cooperation with other religions – to find God together. The religious search has a dialogical dimension, i.e. only together will all religions come closer to discovering the truth of God. The process of finding God is not simply the learning of doctrine; that would be the learning of only the final *product*. The exploration of religion is a *process*, involving the meeting and swapping of perspectives, which leads to a general progression in understanding. In each case, the general theological debate over questions of inter-religious learning inspired a new beginning in the study of religion, which offered religious teaching a new example of how pluralism could be achieved through dialogue. Inter-

114

religious learning presents pluralism in a way so as not to neutralize differences between religions. The religions and their differing claims of truth are not made equal; rather they are the subject of study. Therefore, there is fundamental value in learning the differences. To uncover further differences and to be able to deal with these differences require the ability to change perspectives. These two aspects are discussed in further detail in the following section.

Treatment of Differences and Changing of Perspectives

Pluralism has expanded and become more radical. Oneness is no longer considered antagonistic to multiplicity; rather it is part of it. This insight is often found to be a contribution to theology. With regard to religion, this implies that one is not compelled by the majority, which is to simply say that religions should not work alone, but rather together. If this is agreed upon, then the question arises if there is any claim to singularity at all (see chapter 2). The answer cannot be positive, as an anything goes attitude would amount to a very cynical view of the history of civilization. When one speaks of the single within the many, the emphasis is placed on multiplicity, but one cannot overlook the relationship between the two without putting the idea of multiplicity into danger. Culture and religion appear to us today in the plural sense, and the deeper we look, the richer the diversity, which at the same time complicates the question of how we are, in education, to deal with divergent positions. To be able to deal with life within pluralism, students must acquire the abilities to understand conflicting currents, to comprehend the basis of differing positions, to form their own judgments, and to communicate their opinions. The memorandum "Identity and Understanding" (Identität und Verständigung) of the Lutheran Church in Germany explains in this with regard to ecumenical discussion:

> The challenge of cultural communication and education, with respect to the worldwide view of religious pluralism, is this: in the midst of all the differences, to strengthen the common bonds in an attempt to work through the differences, not overlook them (1994, 65).

The common characteristic does not overshadow the difference, nor does the difference overshadow the common bond. The study of religion is, therefore, concentrated on the relationship between the two.

The Perception and Treatment of Difference

Years ago, Helmut Peukert had already designated *difference* as the central term in education theory.

> For discussion to occur, one must include all unique experiences and decisions, individual history and distinctive identity of both parties, then blend the differing perspectives together in order to reach a

common understanding of differences and similarities with which both parties can work together. Education, as the ability to reach a higher level where one can understand and appreciate others, is attainable only upon consciousness and concession of difference (Peukert 1984, 134).

Peukert founds his proposition, in which he sites communication itself as the deciding medium of communication theory, on comprehending difference – and exceeding it. Communication is based on the possibility of achieving a consensus (i.e. agreement): not to go beyond difference, but to work within it. This communicational framework developed by Peukert corresponds well with the prerequisites of inter-religious learning.

Before one quickly and easily swears by the idea of unity, one must first affirm, at least in principle, the possibility of difference. Despite the position of post-modernists, i.e. that the idea of oneness has disappeared, one must also appreciate the positions that human communication often involves both uniqueness and difference and that this situation can and does occur. Without any sense of unity in a normative perspective, upbringing and education are as inconceivable as a meaningful c oexistence. With r egard to t heology, Paul Knitter s tated t hat w e have, therefore, in our contemporary and plural world the feeling that if a single religion cannot exist, then several religions cannot exist (Knitter 1985). On the one hand, multiplicity is irrevocable. On the other hand, the individual claims of each religion demand representation. There appears to be the need for a concept that focuses on diversity instead of avoiding or downplaying its importance.

In a p lural a nd m ulti-cultural s ociety, d istinctiveness i s n ot something t hat is given; it is produced. Distinctiveness must be found within multiplicity. This finding appears much stronger in process-oriented learning processes as opposed to product-oriented learning processes. Finding distinctiveness means to engage oneself in dialogue – with oneself and with others. Aspects of interaction and communication thereby stress appearance rather than an accumulation of knowledge. Interactionist concepts of identity have made this abundantly clear. Identity is not, therefore, simply the discovery of the internal core, which is based in the person and unfolds in the regular cycle of life, but it rather results from the dispute between expected roles and self-image (cf. Mead 1934). Paul Ricoeur speaks of *Idem* and *Ipse* identity (cf. Streib 1994). *Idem* means the identity line, which is appropriately regarded as the internal core and which highlights the moment of continuity (sameness) through time as the central theme. *Ipse* stresses the reflecting character of the identity directly because of temporality. The state of *Ipse* (selfhood) exists within diachronic dimensions in time and not independently. It depends on the many possibilities of identity. For Ricoeur, t he n arrative self produces the connection, m eaning that t he subject tells itself its history. This is how the synchronous and diachronic aspects are arranged. Hence, religious identity is a process of inner- and inter-subjective dialogue. From an educational perspective, this process structure provides the opportunity to learn about the conflict with difference, achieve further insight into the conflict, and understand the process as a contribution to identity formation.

The notes on conception of identity refer to the second point, which says that singularity simply can no longer exist or be produced in a pluralistic, multicultural society without consideration of the respective others. Cultural identity must take a detour over or around the others. This is why an anthropological perspective can be so insightful, especially if it orientates itself specifically on the subjective: it involves the understanding of others and allowing others to live as they wish, approaching with a moderate attitude. The idea is not to try to make everything equal or to integrate all into one, but rather to recognize and understand the dimensions of multiplicity and then ask the question of which position has been earned and is favored by all. Such questions are concrete, for example, when we speak of the differences between Islam, Judaism, and Christianity with respect to the equality of women, of the differences between Christianity and Hinduism with respect to the understanding of the relationship between God, creation, and humanity, of questions of the legitimacy of violence in Islam, Judaism, and Christianity, etc. All other thoughts aside, the fact remains that the discovery of truth is much more likely to occur with the consideration of many perspectives rather than one; consequently, dialogue can reveal whether and which truths each perspective has to offer the others and which, if such is the case, can be discarded. Not only are the agreements productive, but also, and perhaps more so, are the confrontations. These confrontations for convention may start as beliefs with alternatives, but they usually evolve into argumentative opinions.

It should be noted that in inter-religious learning, the other one is not simply the non-Christian perspective that sits opposite the Christian, as if the religions are seen as a homogeneous entity. Studies on the religiousness of students reveal that the classroom situation itself is a plural environment, posing a significant obstacle to the possibility of instruction under a Christian church-sponsored model (cf. Ziebertz 1993). Already the proportion of those who are believers to varying degrees fill the position of others and serve a purpose in the development of personal religious identity. The treatment of difference covers at least these two topics: the difference between individuals within a Christian context and the difference between the religions of the world.

Experience with difference and the association with different positions and perspectives from the view of those who study education reveals problems. Difference always seems to include incidents of competition and conflict. For unstable students, this can be threatening. This can result in hostile attitudes between students. This explains why inter-religious and inter-cultural curricula attempt to diffuse differences and favor a harmonic model, concentrating on similarities and neutralizing contrasts. The recognition of difference can serve as a testing ground through which to practice tolerance. Tolerance is not difficult to achieve if agreement between parties exists. It is when agreement fails that tolerance is difficult to achieve, but this is when it is needed most. The conflict is the problem, not the agreement. Educational models that seek to help children and youth to develop the ability to deal with the competition of world and life concepts should make diversity their central theme. Children and young people do not need protection from what they experience on a daily basis. Through learning in and with difference, they are well prepared to deal with pluralism. Nonetheless, the development of a religious understanding of difference is often a much more complicated task. Where religion is considered a private matter, it is set apart by itself.

In order to discuss difference in an educational sense, an adequate discourse model is required. Schlüter (1994) advocates a set of discourse ethics that free communication from the obligation of achieving universal consensus or total heterogeneity. Communication should neither subliminally attribute variety to individuality, nor should it be inconsequential because everything applies. The goal of communication is to achieve agreement on partial aspects and to be able to live with a temporal set of arrangements. Also of note are the dynamics of change, which will not allow the freezing of alternative points of view. It is the method of communication that can lead to coherence. Communication in this regard is a final norm or standard from which we cannot extract ourselves. Successful communication requires one precondition: the ability to change perspectives.

The Changing of Perspectives

In religious teaching in the past, the discussion of religions usually focused on world religions. The Christian perspective formed the basis from which to view other religions. This did not exclude a demonstration of how they understood themselves. The comparative standard always remained the *I*-perspective of Christianity. Only gradually in didactic circles was the idea of mutual enrichment introduced. Dialogue, in the sense of a swapping of perspectives between the *I* and the *You*, was rarely realized; the *I*-perspective dominated. This approach is called *mono-religious* (cf. Ziebertz/van der Ven 1996). The direct alternative is a *multi-religious* concept. It is built around the *It*-perspective. *It*-perspective means the taking of a widely neutral viewpoint and viewing the religions from the outside. It frees itself of any religious or theological personality and views all religions from a removed, objective position. Meeting with religion is not a function. Thus, this multi-religious approach reduces the importance of a specific religion and introduces a new dimension: bringing all religions to the same questions: "How do I act in such a way as to include all religions?" "Which of the transcendental stances offered by the many religions is mine?" Furthermore, an objective *It*-perspective is maintained without the possibility of adopting one such position, unless it is sufficiently substantiated. In order to justify taking such a position, one would have to show how situation- and context-free discussion is possible. The contemporary constructivism debate makes this topic a particularly hostile one. In light of this, inter-religious learning seeks to find a way to expand the *I*-perspective to include the *You*-perspective and develop a mutual reference. With respect to the processing of differences, the ability to change perspectives is a crucial principle of inter-religious learning.

When one speaks of perspective swapping in the context of learning processes, one speaks primarily about the acquisition of a twofold ability: first, to understand one's own religion from that perspective and the perspective of others; and second, to understand the other religion from the perspective of someone of that religion and from an outside perspective. This takes time. It is not in any way similar to a mathematical formula that all of a sudden just clicks and makes sense. Instead, understanding is more structured in the form of interpretative circles, forming a spiral that through default leads to the object. This object can be another text or another person – thus, a direct or indirect meeting.

The indirect goal is the *achievement of understanding*: indirectly because the open-endedness of the spiral of understanding cannot be defined like a product. The direct goal is the *process of understanding*: thus, the constant changing of perspectives. The changing of perspectives presupposes, among other things, that the *I*-perspective exists, i.e. that the individual can feel connected with one religion (more or less) and/or that he/she can relate things to his/her own religiousness. The development of an *I*-perspective is undoubtedly a base function of instruction and an *element* of inter-religious learning.

Inter-religious learning is focused on mutual understanding, tolerance, and respect. It also includes self-reflection and self-criticism (cf. Ziebertz/van der Ven, 1995). Religions do not meet in a static state but as social forms and individuals with a concrete history. No religion is idle or uniform, but rather plural and dynamic. Self-reflection and self-criticism are necessary because religions are historical creations, conceived in specific time periods, which, when reviewed, can be worthy of criticism. Criticism involves distance – quite an ambivalent undertaking. That which might be interpreted from a mono-religious perspective as a danger because it can entail the change of religious confessions or even a decision against faith could, on the other hand, set the conditions for the process of mutual understanding, which Dunne (1965) and Knitter (1985) described as *passing over*. This passing over makes inter-religious learning a more provocative experiment – not only for the understanding of other traditions, but also for the deeper insight into one's own religious tradition. The religiousness of the postmodern period will likely always imply inter-religiousness and will likely bring inter-religious learning into the spotlight in the study o f religion. F or practical i nter-religious l earning, a n i ncrease in the number of lectures on the subject instead of a limitation of available courses should occur.

Inter-religious Learning as an Integration of Perspectives

Empirical studies show that inter-religious learning is not simply a process of learning about mono-religious and multi-religious approaches, but rather involves a transformation (Ziebertz 1993; Sterkens, 2001). Inter-religious learning integrates the *I*-position and the *It*-position of the respective approaches. It does not allow the two positions to stand on their own and instead places the *I* and *It* into a connection through educational discussion. Learning is executed by working through the relationship between *I* and *It*. Something special about inter-religious learning is that the existential meaning of the occupation with religion (*I*-position) is not neutralized, but rather it is understood as a precondition. Inter-religious learning contributes to the formation of the *I*-perspective. Equally important is the effort devoted to increasing the understanding of the *It*-perspective. Thus, the criticism alleging an exclusionary mono-religious perspective that does not take into account the alternatives can be dismissed. In the sense of understanding education, inter-religious learning does not simply reduce learning into an accumulation of knowledge over different religions but expands it into the formation of a subjective reference to all religions. Learning through the changing of perspectives describes the process of self-formation by switching back and forth from inside to outside.

Open Questions

This chapter asked some questions about the future of Religious Education under t he c onditions o f a p lural society a ccording t o w orldview. The r eflection over what meaning inter-religious learning had in this context touches empirical, conceptual, and normative levels and inevitably leaves some questions open. Some of these questions will now be addressed.

Empirically, the question is whether the occupation with diversity might hinder the development of personal identity if it is introduced too early or is promoted without a proper introduction and explanation. Proponents of the first position believe that it is important for the individual to have an opportunity to develop a Christian religious identity before exploring other beliefs. Others feel that individual identity corresponds with nature and exists in a comparative state with others. In this case, exploring other beliefs can even contribute to the development of a personal identity. How religious identity development actually functions is something requiring further research.

Conceptually, discussion centered on the society sketch, which asked the question of whether the present religious educational structure would improve if it concentrated more on dialogue. Inter-religious learning was cited as one possibility for dialogical learning. The suggestion is to transfer inter-religious learning not only as a section within the framework of lectures but as the curriculum principle; however, the problem is that it does not satisfy all requirements and leaves some aspects of conceptual development unfulfilled. This applies equally to intercultural education.

From the didactical perspective, there is a clarifying requirement of what a more dialogical religious education can achieve. What does it mean to journey with students in search of some sort of transcendental reference (cf. Groome 1980)? Is it necessary to increasingly ask questions and explore Christianity because appropriate social experiences are missing? What is it called when one includes all of the religions of the world in dialogue? How can these different levels be connected to awaken the question of God, to initiate an understanding for the reality dimension of faith, and to facilitate personal decision-making?

Fourth, one must ask whether the focus on difference and the ability to change perspectives are adequate for the establishment of dialogical inter-religious learning. Under which prerequisites does the handling of differences work in an unsettling manner? Under which conditions does it contribute to self-consciousness and help bring clarity? On the other hand, what would conceptually be missing from teaching if, for example, in view of religion, emphasis was placed on things in common? Is the learning of perspective-swapping sufficient in order to avoid isolation in one position and to allow instead one to work through diversity? Is the changing of perspectives only possible in specific age and developmental stages, and is it at all possible to control how it is learned?

Finally, one cannot overlook the problems that fall into a normative category. To conceive of Religious Education under the conditions of pluralism, one cannot escape the questions of whether and how instruction should and can achieve the existential depth of that represented by the Christian churches. The goal of religious learning in schools must consider its audience. If it is to be successful in the future, it must reposition itself to receive the students being taught more effectively. Clarification is expected from dialogical inter-religious instruction. Theological designs on inter-religious dialogue affirm that the main concern is the common search for reality over the empirically findable reality: for the transcendental, for the Ultimate, for God! It must be considered normatively whether Religious Education, if it gives this question up, is not giving itself up; however, a normative approach will not help to explain how to find the road that leads to this goal. For those answers, one must turn to conceptual and empirical explanations.

8

Teaching Ethics in a Plurality of Values

When students are taught ethics, they are learning about values and norms. The content of ethics is made up of the values held by the subject, the churches, and society. The goal of teaching ethics is to pass on the capacity to carry on a practical discourse on values and to answer responsibly those questions that demand a good sense of judgment: What must I do? What should we do? What is right? What is desirable and realistic for others and for myself? These questions are not limited to a specific school course such as ethics, but are also essential components of Religious Education. Christians use their ethical judgment and common sense just like every one else, but they do it within the scope of biblical Christian tradition. The challenge to ethical learning processes within Religious Education is to help students develop and base their ethical sense of judgment and values in light of the Christian message. This, in turn, takes place within a plurality of values and norms. Four models (value transfer, value clarification, value development, and value communication) will be tested on the way they treat value plurality and on their specific contribution to the teaching of ethics.

What makes the teaching of ethics so difficult?

Those who deal with youth in schools are confronted by a myriad of expectations, worldviews, and forms of interpretation. They have to respond not only to students' interests, which originate in a variety of backgrounds, but also those of parents and the school, as well as those of the administration. It is, furthermore, highly unlikely that a single one of these groupings could be said to be homogenous, not even the teachers themselves. These groups are not always going to get along in a harmonious way; conflicting expectations, interests, and values are bound to come up. In this way, the teaching of ethics mirrors the plurality of attitudes and values that make up our society today, including all its conflicts and opportunities.

Not just religion itself but also specific churches, such as the Roman Catholic Church, for example, is affected by modern plurality. Although the Second Vatican Council excluded questions of faith and morality from the worldly autonomy, there are usually several answers given when a Christian asks how he or she is to behave in a certain situation. Even though church teachings offer fairly uniform answers, theology has become all the more pluralistic in its responses to the Christian core concepts. Among the faithful, there are varieties of attitudes that are only slightly different from the plurality that we see in society.

Plurality is a social fact that perfuses the educational practice. It cannot be deliberately avoided, nor is it realistic to view the teaching environment as a sanctified microcosmos, separate from the social connections that the students have. In the modern differentiated world of media, plurality is a factor that education must take into account. This plurality does not just open up positive opportunities, such as experiencing individuality and freedom; it can also raise insecurities and problems of orientation. The question of *which* values and structures of meaning should be taught and *how* they are to be taught is a topic that requires careful consideration.

The c onsequence o f p lurality i s t hat e mbracing c ertain v iews a nd v alues t hat deserve to be passed on means excluding others. Therefore, it will be expected that this choice can be justified. Teachers are seeing that just referring to the authority of a church when passing the material on to students is insufficient and that when this material is discussed, a single complex usually turns out to suggest not one but several answers. Just calling this dilemma the crisis of passing on values would be too one-sided, especially if this simply refers to interruptions in the teaching process or a negative spiritual or cultural environment. In the practice of Religious Education, the very legitimacy of the imparted values is often up for discussion. This is especially the case when the question of which values and norms are worth being passed on arises. Religious educators are called on to deal with a multitude of knowledge, experience, attitudes, and demands on the part of the students, a challenge that cannot be properly met with the traditional interpretation of passing on values. Many now realize that neither rigidity nor relativity is a good socio-educational solution to the problem, at least not in the end (cf. Hall 1979, 4-20). Whatever the solution is, it has to be comprehensive, teachable, and able to stand up to critique. Young people are demanding to revise and review more than just one specific concept of values. This capacity for critical review is something that is expected of them in many other areas of everyday life anyway.

Religious Education has to do its part in helping to develop this capacity. This is particularly true in view of the fact that the learning of ethics is *intentional* learning, i.e. intentionally planned. It is different from *incidental* learning, by which we mean the processes of internalization and imitation that every child goes through from the day he or she is born. The child does not ask what it is taking over, or what is patterning its life; it simply builds up the worldview that it encounters within its family and peer group's socialization. This form of moral socialization is usually not initiated or accompanied by a reflective educational attitude on the part of an adult – it simply happens coincidentally and independently. Intentional ethical teaching is a planned educational process that explicitly brings up values and norms. The intentional facet will be the primary topic of this chapter. Obviously, incidentally gathered values and norms also play an important role in class; students bring their own values with them and are not blank slates. Therefore, the intentional education of values may find certain incidentally acquired values to be either positive or negative (cf. Moran 1989).

The teaching of ethics should help the students in orienting themselves, but it cannot become a process of indoctrination. The plurality of society must be respected; students should not be pushed in one direction or another. The goal of Religious Education, however, remains the imparting of material such as the teachings of a church; this includes both evocative (responsive) and absolute content. Some particularly challenging issues that will come up are taking sides and freedom of choice, orientation and plurality, and rigidity and neglect.

It sometimes appears that the teaching of ethics is a particularly problematic task in our modern society. The plurality of values and norms appears to be the biggest problem. Conservative authors are of the opinion that plurality is the cause of the crisis in which the teaching of ethics is caught. It is easy to see why: if a single unified value conviction is missing in society, then the ethics being taught cannot steer in any one direction without being challenged by the youth. It makes no sense, however, to start blaming the unavoidable fact of plurality, nor can we conscionably stop teaching ethics in school. The issue here is how to see the problem as a challenge and find the solutions to overcome it.

The Plurality of Values and Norms: Problem and Challenge

The values of today's youth are constantly discussed and subjected to a lot of debate and criticism. At the same time, we must consider the truism that young people's attitudes simply mirror the society in which they grow up. In order to develop processes of ethical learning, we must gain an insight into the values and orientation of youth, as well as the dynamics of the values offered by our society.

The Youth's Orientation of Values

An empirical study was carried out in which students were asked to respond to a variety of value statements (see Table 1). The results reveal that the values that clearly dominate in the minds of the youth are those highlighting personal freedom, supporting a certain degree of hedonism (including a positive view of sexuality), and emphasizing a eudemonism that puts personal happiness in the foreground. As the overview shows, these values are considered especially important by more than 90% of the students. Values that highlight social issues come in second; these include helping those in need, being committed to relationships (marital and familial), and contributing to society. These secondary values also include "making lots of money." The third place is taken up by a mixture of different values, such as getting involved in the making of a just and fair world, climbing the career ladder ("having a high position") – as well as values denoting religion, which, coincidentally, come in last. "Having a faith," which might also mean "having something to believe in") is something 56% of the respondents found important. In those values, however, where the word *God* appears, the approval sinks below 50%.

Table 1: *To which values do young people aspire?*			
(N=723; Responses in percent)			
	not important	important	very important
being free and independent	0.0	4.0	96.0
doing and being able to do what you want	0.5	4.5	95.0
enjoying life	1.0	4.0	95.0
experiencing sexuality	1.0	6.0	93.0
being balanced and in harmony with yourself	1.0	9.0	90.0
earning a lot of money	6.0	18.0	76.0
being a good person	6.0	20.0	74.0
helping those in need	8.0	23.0	69.0
enjoying quiet moments	9.0	25.0	66.0
marrying and having a happy marriage	10.0	23.0	66.0
making a contribution to human society	7.5	29.0	63.5
having children	11.0	31.0	58.0
promoting greater equality in society	11.0	32.0	57.0
obtaining a high position in society	10.5	34.0	55.5
having faith	14.0	30.0	56.0
wanting God to lead my life	27.5	28.0	44.5
trusting in God	26.5	30.0	43.5
(Source: Ziebertz et al. 2003)			

Furthermore, there is a connection between the religiousness of a respondent and the orientation of his or her values (cf. Ziebertz/Schnider 2000). Young people who describe themselves as religious are significantly more positive towards social and family values, as well as values stressing the pursuit of happiness. At the same time, they are significantly more negative towards those values directed at material things and personal autonomy in comparison to those who described themselves as not religious. This connection does not, however, change the hierarchy of the values. Freedom and autonomy are right at the top, even for religious youth. Their value profile corresponds to the general hierarchy of values, though it takes a slightly less extreme form. How should these results be evaluated? Are these subcultural value orientations, or do they accurately reflect the patterns we find in society at large?

Trends and Changes in Values

Value orientations demonstrate convictions that influence human action and interaction over longer periods of time and regulate life in society and at home. Although they do not change from day to day, they are by no means permanent. Changes in values are popular topics of research. The result has produced a confirmation of the sociologist Helmut Klages's theories: orientation revolving around duty and order values has diminished, while the values emphasizing personal development have gained in popularity (cf. Klages 1988).

Klages explains this change with a transition from a nomocentric understanding of oneself and one's world to an autocentric understanding. A nomocentric view of oneself and the world is characterized by a sense of not only being dependent on one's environment, but also being indebted to it. In this sense, a person is reliant on his or her environment because it would be impossible to master one's own life without it. The self-esteem is established through belonging, membership, and duty. An autocentric view of self and world is based on the capacities held by oneself – the individual rationality, the individual sense of judgment, the individual sense of worth, and the need for personal realization. This latter concept is often described with terms like *spontaneity*, *impartiality*, *directness*, *self-realization*, *searching*, *taking advantage of alternatives*, and *expectation of resonance*. The autocentric view of self and world defines itself as independent from the social environment or, at the very least, as having a right to such an independence (Klages 1988, 64 et seq.).

Orientation of Values and Change in Values

When comparing a change in values with the empirical survey results described above, then K lages's theory certainly seems to offer a plausible explanation. Values such as freedom and autonomy contain an orientation of self-realization and could be seen as a sign of an autocentric worldview in which everything revolves around the subject itself. On the other hand, Klages speaks of a balance between values of duty and values of self-realization – today we have to ask whether this balance has already been tipped in favor of the latter.

The analysis of the change in values demonstrates a trend towards values centered on the individual. On the other hand, these values do not correspond to a negative change in social values; rather, they usually correspond to each other, though it may be assumed that the balance can tend to go in one direction or the other in individual cases. What is particularly remarkable is the secondary importance attributed to values connected to religion. This conclusion, however, may not be interpreted as a sign of anti-religious attitudes. The Christian religion also embraces the search for personal happiness and social harmony. Christian ideas are often explicitly referred to within such values.

Besides the content of the values, there is another important point to be made here. The increased freedom of choice based on an autocentric worldview means an increased importance of the individual in deciding for or against certain values. No matter how this is judged, it is undeniable that authority and tradition have lost the privilege of selecting values for the individual person. This fact cannot be ignored when creating a plan for teaching ethics in school. It raises the question of how we can help young people develop their own sense of judgment.

Models for Teaching Ethics

In the following section, four models for introducing and teaching values and norms will be presented (cf. Van der Ven 1985; Ziebertz 1990; 1991; 1992).

Value Transfer

In predominantly homogenous societies, there was a clear sense of the true, lasting, and binding values, values that left no doubt that they needed to be passed on to the next generation. These values were in and of themselves, tried and true. Morality education in school – much like at home – tried to pass on the values that were most common in society. Passing on values in a society of pluralistic values inevitably means picking up values and norms that are preferred by a particular social group. This could mean preserving values that were important in the past, but it could also refer to those values that are seen as a liberation from tradition. Whatever values are given preference, the formal procedure is similar. The aim is to shape the attitudes of the young people and influence their action and decision-making. The central issue is the desire to pass on a certain system of values. The goal of this learning process is quasi built into the values that are being visualized. This process assumes that teachers make a conscious choice out of the various values that are available. This also means that it is clear right from the start which attitudes are to be formed in the students. In other words, a specifically selected choice of values and norms is considered essential; passing on the latter to young people is then legitimated by the goal connected to these values, i.e. the preservation or criticism of tradition. This process can be found on two levels in a church's education of morality: first, in the choice of *Christian* values that stand in opposition to those of the *profane* world, and second, in the choice of *specific* Christian values that stand

128

in opposition to *other specific* Christian values within the *specific* church *itself*. The concept of value transfer quite simply does not differentiate between goals and content.

Value transfer can have a cognitive, emotional, or motivational character. In the *cognitive* character, the main concern is the processing of information, i.e. the acquisition of knowledge and the development of thought. The students' cognitive structure is to be formed through the familiarization, reproduction, and classification of values. The *emotional* character views the learning of values and norms as a process of internalization. Values are thus integrated and made into a personal declaration. In those cases where the emotional character is stressed, the cognitive focus appears as an intellectualization of the morality education. The emotional alternative has a preference for learning through idols, virtues, a nd (shared) ideals. T he *m otivational* c haracter a ims t o i nfluence the direction taken by the young person's own desire and will. This is often connected to the creation of specific attitudes and demeanor. Value transfer, then, is characterized by steering the learning process, i.e. the content of the intended motivation and the attitude adopted by the young person are predetermined through the choice made by his or her teacher. The goal of value transfer can be shortly s ummarized a s f ollows: Y *oung p eople a re t o a dopt t hose v alues a nd norms that have been intentionally pre-selected by his or her teacher out of a range of possible alternatives. These are values that the teacher has found best with r egard t o t eaching a c ertain v alue o rientation for g uiding future a ction and decision-making.*

Value Clarification

The concept of value clarification is a direct alternative to the model offered by value t ransfer. I t i s n ot b ased o n e xisting v alues a nd n orms t hat the students have to internalize but rather on the values that young people have already internalized. The analysis shows a correspondence between the concepts of value transfer a nd v alue c larification. B oth a ssume a s ocial s ituation w ith d iffering pluralistic values, some that harmonize with each other and others that stand in conflict. The main difference can be found in the conclusions arrived at in this situation. Value clarification sees no moral crisis, nor does it assume that particular moral systems suffer under pluralism. It concentrates on the individual and on how the multitude of choice expresses itself through uncertainty, apathy, or aimlessness. The so-called moral crisis is, according to Hall (1979), actually an identity crisis. Therefore, the morality education theories of this model focus exclusively on the individual. Young people have to learn to think about their own value traditions and, through a form of biographical reflection, arrive at a unity of thought, emotion, and decision-making. While value transfer reacts to plurality w ith a p re-selected c hoice o f v alues, v alue c larification r espects t he multitude of choice. Furthermore, the idea of making a pre-selection on behalf of the students and then introducing this in class for the purpose of assimilation is rejected. First, that idea is unrealistic in view of the plurality at hand, and second, it is simply wrong because it violates the students' personal freedom. According to their personal circumstances, the students should be able to develop an identity that is the result of productive self-design and that is not a simple reflection of external expectations. The solution, as offered by value clarification, is to guide the students' exploration of those attitudes and internalized norms that interfere with the unity of thought, emotion, and decision-making. These values should be brought into the light of today and opened up to processing in order to confirm, correct, or reject them. Through value clarification, the adoption or internalization of values (which value transfer sees as the final achievement) is biographically reconstructed and opened up to critique. The goal is to track down consistencies and inconsistencies between the values developed in the course of one's life earlier and now. The question asked is, are the attitudes and values acquired in harmony with the current consciousness and the current emotions? Methodically speaking, this is a process of unfreezing, involvement, and refreezing, i.e. the thawing of acquired values, the opening oneself up to new choices and views, and, finally, the freezing of the new attitudes.

Raths et al. (1966) see their concept, value clarification, as the definite alternative to value transfer. For them, value transfer is the same thing as indoctrination, even in those cases where the internalized values are not connected to negative emotions. First, it means excluding young people from alternatives; second, the legitimacy of the pre-selected values is arbitrary; third, values are relative – just because something is good today does not mean that it will be completely unacceptable tomorrow; and fourth, the development of values as a part of the development of an individual identity is not properly taken into account. The freedom of self-determination is the focus here. The road to an individual exploration of values must remain open; no one objective value is so important that it can be allowed to limit the free orientation of an individual. The goal of the teaching should not be extracted from the content, but should, rather, have a critical function towards the content. The goal of value clarification can be shortly summarized as follows: *Young people should reflectively be made aware of the values and norms that they have internalized in the past and, using the feelings and emotions of today, become conscious of consistencies and inconsistencies. These should then be worked through in order to create a unity of thought, emotion and decision-making that allows them to find and stabilize their personal identity.*

Value Development

The main proponent of this model is Lawrence Kohlberg (1981; 1984), who describes the development of moral judgment as a sequence of six stages that

130

people can potentially go through. A *pre-conventional* stage (which includes the first two stages) is characterized by an orientation based either on punishment and obedience or on instrumental values. These first two stages are further characterized by the threat of punishment or the social attitude that "if you scratch my back, I'll scratch yours."

The Stages of Moral Judgment

STAGE 0 EGOCENTRIC JUDGEMENT (Approx. 4 years)	*What is right:* *Reasons for being good:*	I should get things my way. Get rewards, avoiding punishment.
STAGE 1 BLIND OBEDIENCE (Approx. pre-school age)	*What is right:* *Reason for being good:*	I should do what I'm told. Staying out of trouble.
STAGE 2 FAIRNESS AS A DIRECT TRADE: "WHAT IS IN IT FOR ME?" (Elementary school years)	*What is right:* *Reason for being good:*	I should think of my own benefit, but be fair to those who are fair to me? Personal interest: What is in it for me?
STAGE 3 INTERPERSONAL CONFORMITY (Middle childhood – early youth)	*What is right:* *Reason for being good:*	I should be a nice person and live up to the expectations of those I know and love. I want the others to have a good opinion of me so that I have a good sense of self-worth.
STAGE RESPONSIBILITY TO "THE SYSTEM" (Early or middle youth)	*What is right:* *Reason for being good:*	I should fulfill my duties towards the social system or system of values to which I belong. I would like to contribute to the system not falling apart, and I want to keep my self-respect as someone who does not shirk his duties.
STAGE 5 CONSCIENCE GUIDED BY PRINCIPLES (Early adult)	*What is right:* *Reason for being good:*	I should show the greatest possible respect for the rights and dignity of every individual and I should support a system that respects human rights. Acting according to my conscience and the principle of respect for each human being.

Table: Lickona 1983, 20-21. The description of stages corresponds to Lawrence Kohlberg's Stages of moral judgment; stage 0 was adopted from William Damon and Robert Selman. The references to age refer to children of average intelligence who have grown up in a supportive moral environment.

Kohlberg goes on to define stages three and four as *conventional*, in which conformity and loyalty to the rules of the social group and authorities predominate. That which the majority finds good and the social order finds correct (law and order) is personally supported by the subject. Finally, stages five and six are autonomous, or *post-conventional*. In the fifth stage, we find an orientation around agreements that are based on consensus and the prevailing public order and laws. Stage six contains a universal core. People at this stage orient their actions around abstract ethical principals, the validity of which has to be demonstrated in the best interests of everyone. As an example of these principles, Kohlberg names both the Golden Rule and the Categorical Imperative: Only act according to those maxims that you would like to see turned into a general law.

Models of morality education built on this theory have a particular interest in the improvement of the ethical sense of judgment. To this end, Kohlberg has constructed a number of stories containing moral dilemmas. Youth should then discuss the possible alternatives and weigh the morality of any one course of action. The task of the educator is to render a diagnosis as to what stage the students are in and then use forms of argumentation from the next level up in order to attain a transition into that level.

One of the better-known stories is the Heinz dilemma: should Heinz steal a medicine that would save the life of his wife? Students are invited to discuss this case and attempt to answer this question. It soon becomes apparent whether they slip into the role of Heinz or that of the apothecary, how they reconstruct the story (from the point of view of the protagonists involved), if they are limited to a certain role, and, finally, if they introduce superordinate principles and issues such as legitimate breaking of the law. The interaction is a learning process in and of itself because the students are asked to change perspectives and search for the course of action that they find just. The possibility of other points of view poses the challenge of justifying one's own opinion, rethinking one's position, and possibly changing it. The platform for this educational intervention is the result of the very normative core that characterizes Kohlberg's model. He speaks of justice as the highest principle. Decisions regarding values are to be judged according to this principle. The goal of value development can be shortly summarized as follows: *Young people should ascend through the various stages of moral judgment and, by analyzing various moral dilemmas, acquire the ability to make these moral judgments based on principles.*

Value Communication

In value communication, "interaction" is a decisive factor in acquiring values and norms. Based on symbolic interactionism (George H. Mead), Habermas (1992) concludes that within all interaction, the participants use each other for reference. Students do not just accept the values offered; they develop an opinion on these values and go on to interpret them. Mead speaks of the inner reconstruction of the perspective as viewed by another or a generalized other. Interaction allows a change in position, and the most important medium of interaction is language. In language, we find the basic structures of human action and decision-making: language *is* action! Habermas sees language not only as a medium for coordinating action and socialization but, more importantly, as a means of reaching an understanding (ideally: a consensus) in regards to those matters that have grown into sources of conflict. With this insight in mind, value communication interprets the communication of those particular values and norms that concern what is desirable and correct for others and myself as the very core of ethical learning processes. Students learn to argue by defending the legitimacy of norms in the forum of argumentative reason in a real communication (Habermas 1990). An important principle for using the argumentative branch of language is the concept of *de-centering*. Using the theories of Mead and Piaget, ethical de-centering is understood as the change between the *I-*, *You-*, and *They-*perspective. The youth thus learn to express values not just from their own perspective (and so expect everybody else to agree with them) but also learn to walk in someone else's shoes and see things from the other's perspective. Furthermore, the issue of legitimacy offers a third perspective. This latter perspective asks if others who might potentially be affected by these values would agree to them or not. The concept of de-centering helps to universalize the question of values and norms and brings the analyses out of subjective bias and egocentrism. The important factor is not just the other but also common (universal) interests, the superordinate welfare, and the needs of those who have the least chance to express themselves publicly. This leads us to the normative base of value communication; this concept is not value neutral, but rather it orients itself around the common will as expressed by the Golden Rule and the Categorical Imperative.

From an educational point of view, value communication anticipates the ideal conversation, one in which all partners recognize each other as equals, treat the arguments of the others the same way they would treat their own, and assume that a basic consensus is possible. The question is, how do these assumptions work in real life, where teachers possess more power and competence than their students do? Benner and Peukert's opinion of this *educational paradox* is that morality in young people can neither be assumed nor simply instilled. If one could assume morality, then deliberations on morality education would be unnecessary. If morality could be or were simply instilled, then modern principles of freedom would be undermined. A form of moral heteronomy would then be practiced, and there would be no respect for the other's insights into the workings of moral principles. The paradox, then, is wanting to teach free insight by using heteronomous methods. Thus, what we want is to give youth an imaginary competence that will stimulate them to gain insight and reflect on values through *their own motivation* (Benner/Peukert 1983). This point brings us to the normative base structure of the communicative approach. Freedom and autonomy are not just anthropologically asserted but are also made possible in practice through the dialogue structure of action; in regards to youth, this is reached through giving the advance described above on the (still-missing) full reciprocity, thus assuming its existence. In this way, ethical statements are not excluded from the communication structure, but, rather, they are interwoven in it.

The innovation of the communicative approach is that it turns plurality itself, i.e. the breakdown of assumptions, into a problem. It does not solve the conflict of plurality before class but instead makes it into an issue. In this way, students have to go through the process of weighing and justifying differing values themselves, thereby improving their ethical competence. Students are encouraged to evaluate the current situation, discuss the ideal situation, and practice drawing conclusions about what could and should be. The goal of value communication can be shortly summarized as follows: *Young people should communicate about values and norms and, through argumentative processes, hone a judgment capacity, learning to reconstruct assumptions gone problematic according to their content and justification. The goal is to clarify, from an ethical standpoint, what values and norms should legitimately guide the orientation of concrete action and decision-making.*

Comparing the Models

The following overview is a comparison of the four models according to four principles. The questions posed are that of what the goals of these models are, what methods they prefer, what value orientations they are based on, and how they deal with the plurality of values. Since their formulations are ideal-typical, several models will always overlap in practice. For a general evaluation, the models here will briefly be compared according to the goals they aspire to.

The goal of value transfer is quite simply to achieve conformity using established views. The ethical quality of particular views is considered proven, which directly legitimates their being passed on. The factually present plurality of values is not brought up, seeing as the students' choice has been made for them.

In contrast to the deductive character of value transfer, value clarification is inductively oriented. The latter considers the methods of value transfer to be indoctrination, since young people never really have the freedom to establish their value orientation themselves and thereby bring their thoughts, emotions, and action into harmony. This is the main goal of value clarification. It sharply criticizes every form of paternalism. The quality of values and norms is determined by their worth to the individual.

Value development aims to improve the ethical sense of judgment, which is to progress through different stages into a thought process guided by principles. From the point of view of value development, value transfer aims for goals within the pre-conventional and conventional stages. On the other hand, value development runs the risk of instrumentalizing real conflicts of values in order to progress to the next level.

Value communication uses real conflicts of values as opportunities for testing the ethical desirability of conflicting values in an argumentative way. The goal is to isolate, from the point of view of the other (or, of all others), those values that deserve to guide the orientation of action. Bringing about ethical maturity here means assuming that youth already possesses this maturity during the communication about values. Maturity must not only be asserted but also practically applied within the structure of dialogue. The value orientation in this model lies in recognizing students as morally autonomous subjects. Those values and norms they actually follow are the results of a learning process and not, as with value transfer, the point of departure.

Summarized Comparison of the Four Models				
	Value transfer	Value clarification	Value development	Value communication
Goal	Youth are to adopt pre-selected values and norms	Youth should recognize already acquired moral attitudes and (potentially) reject some	Youth should gradually improve their moral sense of judgment	Youth should determine the desirability and potential of values and norms through an ethical point of view
Method-Process	Straight passing on of values through cognitive, emotional, and motivational methods	Being made aware of and confronting acquired values and norms	Discussion of moral conflicts using stories of dilemmas	Participation in argumentative processes of discussion with various changes in perspective
Value orientation	Lies in the content ("the worth") of the values and norms to be passed on	Lies in the optimization of subjective thinking, feeling and doing	Lies in the construction of ethical judgment guided by principles	Lies in the youth's ethical maturity, which is both method and goal
Value plurality	Is reduced to those values that are to be adopted by youth	Is reduced to the values that have individual importance	Is brought up in selected dilemmas for a functional purpose	Is the point of origin and an issue of discussion regarding values and norms

Whatever model teachers actually end up using, ethics education in school must avoid two extremes: rigidity and permissiveness. Moral rigidity in ethical learning processes implies monopolization and conformity. A rigid ethics education

135

might have well-meaning intentions, e.g. not letting any insecurity show and always having the right answers, but those learning processes run the risk of turning into indoctrination. On the other hand, permissiveness can create a social vacuum. In that case, students do not learn to make a judgment and defend it. Even with the best of intentions, such as respecting the freedom of opinion of the youth, permissiveness has a tendency to turn into moral neglect. The challenge is to transcend the dilemma of having to choose between one extreme and the other. The best chances to respect the students' freedom and at the same time give them the skills to interpret and judge values are provided by the models of value development and value communication. Value development highlights the questions of age and developmental lags, while value communication realizes the educational importance of practical negotiation processes. The motto "test all and keep the best" is imperative and encourages one's own personal judgment and decision-making, thus rejecting the straight adoption of others' decisions. These are the theories that must be implemented in class.

Sense of Judgment within the Horizon of the Christian Tradition

Traditional concepts within the teaching of ethics put the conscience at the center of attention; in this chapter, the students' sense of judgment stands in the center. For this reason, we have to clear up the relationship between the two. The emphasis on the sense of judgment implicates a conceptual preference for process oriented learning. This learning is different from product oriented learning. A specifically Christian teaching of ethics will now be presented.

Conscience and Decision

The first question is, how much does the teaching of ethics in Religious Education depend on the concept of conscience? The moral theologian Bruno Schüller (1980, 40-57) begins his moral theology with a discussion of "conscience." He introduces different uses of this word and concludes that it can be done away with; there are better synonyms for it. If conscience is used in the sense of moral, then we mean the attitude of not orienting ourselves around usefulness as such, but around moral duties; if conscience is used to mean the inner ruler or the heart, then we are talking about the perception of our own feelings and inner voice; and if conscience is used as cognitive faculty, then there are better ways to describe it than with the word *conscience*. The word *conscience* has a role to play in everyday life. Yet when we are discussing how the conscience works and is to be educated, then he believes this interpretation is imprecise and ought to be avoided. When talking about the conscience, we are really talking about a person's cognitive faculty. This should not be defined through reasoning found deep in the soul, but rather through the moral insights and decisions that a person arrives at.

Education of the conscience is education of ethical insight, an ethical sense of judgment, and the reflection of ethical action. Because a particular action does not follow directly from a particular way of thinking, Religious Education is especially interested in the creation of insight and the promotion of the sense of judgment, i.e. how ethical decisions are made, where they originate, and if they stand up to general common sense. This goal would suggest cooperation with that branch of moral theology that Alfons Auer calls "autonomous morality." This branch within moral theology does not represent a concept of autonomy in the sense of individualistic arbitrariness but instead radicalizes the view that a person using his common sense can recognize that which is supposed to come from free insight. Auer clarifies, "The concept of autonomy contains the perception that Man is, himself, Law; that moral norms are not placed upon him by the exterior in the form of heteronomous obligations, but are developed by him using his own common sense" (Auer 1984, 206).

Product and Process

The next questions are, how and why should a formal-ethical approach in Religious Education, such as value development and value communication, be given preference before a material-ethical approach, such as value transfer? While value transfer makes material-ethical decisions as to what values are worth passing on, formal-ethical models appear to be free of any content. It could be argued that this promotes moral neglect. Such a critique would, however, overlook the fact that these models are not value free. The normative basis of these models does not measure itself according to any selection of particular values, but rather according to the possibility of gaining a free insight by optimizing the sense of judgment in a practical dialogue structure. Determining *how* and in *what manner* young people learn is the responsibility of the ethical-normative educational plan. This also corresponds to Immanuel Kant's principle that a person must always be the *end* and never the *means*. For the teaching of ethics, this means differentiating between process and product. Ethics education that starts out at the product begins by setting out a certain understanding of ethics, which, at the end of the learning process, is to be shared by the young. Ethics education that starts out with the process wants the young people to get familiar with ethical principles, which they can then use to differentiate and judge various understandings of ethics. Furthermore, the normative basis for this process correlates with the *democratic principle* guaranteeing freedom of choice, but which, at the same time, assumes the ability to make a choice (cf. Peukert 1984). It also correlates with a great tradition in ethics – that good action is tied to free insight. Ethics education must create or improve the conditions for learning that empowers students to come to a free realization of what is good; ethics education

137

must not indoctrinate the students with the good. A consequence of the process orientation is the fact that the final "product" that ends up being chosen by the students is unknown. The models of value development and value communication have a concrete material base norm: the autonomy and freedom of humanity. The assumptions behind this base norm are that nothing rational speaks against it and that no other norm supersedes it in ethical quality. The criticism that formal-ethical concepts are arbitrary falls apart against this argument. In 1949, while still influenced by the war, Jean Piaget wrote (quoted in Bertram 1986, 123), "The problem that has to be tackled by international education is not guiding the young to pre-determined solutions but giving them the means with which they can develop such solutions themselves. At this point, we must refer back to two connected basic principles that an education based on psychology may never neglect: first, the only truths are the ones you have developed independently yourself, and not the ones you receive from the outside, and second, that which is morally good is essentially autonomous and cannot be prescribed."

Leaving product placement out of the picture does not mean that important cultural and Christian positions should be left out of the educational plan if the students do not bring up the topics themselves. In fact, they must be brought up, since norms and values cannot exist without tradition and history. The only thing that changes is the pretence with which they are introduced. They have to be communicable and open to criticism. In order to stay communicable, they have to be treated as hypotheses of truth. All objectively presented statements are based on subjective reflection – meaning these, too, are always open to new insights.

The Teaching of Ethics within the Horizon of the Christian Faith

The third question is, what makes the teaching of ethics within Religious Education different from the teaching of ethics in other subjects? Alfons Auer formulates an important condition: speaking about the basic Christian values (*proprium*) does not mean that Christians have a particularly structured cognitive faculty or rationality that is different from the common sense of everyday life. When Christians make ethical decisions, they are using the same common sense that every other individual uses. For Auer, the basic Christian values (*proprium*) are a horizon of meaning made available to humankind through the revelation of God through Jesus Christ, a revelation that calls upon Christians to act a certain way. This calling is not so concrete that today's Christians simply know what the right thing to do is because of their observations of what the Christians during the life of Christ did. The ethical principles of Jesus, available to us through the Bible, must be mediated.

We have to ask if the implicit horizon of meaning included in value development converges with the horizon of meaning of the Christian message. Kohlberg names justice as the norm for his concept. Judgment guided by principle is higher than the stages that precede it purely because it is directed at an ever more universal form of justice. With a view to the biblical tradition (cf. Marino 1983), justice is often named as the sum of the Old Testament, something which is then concentrated through the commandment of love (Matt 22:36-40). Value development is right at home within Religious Education when you take a fair sense of judgment to mean the norm for a community, such as what the prophets fought for and how Jesus Christ lived.

Similarly, we have to ask if the implicit horizon of meaning included in value communication converges with the Christian message's horizon of meaning. The norm of value communication is the Golden Rule: "Do unto others as you would have them do unto you" (Matt 7:12). Immanuel Kant further developed this rule in his Categorical Imperative. Value communication tests values in light of others, all others. Promoting the competence of the students in order to give them the capacity to do just that is a task native to Religious Education. Love of God, love of oneself, and love for one's neighbor are inextricably linked to one another, so much so that one could say that the love of God appears within love of oneself and love of one's neighbor. Value communication operationalizes this love as a process of communication in which unequal relationships of dominance are broken up and reshaped to form symmetric communication. This process also includes all those who have no voice of their own.

Quite apart from this implicit compatibility test of value development and value communication with Religious Education, we also have to clarify how the Christian horizon of meaning is explicitly brought into focus. This horizon of meaning is available, among other things, in the Ten Commandments, in the Sermon on the Mount, in similes and parables, in the many testimonies of Jesus acting on behalf of those who counted as society's worst-off, etc. It is also available in the Old Testament, from the story of Creation to Abraham and from David to the prophets (an example to follow).

> In the context of world religions, the class will touch on dealing with strangers. There are any number of media articles regarding questions of immigration and asylum politics. Students are given access to this article and other similar material and are then asked to formulate their own opinion. The concrete article deals with an incident where the police broke up a church asylum. Some will say the asylum seekers have to be deported because their application to stay was turned down; others will feel that generosity is called for. From a Christian point of view, there is no one right answer. Nevertheless, biblical texts offer a horizon of meaning in order to form an opinion: the experience of be-

ing a stranger in Egypt (Ex 23:9); the commandment of love for your neighbor (Ex 20:2-3; Lev 19:33 et seq.); the reference to the stranger in the parable of the Samaritan, the one who is my "neighbor" (Luke 10:25-27); the unity in Jesus Christ and the equality of every person (Gal 3:28); the growing together into unity within a greater variety (Acts 2); the treatment of a stranger as a criteria for the salvation of humanity (Matt 25:31-36), etc. Yet not one of these references offers a direct solution to the problems associated with immigration or asylum. Promoting an ethical sense of judgment in Religious Education does, however, mean getting familiar with this horizon of meaning, learning to tie it to ourselves, or even making judgments and decisions based on it.

This example demonstrates that it is not easy to isolate the basic Christian values. One can only formulate such obligatory values (without receiving much opposition) if one formulates them abstractly (e.g. as justice or love). Yet abstract formulas have the disadvantage in that there could be a great distance between them and actual application. For this reason, the basic Christian values demand new interpretations all the time. This task is up to all of theology to fulfill – and, as far as ethics is concerned, up to the moral theology to explore. Theology, however, speaks in many voices. Therefore, the reference to the Bible alone as a source of faith is not enough. According to Catholic tradition, neither is the sense of belief held by those who are baptized and confirmed. This sense of belief definitely allows them to emphasize their sense of judgment, even though – as in the case of youth – it must first be formed, which, in turn, means anticipating it. The Church does, however, point out that moral judgment should also be measured according to what the Church teaches. It is a particular trait of the Catholic faith to see the teachings of the Church next to the Bible and the sense of belief as the source of faith (*sensus fidei, sensus fidelium*). According to Alfons Auer (1984, 185-197), Church teaching can guide ethical judgment in three different ways:

- the Church teachings should present the Christian message in an *integrating* fashion, where many voices can be heard;
- it should bring up the message in a *stimulating* way, in order to ascertain the Christian horizon of meaning; and
- it should introduce the tradition in a *critical* light, even in those places where human social development threatens to exercise sharp criticism.

The teaching of ethics in Religious Education is a communicative action. The goal of this field of Religious Education is not so much the *result* of the consensus aimed for, but more the process that leads to the consensus. Communication is not just talk, dialogue, or conversation; it is about the meaning created by the force of communication. Learning about ethics in Religious Education is communicative learning. Value development and value communication are tied to the Christian horizon of meaning by

- activating one's own sense of what is good, accessing the biblical horizon of meaning, and introducing the voice of the church teachings;
- asking for the desirability and possibility of value judgments in real communicative situations while taking issues of age and development into account; and
- letting students "learn by doing" (communication is action!), i.e. sharpen their sense of judgment by developing and exchanging arguments and perspectives, all the while trying to come to an understanding.

The main issues involved in morality education are first, assuring an adequate preparation of the content of ethics education and second, finding the best method of introducing values and norms. As far as the method is concerned, value development and value communication offer the best courses of action for guiding young people in the understanding of values and norms. They take the plurality of values seriously and aim for a sharpened sense of judgment on the part of the students. As far as the content is concerned, there is no need to protect the young people from plurality, which society exposes them to anyway. Taking into account their age and development, it is more productive to confront them with value conflicts, letting them practice arguing for and against conflicting values and taking up a personal opinion. In this process, they are made familiar with Christian principles that are then introduced to back up their justifications.

Part IV

The Dimension of Space

Educational Space Inside and Outside of School[*]

The spaces in which we learn only occasionally come into consideration when we reflect upon learning processes of Religious Education. The rectangular classroom (with the typical desk arrangement, traditionally staggered, in a semi-circle, etc.), the arts and science rooms, the music rooms, the laboratories, the school corridor, the break-hall, the school playground, and also perhaps the adjoining sports field are all naturally taken for granted as spatial conditions for school education. Concerning the didactics of Religious Education, further types of space are given attention. Thus, if we take an anthropological approach, students and teachers are themselves space in which and with which education takes place. The church spaces tell a story, emit a certain aura, and are significant places for specific rituals. Virtual space has a religious charge from which and with which we are able to learn. Space is not just pre-determined but is also created. It is filled by life and spirit; it conveys a certain message or can take on a special meaning.

Religious Education cannot be adequately described without referring to the dimension of space. Therefore, a reflection on space belongs with a reflection on Religious Education. The multifarious nature of space must be explained by means of selected examples. In regards to the didactics of Religious Education, we first think of the school building and the classroom. Space in this context has, among other meanings, an architectonic meaning; it is also about the space of school, which must be filled with life. We want to address this type of space and look for its connections to learning processes of Religious Education. Furthermore, space can have a corporal meaning, since everyone is himself or herself a type of space. The question will be how the space of the body can become a topic in learning processes of Religious Education. Third, there is space that has direct reference to religious meaning: sacred space. It must be investigated as to which types of sacred space can be included in learning processes of Religious Education. Finally, students come to school with numerous experiences of different types of space. Aspects of virtual space should be examined and used for the benefit of learning processes of Religious Education.

---

[*] This chapter was written in cooperation with Andreas Prokopf.

Developing Space as an Exercise for the Teaching of Religious Education

First, what do we understand the term *space* to mean? There are types of space that we come upon and types of space that we create; space in which we learn, and space by which and with which we learn; space that releases a religious aura, and space in which an encounter with the religious dimension of reality is made possible; there is local space and spiritual space. Space is also far more than just a room or a building. The questions of how, where, and what space might be are closely connected to human perception. Gestalt psychologists point out that an internal and external, a time and space, exist only within human perception. The cognitive world is the spatial and temporal reality of the discerning human being. Cognitive space-time concepts are not a reality in themselves but rooted in human perception. Even the space of school, which exists objectively for both teacher and student, is not experienced in an identical manner. The meaning attributed to these types of spaces can span from the place of oppression or the place of necessary bread-winning to the place of creative development" or the place of completion of a life-task. Consequently, the same space can sometimes be experienced very differently. There is a visible surface structure and a hidden substructure. Space can also be transcended. In the space of school, new types of space are constantly being accessed and created: technical space, virtual space – and also religious space in the different spaces of the world.

From a cultural-anthropological point of view, a space can even have a religious charge. A continuously recurring basic pattern is established in our dealings with space. People tend to fence off spaces in the local and spiritual spheres of their lives. Seen anthropologically, the fencing off of spaces has the function of bringing a seemingly chaotic world into order. Here, it is necessary to mention sacred space: this too is fenced off from the other spaces of our life. In religious phenomenology, sacred space within the boundless space is seen as an act of constituting a holy space to confront the formless expanse of the universe. This differentiated holy space makes it possible to construct an ordered world out of the chaotic cosmos. Even within sacred space, we can observe delimitation: space for the people, space for the clergy, space for silent prayer, etc.

Education in the Space of School

Surface and Subsurface Structure of Spaces

Students who reach their last year of secondary education will have spent many hours of their lives in a school space. In this way, they share a large part of their lifetime with each other in a confined area. Perhaps more clearly than in the past, it is now understood that school cannot simply be seen as a learning factory, but rather that it is, for better or worse, a living space. An inventory of the school spaces would include the classic lesson space (classroom), function spaces (for physics, chemistry, arts, music, I.T., etc.), special spaces (administration, library, toilets, etc.), and miscellaneous spaces (hall, cafeteria, etc.). Multifarious experiences are connected to spaces: smell, condition of the walls and furniture, lightness and darkness, decorated or bare, homeliness or non-homeliness. Many of these experiences are based on sensory perceptions, which, even if not reflected specifically, can play a decisive role in the students' feeling comfortable at school. Aesthetically pleasing spaces promote well being; non-pleasing spaces prevent or weaken it. Spaces can also be felt as filled with spirit or spiritlessly dull; spaces can inspire or imprison; spaces can awaken and drive strengths or overpower us, making us feel small and helpless.

It is not enough to look at a space with regard to its outward appearance. Spaces have a surface and a subsurface structure. Surface structure means the discernible amount and physical form of the space. Subsurface structure is understood as the rules of use and ritual that apply to certain spaces. We could also say that through inquiring about the subsurface structure, we are asking about the meaning that a space might have. Meanings are largely handed-down – students and teachers come across them as unwritten rules and adjust themselves accordingly. Meanings also have a history of tradition, i.e. they are susceptible to change. For the didactics of Religious Education, the subsurface structure of spaces undeniably takes precedence. If, for example, a school has a quiet-room at its disposal that is then gradually filled by material boxes, the subsurface structure of silent, reflective contemplation is lost. The room or space has forfeited its atmosphere as a quiet-room. This aura can only be maintained if the configuration of the space and the intended use remain congruent.

In the Bible, we often come across space as a metaphor: God created spaces (Heaven and Earth); God breathed spirit into the human body (space); God cast man into the space of Creation (Earth); Jesus visited symbolically enriched space (e.g. the dessert, the mountain); Jesus goes into the spaces (houses) of the people; and the churches are spaces in which faith lives on and is promulgated. These few examples show that spaces have meaning or that meaning can be connected to spaces. In these spaces, activities take place that constitute people as people according to the image of God. It is about the salvation of the people: "Today, salvation has befallen your house" (Luke 19:9).

Learning to Shape the Space of School

When someone thinks about school spaces, he or she first considers their functionality and then perhaps thinks about the sterile PVC floors or the often-penetrating smell of cleaning supplies. Within the realm of pedagogy, the extent to which it is possible to shape the school space so that it has a more homely feel, to which students as much as teachers are accustomed, is being increasing considered. The saying "you eat with your eyes first" could be modified to "you learn with your senses first." The metaphor of the setting is present in the story of Creation. Man was put on Earth to shape it; Man should establish himself domestically and in a homely manner, rejoice in the Creation, sustain and develop it, and pursue the act of Creation (although anthropologically this idea is constantly being narrowed down to the permission to rule over the world). If we transfer these ideas to the school space, then it is not a question of interior architecture, but more comprehensively, it is the question about the life that happens in this space. The particular opportunity of Religious Education lessons lies in its recognition of the subsurface structure of school space and its contribution in bringing soul into this space. A local view on spaces must be distinguished form a communicative view.

First, the local aspect. If a contribution towards developing a homely feel within the "school building" is to be included in the framework of Religious Education, then types of project work are suited. Students and teachers first look for a central idea and then base a plan of organization upon it. Central ideas can be "What we see as holy" (students collect photographs and objects that demonstrate their understanding of holiness), "Happiness has a name" (the Christian hope for salvation and redemption has dimensions both of this world and of the other side; pupils consider what their hopes for the future might be and how those hopes are founded) or "Where we like to be – where we would rather flee from" (students turn the types of space to which they attribute either negative or positive meaning into topics; they draw the spaces in which they feel at home and those in which they feel put upon – spaces in which peace prevails and those in which conflict prevails). Naturally, this is not an exhaustive list of possible central ideas. In these examples, lending soul to a space implies tracking down nodal points in our lives, intensifying them, and visually processing them through symbols. Symbols turn life into a topic and prompt us to reflect. In this way, Religious Education lessons can act as a stimulus to select the space of school as a central theme. When this occurs, the school space can become part of me and promote a sense of feeling at home while at school.

Second, the communicative aspect. Teachers and students do not just use spaces but create them through interaction. They follow codes that apply to certain types of space and allocate one another to a position in that space. Two examples of this:

- In one class, the teacher slowly paces up and down the rows of desks as the students scribble away. The students seem to be tied to their seats with their sight fixed on the work sheet. The teacher strides through the space, which she rules in this hour.

- In another class, the students are working in groups. Individual students go to a neighboring table and borrow glue and scissors. Work is compared, examined, and discussed. The teacher asks questions, supports, and advises. The space for communication is not concentrated upon the teacher but has many nodal points.

In both cases, the space is shaped according to communications relations. We can distinguish between linear communication and network communication. In classroom space, linear communication in the sense of the transmitter-receiver model is presumably more predominant. In linear communication, teachers occupy the key position in the lesson. They are the point of reference for courses of communication, for authority, and for power, and they allocate students their places. If this claim were unrealistic, teachers should loose their key positions in integrated communication. In fact, they see their roles very differently and, accordingly, apply their powers differently. In integrated communication, there is not only one center, but several. Teachers are the directors of the processes of communication. To the extent that they cede a part of their space dominance to the students, the frequency of interaction of the students increases – both as a whole and with one another. The space comes alive and receives a new structure. Undoubtedly, not all lessons can always be conducted through integrated communication. The question is, however, whether there is a theological reason why teachers who are sensitive towards the space dimension of education should employ network communication. The reason lies in the meaning of the word itself: *communio* or *communicatio* stands for relationship, community, and exchange. God speaks to the people *in relation to them* – namely through Jesus Christ. The medium is the message; the contents of Religious Education lessons and the form of class communication must correspond accordingly.

The Individual's Body as Space

A quite different educational space is the individual's body. When we look at the body with respect to teaching Religious Education, it is not a matter of content foreign to theology. In Christendom, the body (corporeality) has always been regarded highly – though in an ambivalent way when dealing with sexuality. The incarnation of God in Jesus Christ and his corporal resurrection refer to the fact that from a Christian perspective, the end of life always incorporates the end of corporeality. The body, which everyone has, is the stage and the starting point of human experience; it is existentially interwoven with human identity. Concerning the body, we talk of a basic mood of human existence that is still given as a foundation for how to conduct ourselves and that has advantage over every perception. With their bodies, people live in the "shrouded existence" (Husserl 1973). They experience the world through the medium of their body (Kruse 1974, 45). The body is the spatially comprehensible stage of self-consciousness, of the emotions, and of the mind.

In the Catholic tradition (but it is certainly not exclusive to Catholicism), the body is regarded as the symbol for the ability to communicate with other people and collect stories. Corporeality facilitates speech, hearing, sight, a conveying of ourselves, and a perceiving of others. In the Christian point of view, the Resurrection stands at the center of body-symbolism; that is to say, Christians believe that the body is reproduced as an expression of communicative and historical spatiality of the human being. Moments of joy and suffering, ecstatic and painful experiences, the life-long process of having been born, maturing, and reaching death are all internally associated, and they are part of the hope for resurrection (cf. Lohfink 1974, 136). For this reason, it is important to conceive the body as a learning space: the destiny of anyone in his or her fragility and restrictions, but also in his or her uniqueness and beauty, receives a face and a name through the body.

The space of the body is a place for many basal experiences. Seen biologically, a healthy heartbeat and a regular breathing pattern make human life possible – the heart and breath (*odem*) are also important concepts in a religious sense. People can express their joy and enthusiasm with their body, but the body also indicates defeat. The external act of praying expresses an internal mood, however varied it might be. Sexuality, one of the most intimate areas of corporeality, requires a responsible way of dealing with one's self and with others. The aging of the body is a constant *memento mori* through which people must learn to handle themselves.

Learning processes involving the anthropological space are, metaphorically speaking, about the aim of getting to know the individual's body as a source from which we can drink. The mood of this space must be perceived and understood, and dimensions must be opened up. Some didactic stimuli are offered for these three aspects.

Perceiving Corporeality

Perceiving corporeality with students implies getting a feel for their respective moods. It is about these questions: how do I feel in my skin? How do I feel in this class, in my body, next to my neighbor? How does the atmosphere affect me? How do I feel in Religious Education lessons; what stimulates me? The teaching of Religious Education can work towards letting the traces of symbolic traditions and religious customs appear in everyday embodiments – with the physical-spatial experiences of standing, sitting, and lying, for example. Standing, sitting, and lying are all elementary positions. Students learn to perceive what is available as existential experience. Vivid examples of this bodily behavior can include the pre-existence and pre-reflexivity of spatiality (human existence is always spatial), the definition of identity over the space (tracking down my location), and the role of the body as spatial-religious carrier of meaning.

Interpreting Perceptions of Corporeality

Through their own perceptions, sensitive students receive important information about their present (also existential) situation. For example, once the students have perceived their positions in the class (e.g. the center of attention or a minor figure), they can continue by questioning and assessing how the assumed positions influences their lives. Do they feel secure and in safe hands in this room, or do they feel fear, a distance from God, and a sense of hopelessness? Are they, symbolically speaking, wandering through a desert, or do they find themselves in the Promised Land where milk and honey flow? With the aid of bodily-spatial symbolism, life can be interpreted on a continuum of salvation and damnation. Methodically incarnate situations can be taken up as crisis or decision in role-playing, e.g. with the exercise of being balanced precariously. How is a will to live to be achieved if life has crises (i.e. is balanced precariously)? Disappointments, doubts, and phases of desperation and despair can be bodily reconstructed in the class space: how we continuously lose secure grips on the world, do not overcome restriction, experience alternating highs and lows, etc. The balancing beams, the horizontal bars, a wooden cross, shackles, shrouds, and blackout devices can be used to insinuate such crises in our corporeal dimension and in this way to concretely visualize them spatially. Here it would also be fitting to enact the return home of the lost son in the class space as a balancing act between hope of acceptance and hopeless self-accusation (Luke 15, 11-32).

Acting with the Body

This idea was introduced by the preceding examples. Nevertheless, the dimension of action can also be made in direct relation to the topic. The aim is to take possession of the space offered to us and be (or become) capable of acting within it. Students learn how to define goals and how to develop strategies in order to shape their lives. Sovereignty and freedom of human existence are basic values, but students must learn about them both. Paul's message is (Gal 5:13): "You, my brothers, were called to be free!" That message can serve as a background against which one can develop spaces of formation in the Christian context of loving oneself as our neighbor. In this way, meaningful structuring of our own life is deduced from a living knowledge about the Christian faith. The acquisition of this ability to act has corporeal dimensions. Methodically, we can resort to Bible-drama (enacting scenes from the Bible). Gaining freedom can include rising out of depression, crying for help, or rolling up our sleeves. In

Bible-drama, existential experience can be understood in direct relation to corporeal experiences in religious practices. Suitable epilogues would be the possessed man of Gerasa (unclean spirits, which drain us of our freedom, are driven into pigs) (Mark 5) or the resurrection of Lazarus with the concrete corporeal demand, "Lazarus, come out!" (John 11:43). Students can experience differing possibilities of overcoming imprisoned existence and feeling inferior: rolling up sleeves, breaking ties, recovering strengths, crying for help, resigning oneself, or believing in themselves and in God. The Christian religion wants to offer aid and support, as well as provide new energy and motivation. In such exercises, we experience how belief can move mountains, open boxes, remove or displace boundaries, lift restrictions, stand things upright, and expel unclean spirits.

Bringing Tradition to Life: The Sacred Space

Alongside the school space and the space of our own body, the sacred space is also a place of Religious Education. What role do churches play for modern people? Will they transform into museums and permanent exhibitions of the history of Christian architecture, image, and music? Alternatively, can churches be seen as spaces of the experience and conduct of existing belief?

In the context of modernity, church spaces can be made "use" of as places of retreat, even by those teenagers who have no particular interest in the churches as institutions. For the teaching of Religious Education, the question is, how can churches, being sacred spaces, become educational spaces? Churches *embody* several dimensions.

- *Transcendence.* Churches differ from the spaces of everyday life. Their different quality in construction and function distinguish them from pragmatism-filled function spaces. Churches symbolize and transcend everyday life and yet stand at the center of it (Soeffner 1998, p. 45). They refer to a world beyond functionality and purpose-rationality.

- *Tradition.* Churches are guarantors of a tradition. By means of their shape and design, they convey a symbolic knowledge about the beliefs and the experiences of past generations (Soeffner 1998, 48). Churches lend a traditionally nurtured richness to religious forms of expression. For Klie (1998, 14), the church-pedagogical value of the reconnaissance of sacral space lies in the fact that participants were re-linked (*religare*) to the Christian narrative and commemorative culture, in whose center stands the attested belief in the incarnation of Christ.

152

- *Rites or Rituals of Passage.* In churches, meaningful life customs are ritually organized: baptism, communion, confirmation, marriage, death, etc. Churches are sacred centers of a community in which life is intensified (cf. Turner 1982). Our house is the spatial inner against the outside world; the temple analogy stands for mythical space in which a community finds it center in an all-encompassing cosmos. The examination of customs finds its adequate space here.

- *Recurring patterns of routine.* The rite that is unceasingly repeated in the church space aims towards a continuously performing, mimetic revival of handed-down religious (also mythical) patterns of routine (cf. Soeffner 1998, 44). The rhythm of nature is reflected in the church calendar and the Christian story of salvation.

Religious Education in the church space (also called church pedagogy) assumes that churches are not museums of a past culture but can be seen as places of a still-existing religiousness. The drafted dimensions of sacral space, transcendence, tradition, rites of passage, and recurring patterns of routine, are not specifically Christian but have always existed. For church pedagogy, it is just as much a matter of pointing out the basic dimensions of sacred buildings as it is a matter of learning to see and interpret concrete evidence of Christian faith. In a time fixed in the present, churches are spaces in which students can meet with their past and thus the foundation of the present and the future. For the teaching of Religious Education, a competency in perceiving, interpreting, and acting can be broadened in learning processes.

Perceiving Church Space

In view of the negative attitudes towards the churches as institutions, it is important that students learn to perceive their feelings about a church and about the moods and atmosphere they sense in a church building. A visit to a church can begin with walking around the church at the students' leisure and taking in the surroundings as they come. They must decide whether they feel welcome and safe or alien and uninvited. Silent viewing of the objects and pausing to take in the environment fully is called for here. Afterwards, they can be told to find their favorite place and, if appropriate, to shut their eyes and absorb additional sensations. Furthermore, attention can be drawn to the play of light, the layout of the church, the position of the altar, the style of the seating, the sound and echo of hymn and organ, the raised pulpit, the liturgical colors, the baptismal font, the dead lying in state, the holy water, the inner sanctum in its spatial realization in the tabernacle, and any number of other things. In this way, students are not filled with verifiable knowledge as with organized church tours, but rather, they first have the opportunity to experience the space of church in their own way and to establish an internal relationship to it.

Interpreting Church Space

Obviously, not all churches are comprehensively equipped and suited to learning about all the stories they might tell and all the elements of faith they symbolically represent. Nonetheless, it is still possible even in simple churches to search for and discover what distinguishes them from profane space. For example, students can learn how to interpret their impressions by being asked which images and presentations of basic life events can be contained within a church and which personal experiences can be linked to it. The church space cannot be sufficiently academically discussed without reference to the worship or service. During a group visit of the (not always the same) liturgy with inauguration, sermons, Gospel, and worship service in general, a church can be perceived as a space in which something significant takes place. All activities are related to these questions: what is worshipped and who blesses whom in whose name? There are many methods to interpret church space. Next to the organized church tour of the history of the construction and art of a church, a tour with an open door can be chosen. Here, students are motivated to walk through the church and make note of things that they might want to ask about, and afterwards they can put their questions to an expert (sextons, church leaders, pastor, priest, etc.). Another possibility is the blindfolded tour. Two students form a team; one leads the other through the church, the other being blindfolded. Ornaments and sculptures can be touched and later impressions exchanged and interpreted.

Action in the Church Space

Lastly, the aspect of action should be taken into consideration. Students are told to walk around the altar. They should incorporate the before-mentioned dimensions of the holy space of the church into their person. Contrary to the otherwise passive role of the laity found in some churches, for instance in the Catholic Church, church pedagogy is meant to make it possible to present religion as a system of signs within the sacred space so that its special 'grammar' can be learnt and the opportunity to 'utilize' religion can be developed. Students occupy themselves with the questions, "How can I authentically deal with my life history in the church?" and "How should I behave in the church according to tradition?" The aim is that teenagers discover the church space to be a space for silence and tranquility – but also the space of the world-encompassing Christian community. They can learn to discover it as the sign of God's proximity.

Transcending Everyday Life – Virtual Space

The virtual space of modern computer games, which we will be dealing with at the end of this chapter, is probably much more familiar to many students than it is to most teachers. On the one hand, virtual space can adopt a religious quality in itself; on the other hand, several types of substance that can explicitly apply to religious topics are found in the virtual space.

The Religious Quality of Virtual Space

The finding that even virtual space can have a religious quality assumes a broad religious concept. The teaching of Religious Education has been inspired by the idea that functionally, the everyday foundation of the meaning of life, and the transcendence of everyday life fall in the field of religious experience. Analyses of the world of teenagers show that symbolic worlds of meaning, which perform the function of forming an identity, are continually established. This also applies to adults. Thomas Luckmann (1967) denotes this "inner world religiousness" (Max W eber) as "invisible"; i t is not directly based on institution, denomination, or tradition. Victor Turner (1982) described how spaces arise from ruptures and crises in the world of everyday living, which, from a cultural-anthropological perspective, deals with an ancient principle: it leads to the fencing off of a "holy" field from the normal, profane world. Mechanisms to manage everyday problems are spatially set in motion and stage-managed, i.e. space is sought which can be filled with the meaning of the securing of identity. Such space still has the function of facilitating experiences of transcendence as well as that of helping orientation, regeneration, a nd l ife r enewal. In the space i n which customs are symbolized, we can observe a special characteristic of human existence. According to Turner, the human is not complete at birth, not yet ready, not yet at his full prime, but this also applies to the cosmos as a whole: it is not yet ready and is also still susceptible to chaos and barbarity. That is why there are thresholds, gates, pilgrimages to the holy centers, customs rites, and conversion rituals. For many teenagers, virtual space possesses the ability to surpass the everyday world. In the dimension of time, virtual space already embodies spatial infinity and the capacity of around-the-clock global communication. In virtual space, all the rules and restrictions of everyday life can be forgotten and left behind. In virtual space, the frontiers to the world beyond the everyday can be surpassed. This broad religious concept draws attention to basic anthropological findings: the interruption of the everyday routine in the modern world i n which people must live is a ccompanied by traditional a nd religious bonds. A religious dimension is found in the structure of everyday life. Thus, virtual space also has its own religious quality because it offers similar interruption.

Religion in Virtual Space: The Adventure Game *Zelda*

There is also religion *in* virtual space, as, for example, in *Zelda* (http://www.zelda.com). When this game is tried out with students in computer labs at school, it can be established that the players quickly identify themselves with the protagonist of the game, "Link." Link (a.k.a. the User) must follow an adventurous path to reconnoiter the three-dimensional space of the game world ruled by the Princess Zelda, from whom the game series *Zelda* takes its name. In different virtual spaces, Link learns more from other figures about his quest. Each space holds many hidden dangers against which Link must fend himself. The analogy of the game with the Christian message of redemption is not difficult to recognize. Zelda also uses several religiously charged notions and symbols. In one game in the *Zelda* series, a magic "Deku Tree," which is presented as a descendent of the gods, discloses to Link the mission that he must complete. The tree reveals to him that the diabolical powers and dark forces in the world are becoming ever stronger and that Link belongs to the group of the chosen ones. He should be aware of his selection and explore his magic powers. Link has to carry out the principle task, which consists of finding the "holy Triforce," the legacy of the gods, and guarding it from the hands of evil. If he succeeds in his quest, he will representatively guard the whole world form the clutches of evil.

Learning to Perceive: Virtual Reality and the Bridges to Christian Religious Symbols

The world of computer games and interaction with fictional heroes such as Link in *Zelda* are so second nature for most teenagers that often the borders between reality and virtuality are frequently not perceived. In class, it can be worked out where we are actually moving around in *Zelda*. What do the different spaces in the game mean? What effect do narrow, dark spaces have? What messages do wide, light spaces have in the game? Which colors appear in *Zelda* that make me feel calm and reassure me as a player, and which colors leave me feeling nervous and panicked? Reflection on the game can show that certain spatial layouts can affect the players. In addition, the atmospheric character of the virtual space in *Zelda* is heavily charged with myth; hence, we come across temples of fire and water, as well as mountains of death, etc. Students can be made aware of this everyday interaction with the mythical in virtual reality through dealing with the topic in class. The aim is to establish that there is a surplus of reality available in virtuality, which expresses itself in the sympathies of the individual player in reference to the colors, form, and design of the computer game. Everything that virtually creates fear in the computer game, that brings about joy, or that promises hope of liberation can find a counterpart in the sensations felt by the player. The virtuality meant to be conveyed corresponds to the inner hopes and fears of the player. In this way, it can embody a reality that finds itself in the User. The dramatically intensified experiences of the computer game correspond to a series of important life matters during adolescence (breaking away from childhood, fear, threats, etc.). Virtuality can be experienced as a facet of reality that is significant to everyday life; it was part of the world long before the age of computers.

Learning to Interpret: Distinguishing Between the Religion of the Computer Game and Christian Religion

Christian Religious Education lessons must take care in enabling differentiation for the religious innuendoes in *Zelda* and in establishing the difference between the religion represented in the game and the Christian tradition. Due to these religious innuendoes, it is necessary to examine critically whether the world of *Zelda* does not simply take over the real world and alter it so that narcissistic dreams of power, success, and fun can be fulfilled. Such a utopia, which holds no new perspective and only adapts the situation in the interests of a small minority or which seeks to fade out the difference between God and man in its fantasies of omnipotence, destroys the consensus between itself and religion. Further aspects can be explored: how is religion fused with magic and myth in Zelda (and in other games), and what does Christian freedom mean in comparison? For example, one could compare Link's charge in *Zelda*'s instruction booklet with the Lord's Prayer: "the kingdom come." Students can learn how to examine the kingdoms critically; the kingdom of the three gods, the kingdom of the Deku Tree, and the kingdom of Link's striving for everlasting life – and in contrast to this the message of the kingdom of Jesus and God with the promise of salvation for all humankind. Whose dialectics (already ... and not yet) can be compared to *Zelda*'s one-sided vision of salvation, which is solely projected on Link.

Ways of Acting: Computer Games as Incentive to Move in the Space of Religion

Students should be sensitized in class to the fact that virtually appearing symbols, rituals, and ciphers have a relation to their own existential situation. If we use computer games for such an approach, then we must no longer work with more or less abstract examples but can rather directly adopt the teenagers' experience. The inclusion of computer games in Religious Education lessons and in the examination with virtual (religious) action can be made fertile for traditional religious spaces. He who recognizes that much reality is hidden in the virtual world can be sensitized to a recognition of reality in symbols – also in religious symbols. It is only through symbols and signs that we become aware of the secret of the Christian faith. It eludes the grasp of man and is yet very close to us all. He who acts by playing acts with the reality of religion (*homo ludens*). Computer games are a native place of learning for teenagers of today. With a corresponding critical attitude in view of the restrictions of this medium, computer games offer several new learning opportunities.

Conclusion

The presentation of the different learning spaces – school space, the individual body, sacred space, and virtual space – should sensitize us to the fact that space is an important factor in Religious Education alongside the concentration on goals, content, and method. We exist spatially and can get rid of space only to the extent to which we can get rid of the culture in which we have been social-ized. Spaces have a transcendent dimension. In one respect, they are of use as pretexts in their pragmatism, and in another respect, they have a far deeper meaning. Reflection on space dimensions draws attention away from the normal didactic principles and to basic experiences of human existence: limitation and surpassing, restricted existence, and shaping – as well as the capability to sur-pass everyday life. Students undergo these experiences at school, with them-selves (their own bodies), in special (sacred) spaces, or, and certainly in increas-ing measure, in virtual spaces. According to didactics of Religious Education, space can be treated as a topic, and it helps to unlock the doors to new worlds.

10

Religious Education and the Public

Reflection over possibilities and boundaries of Religious Education take place in relation with the public. The modern understanding of public is far too complex to enable us to treat it exhaustively here. After first clarifying what public means, three selected public areas are highlighted: culture, media, and politics. Certainly, there are wider areas that could be considered, and within these areas, many specific facets could also be named. We must, however, limit ourselves in this chapter to exemplary representations.

Students are closely tied to the public. They act according to culture, live within the world of media, and are involved with affairs in the political arena. Education and Religious Education are no longer conceivable as existing outside this public sphere. If the school of Religious Education considers religious learning processes with conscious regard to its more public context, a three-phase reflective perspective is offered.

- Religious Education as a scientific discipline examines how the field of Religious Education is influenced by these public areas. This reveals what, where, and how learning can take place, along with how Learning processes, pupils and teachers are influenced by the public before the teaching and learning processes even begin.

- Furthermore, Religious Education examines how it, as theory and practice of religious learning, can have an effect on these public areas, e.g. through publications, research results, surveys, etc., with which it has a share in public discourse, and how, through the practice of instruction and education, it clarifies society, culture, media, and politics and increases the ability to function within these areas.

- Finally, Religious Education reflects on the possibility of showing how the public itself can be made the central topic in religious learning processes in order to help students become conscious and responsible to others and themselves in their capacity to function within these public areas.

This three-way reflective perspective operates thus *from the public, to the public*, and, when made the central theme, *about the public*.

The public reference in Religious Education is not simply one topic among others. It is essential for a contextual reflection on Religious Education. It looks at the education of individual subjects, but within the context of the culture of a society. For all education and educational processes, the term *socialization* expresses this well. This term refers to two dimensions: the development of self (individualization) and becoming a member of society (socialization). With this distinction, one realizes that the development of the self is directly connected to the reality of a certain culture. Individualization outside of this reality is not possible. The meaning of public (above all, non-church) will be discussed in the following section.

What does *Public* mean in Religious Education?

The first thing to clarify is what we understand by the term *public*. Since antiquity, the term *public* has marked a realm that is effectively defined as the open and manifest, as separated from the private and not openly accessible areas and spheres of life (Honecker 1995, 18). Early Christianity placed itself within this concept of public. From the beginning, it was based on open presence and properties. The pronouncements of Jesus give an example of the association with public and the many demands on public representation of faith. As simple as the public reference of Christianity is, the term *public* did not become relevant as problematic, in reference to cultural history, until the 18th century (cf. Sennet 1976). What we today understand under the term *public* has developed with modern times. Unfortunately, we cannot at this point go into detail on every facet. Worth mentioning in this connection, however, is the classic study "Structural Change of Public" by Jürgen Habermas (1990). For the religious educational approach to public, a brief classification should be all that is necessary. Three developments have contributed to the way in which practical theology and Religious Education in particular are related to the public (cf. Drehsen 1991).

Phases of Development

The emergence of the public in today's sense is closely connected to the formation of civil culture. This civil culture has roots stemming from emancipation, roots shown in the overcoming of the absolutist, feudal social structure and the implementation of democracy and the rule of law. Public was not an issue; everything official, national, and general all coincided with what was public. In civil society, new individual orientations destroy the rules of obedience and obligation orientation in relation to the national authority, church authority, or both. An important new orientation is the right of self-realization (see chapter 8). It revokes the collective association. With this claim, there exists an individual space within the space of the masses.

160

The second important developmental step is the differentiation between *system* and *Lebenswelt* (meaning the sub-conscious, preconditioned socio-cultural way of v iewing t he w orld a nd l ife) in c onnection w ith civil c ulture. F or religious worship, this development has many consequences. In central Europe, Christianity characterized the uniform society; institutionally drafted religion and individual worship were simply two sides of the same coin. If one calls the implementation of civil culture a process of emancipation, the question then arises, emancipation f rom w hat? The a nswer is e mancipation f rom t he m onopoly o f Church-written Christianity on a global scale in t he micro, meso, and macro domains. With the development of civil culture, thus developed that which we today understand as public: a free flow of thoughts, worldviews, and beliefs, of preferences and dislikes, and of the values and standards that regulate our lives. Church-represented Christianity did not, however, disappear as a result; rather, it is no longer the basis of culture but instead a sector of public culture. In this public realm, confessional Christianity must compete with other Christian and non-Christian churches, as well as (although not always) with religiously motivated communities for normativity, i.e. over the occupation of topics that influence and dominate the conceptions of t he world and, ultimately, power over what is defined as religion. The development of pluralism is inherently connected to the development of civil society. Its implementation was difficult and rich with conflict, and the management of pluralism remains an enormous challenge to this day – for the churches, but also for society.

Currently, there is a third development to add to the birth of civil culture and its principle of *competition*. According to Drehsen, there is a universal principle inherent in civil culture that does not stop at the walls of religion, but rather penetrates it. Religion is not another world on its own, separated from reality and the world of flesh and bone, as discussions of church and world in which the two are differentiated would propose. If one understands religion as a part of culture, one identifies it as part of the culture of a society. This means that the purification of religion will become more difficult and that civil values, norms, and attitudes will increasingly infringe on the religious sector. The consequences are that Christianity loses its unique shape and that religion and churches are pushed further apart. Probably no church can continue to integrate its conceptions of the world together with its church-written Christianity. It does not, however, only concern general conceptions of the world and attitudes. There are also religious elements that have their roots in Christ but have also become openly and independently active, and therefore, they operate beyond the control of the churches.

The Public and Identity

The main point of these reflections is this: with the recognition of these shown differentiations, the need of the foundation and assurance of identity originates. A church as an institution has this need in the same way as the individual does, no matter what type of conception of the world he or she has. If, for example, the personal conception of the world stems from the church-based Christian view, it is required that the assurance of identity take into account the obvious possibility of non-belief, religious pluralism within and beyond the church, etc. If in a non-traditional sense the personal conception of life is unattached to a church-based Christian view, then the assurance of identity is directed under the circumstances of a rational and emotional verification of separation and of arguments for a different view, perhaps also for a supposedly viewless life perspective. What is being discussed here is the moment when cultural uniformity is no longer synonymous with the *corpus christianum*; where differentiated segments are in competition with or perhaps even against the church-based Christian normativity, where church-based Christianity perceives itself in a religious setting with Christian claims being represented outside the Christian institutions, and where the boundaries between inside and outside are no longer easy to distinguish, the question over identity becomes a critical problem. Becoming conscious of the differentiation of worldviews results in the need of identity assurance, particularly the development of a foundation in *reference* to the public. At this point, reflection over functions and objectives of Religious Education can hardly be limited to the existing space of the stable holy community and still be successful. The glaring light of the public shines in the windows of the classrooms and church centers.

This is where the question of which path should be taken becomes virulent. The crisis is one of positions – whether the identity of church-represented Christianity becomes more secure *with* or *against* the public. With this decision, some very different demands are connected to Religious Education processes. One can limit oneself to the segmented realm of church-drafted Christianity and make honorable motives valid. Such a form of theology can at the very least be interested in functioning in the religious sector of society in order to maintain the distinctiveness and profile through appropriate normativity. Nevertheless, this can present a completely new set of problems. One problem can be the lack of exchange with the civil culture altogether. If a church does not want to become a sect, it must make a permanent effort towards communication, exchange, and disputes over meaning. Another problem is that a believer's world is only very rarely broken into parts. Different humans' lives run in different sectors of society, and in order to do this, they construct linguistic and symbolic bridges. The stability of the bridge construction is threatened when the divergent codes become disarranged.

162

The alternative orientation gives its attention to publicly present religion, including publicly active Christianity. From this perspective, the dangers of becoming absorbed in civil culture and yielding to the civil religion of the community clearly exist. These dangers are real and must be kept in view. To get involved in the public sphere inevitably means becoming partially equal. Without moments of agreement, there can be no understanding. These dangers must be taken into account, but the risk is justified by the chance to participate in the open discussion over the religious dimension of reality, or perhaps even just to bring this dimension into conversation and making it a public dimension (see chapter 4).

The public is a place of religious learning. Next to family, school, and parish, it is worthy of the highest attention. As will be shown, the public does not only have educational, theoretical relevance when identified as Christian and, therefore, can be claimed as a reinforcement of a religious socialization processes. The blending of individual forms of religion, of institutional presence of religion, and of cultural religious patterns already makes the public a place for education *par excellence*. In reference to the public, Religious Education stands by the claim of achieving processes of understanding and communication. Thus, it fulfills a crucial part of its function. Ordered Perceptions, Recognition of Differences, and Understanding and Interpreting are neither conditions nor exclusive consequences of learning processes but are instead dimensions of learning (see chapter 2). We turn now to the following three areas of the public and will show in practical interest some connecting lines between Religious Education and the public.

Culture

When we attempt to provide insight into the cultural dimension of religious learning and education processes, we need a working definition of *culture*, without our interest being to achieve a scientifically precise and elaborate one. For our purposes, it is sufficient to understand that culture is all of the expressions of a given society, which, in the broadest sense, establish a set of values and norms in which the individual can find a foundation of sense and meaning. Is our society at all Christian, or has it already reached a state of "post-Christianity"? Does Christian religious discussion focus on a rudimentary topic, which for the most part is no longer relevant? Has the reflection of the religious dimension of reality become a special domain to which only few have access? These questions provide an adequate assessment of the cultural requirements of Religious Education. With them, we can clarify how processes of education are pre-formed before the education begins.

The social differentiation processes of the last 300 years have generated a crucial modification to the position of Christianity within Western culture, reducing it from the overarching position it once had (the "canopy," as P.L. Berger called it), to one of several realms of culture. Present analysis continues to explore this and has come to the interpretation that there no longer (or scarcely) is a religion in Western culture. If religion is still found from this perspective, it is quasi religious, lacking explicit substantial (Christian) content. Without degenerating towards the other extreme of a Christian saturated culture, a sober view must recognize that the current situation is much more complicated. The search for clear boundaries is useless. Instead, we will try to identify some aspects.

Cultural Imprint on Religious Learning Processes

Religion is present in culture. First, we turn to the surface of the religious presence in discussion. Culturally, religion usually appears as religion connected to a church. Some examples bring a positive public interest in religion while others create a negative connection. The presence of controversy often seems to accompany the appearance of the churches. This wide span of opinions seems most common in the Catholic Church.

On the one hand, the Church is very much in the public eye, especially when Pope John Paul II undertakes a pastoral tour. If his attendance in foreign countries is planned, reports will appear in most newscasts, usually with live coverage. It is shown how the Pope meets with all of the powerful figures of the world and how he freely celebrates the liturgy and all it represents before inspired groups of people. Even while hindered by age and sickness, the Pope is shown as a courageous man who is not afraid to face and criticize ruling world powers and governments. He has the courage to speak out against unfairness, racism, and torture – remarks that receive much support from Western countries. At the same time, he expresses the Catholic position against birth control and abortion and advocates for sexuality to be directed towards marriage and family. He disciplines bishops and local churches and disapproves of certain theological currents. These positions not only lessen the Pope and the Catholic Church's popularity, but they are also the cause for open aggression, mockery, and jeers.

The Christian churches are also present culturally in the search for values and standards and in the attempts to answer general questions about life and the future. Church-based Christianity is still a source of influence on a greater level. It often performs the function of mediator for unions and politicians and contributes to ethical commissions and at international meetings, etc. There are also many artists and politicians who do not hide their faith and are well known as religious people. These people are not insignificant in the public picture of religion. Conversely, the public perception rarely reaches any depth. When the

Catholic and Protestant churches argued over the teachings of salvation in 1999 and 2000 and finally signed an agreement, the public was aware of the conflict and the resolution, but few actually understood the concrete theological problems. Theological arguments are reserved for the inner niches.

On the surface, the cultural presence of religion is set by the Christian churches, but below this level, the picture is more multilayered. As history shows, there have never been so many believers as there are now in this time of disbelief. What is meant by this is that never before has there been such opportunity for those promising new and different routes to salvation. In the meantime, New Age and esoteric groups have developed at a considerable rate. The offers range from Far-Eastern healing methods and meditation techniques and painting and self-experience in Tuscany to sense extension by sitting on hot rocks, for which one must go to the Canary Islands – Lanzarote, to be specific. This new religious subculture maintains its own marketing system independent of the churches. Even if a hoax (on the supplier's side) and naivety (on the consumer's side) often explain the situation, one cannot overlook the need for some sort of religion, expressed in the Latin word *religare* (see chapter 4). This shows up as the central theme in personal individual religious questions. This becomes clearly visible when reading autobiographies and other literature. Most people would n ot d escribe t hemselves t his w ay, b ut e mpirical s tudies p rove t hat t he question of where we come from and where we are going remain vital. As a central topic in much rock and pop music, it is clear that this is true.

When Religious Education looks to society for answers as to how students assume and process religion on an individual basis, the findings will be mixed. The presence o f church-based C hristianity i n c ulture i s n ot just c omposed o f reports of scandals, but it also has a positive side. From the position of young (and older) people, a sense of a church is visible, although this is dominated by a more reserved approach. In particular, the Catholic Church is seen as old fashioned and less attractive. If one looks at it from the other side, e.g. as a provider of answers to vital questions, the restraint often yields to curiosity. At the very least, people want to hear what theologians and the churches have to say, although the hope that something enriching will be taken from this is less certain. This ambivalence, however, shows no signs indicating that religion is accepted as something necessary or that the churches could be eliminated anytime soon. It is connected to the differentiation of religion. The discussed facets explain only a small part of this large field, but they do suggest that students bring along certain predetermined cultural elements, which Religious Education cannot leave unconsidered. The culturally acceptable public influences both style and environment – also in the area of religion.

Effect on Culture

What effect can theology and Religious Education have on culture? The scientific study of Religious Education is itself a part of culture. It stands, as the churches, no longer for the cumulative collection of religious knowledge, experiences, and attitudes. It is confronted primarily with the demands of being able to participate in cultural discourse, not to lose sight of the multiple forms of religion, and to accept criticism – but also to create opportunities for a religious existence in today's society. Its main tools are scientific discourse. In good theological tradition, theology speaks about the rational responsibility of a religious life and the solidification of Christian faith. Probably no other Roman document showed the function of the task of developing culture better than the encyclical *Evangelii Nuntiandi* (1975). This document, signed by Paul VI, tracks religious colonialism and relies on amalgamation (connection). The research of Religious Education can illustrate the conditions and show the possibilities and boundaries. As an empirically based discipline (see chapter 11), it brings proven expertise into the discourse of theology and church, thereby helping to prevent the loss of reality. As a theological discipline, it regulates the clarity, interpretation, and sense of the contents of discourse, which it incorporates in its public message.

Culturally Mediated Religion as the Subject of Learning

How should religious teachers teach culturally influenced religion? Current forms of Religious Education acknowledge cultural tendencies, events, and developments. In the best sense, it will not disregard any enlightened tradition, namely striving for religious autonomy and methodically working not to counteract this goal. He who wants maturity must also make this an element of the learning process and accept the challenge. *First*, that means to be open to the perceptions the students bring with them and not to tamper with the many different perceptions. If students express perceptions, these are inherently correct in their subjective understanding. What students know, feel, and believe about certain religious questions does not only have instrumental value to education by showing how one can most effectively make connections to the meaning; it also shows how religious questions are effected by today's culture. *Second*, it aims to thaw the perceptions (i.e. to deconstruct them and reveal the contents) and to confront them with alternative points of view (to which other pupils often supply the appropriate counter example): where some might consider the Pope a dictator, others will place his charisma at the forefront. The classroom is itself a microcosm of culture. The deconstruction helps to free the intentions of the declarations, to differentiate them, to arrange them, and to accommodate their treatment: is criticism directed at individuals within the churches or at the churches as institutions? Are we speaking about traces of Christianity on society, about institutional or personal questions, etc.? The crucial *third* point is to exceed the perceptions. Hypothetical questions such as, "What would it be like if the 10 Commandments never existed?" or "Would the world be missing something had Jesus not given 'The Sermon on the Mount'?" or "What are the 'gods' that we believe in like, and what comforts do they provide us with?" can be helpful.

When considering the cultural dimension of Religious Education, other crucial questions arise: is it enough in religious learning processes to simply display or maintain a sense of the deeper layers of life? Is it enough to secure or develop an interest in transcendentalism? Is it enough to acquaint students in religious instruction with a reflection of life and the world, which blends the broadness (and often flatness) of the many attitudes towards life? Is it enough to generate an enthusiasm for religion? In the context of these efforts, it becomes abundantly clear that a general religion is insufficient. If these questions can be answered to some extent in the affirmative, then it becomes a personal decision of whether or not to engage oneself as a religiously sensitive person in a historical traditional system of faith.

Media

The strongest influence in public is most certainly the media. The media play the deciding role in structural changes of the public (cf. also Habermas 1990, esp. 275-343). Teachers report that many of their students have greater exposure and access to media than they do. It is not only the older teachers, who still perhaps remember the revolution of the introduction of the television, who must struggle to keep up with the technological advancements being made in media. There are no classes about increased contact with media for adolescents to take. They are surrounded by it, and it is readily available. In the following section, we ask how students are shaped by the media, what effect or influence Religious Education can have on the media, and how Religious Education can incorporate the media into the learning process.

The Shaping of Religious Learning Processes by the Media

Statistics on the viewing of television by young people reveal that the television belongs to the most beloved forms of media. It is not uncommon for a youth to spend two to three hours (if not more) per day watching television. Explicitly religious topics are rather insignificant here, as young people make up a small fraction of the viewers watching programs covering religious associations, religious communities, churches in foreign countries, etc. Furthermore, series about the history of Christianity do not attract young viewers. If religion is offered within the area of entertainment, the numbers are somewhat higher. Thus, there is rarely a time when at least one television station is not featuring either a televangelist or a clergyperson on a talk show.

To a considerable degree, young people satisfy their viewing interests with private stations. As opposed to the lame and boring topics found on public channels, youths turn to private channels for cool programs. Daily soaps and music programs are those most frequented. The daily soaps offer a view of family life that knows only extreme fortune and tragedy and shows that in the end, a fighting spirit and the will to live are the keys to survival. The family life shown apparently meets the wishes, fears, and desires of its audience, even when some of the most detached viewers feel that the pain threshold and superficiality are excessive. Nevertheless, there must be some deeper attraction to these programs. Do they show the picture of a family that is less and less common in real life, in which people cry and laugh, in which feelings still play an important role, and in which communication between family members still takes place?

In addition to these programs, younger viewers are particularly attracted to the many music stations. VIVA in Europe, VH1 in the US, and MTV are definitely the most popular. Although the concept of the stations is very simple (practically monotonous), it is enough to get young people hooked. Music is the focal point, complemented by video clips. Music channels form styles and trends to a considerable degree, and while not always explicitly, surely implicitly. They present what fashions are in style – what is "in" and what is "out" with respect not only to fashion, but to attitudes and opinions as well. These channels also establish a direction for consumer interest and set forth the criterion by which one can present oneself effectively in public. To a certain extent and in opposition to a trend of individualism in society, new standards are presented, and so in this sense, the music channels are fulfilling a unifying function. If one lives by the codes established by the music channels, you will recognize and be recognized by like-minded individuals. The function of peers is thus virtual.

Next to television, the radio remains a very popular medium. Regional radio programs are particularly popular. For example, someone can simply call the radio station and use it to spread information to other listeners that the traffic light at Main Street is not working again, the swimming pool is closed, and swimming lessons are cancelled, or because someone wants to invite all the cool people in town to his birthday party on Saturday. The regional station informs everyone about the people and events close by, relies on an emotional affiliation, and tries to provide a neighborly atmosphere. Music selection is usually pop and hits, which most listeners can sing along with. Traditionally, family, neighborhood, and youth groups were the heart of the community. There, people shared views and thoughts, sang, danced, and celebrated together. It appears as if regional radio can now fulfill these roles.

Lastly, the internet. A growing percentage of young people have direct access to the internet at home. The numbers are continuously rising, although the fact that these results a re o ften class-specific cannot b e overlooked. The frequency of surfing corresponds to levels of education and wealth. The internet serves various functions. Besides fun and games, the internet offers young people a platform for communication, giving access to a wide range of topics. Both sides of communication, specifically content and relationship, are also important to internet usage. The internet houses knowledge; it is a fountain of information and unique questions. Young people are realizing the increasingly important role the internet plays in personal development. The internet, however, also acts as a founding agent for relationships and communication, often with unfamiliar people. Love and sex may play important roles, but not exclusive ones. Additionally, the internet allows for the construction and maintenance of an entire communications network that allows people to share experiences, close thoughts, and feelings over great distances, something which some may not be able to do in face-to-face communication. The internet can help one escape a boring and rainy day in the country; the fact that this world is virtual does not matter as long as it feels real.

What does this all mean? The importance of media in our lives will only continue to increase. In the future, everyday life will be ever more controlled by the various forms o f m edia. S econd, the number o f d ifferent t ypes of m edia and their effectiveness is also increasing. Third, new ways of linking different forms of media together are being created. Since the not so distant introduction of television, the development of the media has made rapid progress. We can only make insufficient estimates of how far development can go and what new forms of media will be used. The crucial insight for the educational and religious-educational connection is that as a concept, the influential power of the media has not been sufficiently studied. It is well known that the media influences adolescents and that for a long time, there has been a branch of education that focuses on media. Yet the school of Religious Education profited from this only marginally. The concentration on form and content of media must move into a new phase, one that likewise considers the global networking of media and the increasingly autonomous use of media directed towards young people. It is difficult to assess the influential power of media and their importance in comparison to family and school adequately. Perhaps one cannot place enough importance on its influential power. Above all, it is very difficult to supervise direct and indirect agents of teaching and their messages. Which styles, environmental imprints, forms of values, and life orientations shown and encouraged by them can usually only be realized *aposteriori*.

Influence on the Media

What influence can Religious Education have on the media? It can assume an opposing stance against the world of media and, above all, can identify the dangers r esulting f rom t he u se o f c ertain f orms o f m edia. A lternatively, i t c ould highlight the good side of the media and emphasize its positive uses. There are arguments for and against either perspective; thus, perhaps the best course is to adopt an approach of constructive criticism. Religious Education must discover that the media is relevant to religious learning. For example, many handbooks on questions of religious upbringing focus on the fundamental function of the family, to which school and catechism are connected. A young person registers what the family no longer provides and accordingly seeks the remaining possible places of learning. Outside of the family, however, children and young people are only partially socialized. Where a deficit of family is identified, there is not simply a gap in the child's character; rather, some other socializing agent, most likely the media, has filled that gap. It appears that a new justification for Religious Education as part of the process of socialization is necessary, one that can process and digest the displaced classical forms of upbringing on the digital heartbeat of the media. The media have created milieus, which function as communities of world interpretation – and work across the differentiation of society.

Religious Education can have very little direct effect on the media. It uses the media itself. What then does it mean to have a constructively critical attitude towards the media? The constructive association with the media is surely based on the multiplicity of ways to use the media for presentations to the public. Most search engines in the internet have a category for religion. Religious questions and theological problems are addressed not only in religious newsgroups or listservs; they also stand in public discourse despite all of the ideas of secularization. Religious Education as a science can take part in this discourse. It can present itself in teachings and research, which provide colleagues and other interested people with information that can inspire debate and communication. It can contribute through references to the establishment of a web of communication, offering other visitors an attractive view into the world of religion.

The critical aspect of reflecting on the media comes in respect to research when one speaks of the role of the media in the process of socialization and when one asks, "Who are the most effective and important educators in the media?" "Which values and acknowledgements of faith do they put forth?" "What are the bases of curse and blessing?" Next to the millions of euros, dollars, pounds, etc. that the media can spend on research and on wooing its clientele, the opportunities for science are relatively limited. This suggests that religious-educational projects on media research require interdisciplinary cooperation.

Religion in the Media as the Topic of Learning

Which learning processes can Religious Education use with regard to the media? Let us now look at the contents of television, radio, and internet, the subjects dealt with in this section. "Religion inside" applies to all three. Through media, we are introduced to a multiplicity of religious contents, content with a clear church connotation and content that is implicitly religious. In television, explicitly religious programs are easy to identify. The quality of many of these programs is excellent and with regard to professionalism offers the same high standard as any other program. They can be and are used for application in classroom instruction. In radio, the respective programs are broadcast from fixed stations to ease orientation. Admittedly, radio programs do not have the same attractiveness as visual media for use in classroom instruction. As for the internet, it should become easier to incorporate this medium into classroom instruction in the future. This does not only apply to computer science instruction. In the meantime, the amount of information available about religion and faith is so extensive that religious instruction relies on the help of the internet to work through certain themes and topics. Sometimes, teachers will provide students with maps that the students use to unlock predetermined treasures of information; other times, students are requested to independently retrieve information that is more specific. The goal is to incorporate the medium of the internet in religion, in addition to the schoolbooks and catechumens.

In addition to using of the contents of the media, education must also lead adolescents to question the media critically. For example, religious instruction can address the question of whether people still speak about God in our modern society. It can differentiate and examine the God of religions and other modern gods and uncover "where mankind places its heart" (Martin Luther). Students can themselves investigate how God's code applies to modern society. They can ask which powers, hopes, or illusions of this code are fading away. Thus, as users of the medium, they are always the subject of their own study.

With our work, we have pointed out the contents of the media and emphasized the necessity of critical analysis. Furthermore, the possibility of cooperation with the media should not be overlooked. In particular, local radio stations are expected to provide local listeners with a specific program at specific times. In cooperation with the media department in a particular area, each respective church could prepare its own program, and this preparation could take place within the context of religious instruction. There are numerous opportunities open to Religious Education in connection with the internet. The results of religious projects or experiences of religious events can be provided over the homepage of a school or a community, along with reflections on sociopolitical and ethical questions. The consideration of such projects for instruction has nothing to do with activism. It also has nothing to do with the activities taking place in other subjects, which may in fact divert from the function of religious instruction. Conversely, the challenge for Religious Education regarding media is finding up-to-date ways of helping to spread the word of God (1 Peter 3:15).

Perhaps the media today offer a more practical setting than Corpus Christi processions to motivate youth for such debate.

Politics

Politics is the third domain of the public with which a pluralistically capable system of Religious Education must struggle. Under the term *politics*, we understand not only the party system and the parliamentary structure of democracy, but also the comprehensive span of opinion formation and decision-making in society. The political parties play a central role, as do the social forces of the churches and trade unions. For theology and the churches, the openness of politics has special meaning. Church-linked religion, particularly in German speaking countries, is a *res mixta*. To name only a few aspects of churches in Germany, for example: churches are public bodies, which means that they are given special rights but also are subject to special duties; the state collects taxes for the major churches; religious instruction is the responsibility of both the state and the churches; *Diakonie* on the protestant side and *Caritas* on the Catholic side are recognized welfare organizations and, in the state's interest, assume a substantial portion of social care. The churches in Germany, Austria, and Switzerland are thus integrated politically and, to a considerable degree, socially. At any rate, they are far from being private associations. This model can continue to function in this way as long as it remains useful to both the state and the churches. This *res mixta* model is always based on give and take. For these reasons, the state is committed to protecting the churches and their roles in society. The churches, for their part, must make clear that their commitment is widespread and that they will assume responsibility for harmonious coexistence. The school of Religious Education stands in the middle of these two interests, as it must consider questions of school policy and religious instruction. It must pursue a two-part understanding of education developed by Karl Ernst Nipkow: the unlimited responsibility for the continuation of Christian faith and the "shared pedagogical responsibility for the public education system" (Nipkow 1990, 59). This understanding became generally accepted in Germany and has functioned well, although the idea of shared responsibility has proven more troublesome in other European countries. We turn now to the interests of Religious Education and ask ourselves where and how Religious Education is influenced by politics, which effects it has on politics, and how politics can become a topic of religious learning processes.

Political Influences on Religious Learning

The dimension of mutual dependency of church and politics, central in the perspective of Religious Education, is founded by education policy and the basic worldview of the general education system supported by federal laws and state

172

polities. Further areas of interest include the publicly promoted church academies, continuing and completing education facilities, adult education institutions, church-sponsored schools, and, naturally, all aspects associated with religious instruction (curricula, the relationship between teachers, alternative instruction methods, etc.) for which the state and churches are responsible. The example of religious instruction makes the dependent relationship between the state and the churches quite clear. Current debates show that traditional structures, even if supported by federal law, continually come up in discussion. The reason for this is not an antagonistic attack on the churches; rather, it is a reaction to the growing pluralism in society and the search for a more suitable model of Religious Education in schools.

This shows that the shared responsibility for education of the churches discussed above cannot, in the political arena, simply be taken for granted. One can agree with this assessment or not. The fact is that in any case, the circumstances demand that the churches and Religious Education emphasize their responsibility to education and show their relating benefits and results. The participation in the debate over religious instruction has other facets, and the church-theological side should make an effort to form a united front. The churches and Religious Education must not, with all the concerns focusing on the specific responsibility of *religious* learning, neglect the perception of comprehensive responsibility for education, thereby exempting themselves from a cooperative approach to this question. These questions are critical because they concern enormous social change that has altered the role of Christian churches.

Effects on the Political Arena

Religious Education, if capable of handling pluralism, will sensitively observe both the political plane and its contribution to the forming of opinions. Yet how can it influence the political arena? Its means are limited to the founding and maintenance of discussions, publicly, politically focused research, and the questioning and support of innovative practice. The inclusion of questions about Religious Education in public discussion is essential. The school of Religious Education reduces its own importance and is itself at fault for some of its missed opportunities for development if it does not pay critical attention to the basic conditions of education or involve itself in discussions about the general problems and goals of both Religious Education and education in general. This obligation stems from both the general function of the university to promote public welfare and the special religious ethos of the Religious Education as a discipline connected to the Christian tradition of a church that does not promote seclusion. The participation in public discourse has a positive-constructive goal. This shows that and how religion does make a contribution to personal development in becoming human, and it also shows what religion can contribute to the evolvement of a fair and human world community. The churches' contribution to education, to Religious Education, and beyond is the promotion of the idea of living together in solidarity for the future and is, therefore, a service to society as a whole. It should be open, so that even those who do not belong to a Christian church can access it.

The school of Religious Education itself pursues educational policies only in exceptional cases, but it avails itself of parameters from which it is able to assess political-educational decisions. Consequently, it requires the development of conceptual designs, argumentative strength, and the ability to engage in dialogue. The participation in public discourse, however, works counterproductively when it is seen as an effort to secure the churches' position.

Discussion partners in the political public are not only party representatives and special interest groups. There is increasing pressure for interdisciplinary discussion. It is important to realize interconnecting relations. One cannot dismiss the obvious fact that the established school of Religious Education pursues certain interests. It cannot, however, take on a lobbying function. As a scientific discipline, it strives to enhance decision-making processes through solid knowledge. For that reason, it bases its arguments largely on researched correlations. Religious instruction is required to do empirical research in which researchers must investigate the factual forms of cooperation between denominations, possibilities, and boundaries of inter-religious learning, the effects of the curricula, etc. In the best case, it succeeds to develop new theoretically and empirically justified models of religious-educational practice. It is the backbone of the theoretical and political arguments on education.

The Political Arena as the Subject of Learning

When we finally ask how the political arena itself can become the subject of learning processes, we move to another level. Students are, to a certain extent, beneficiaries (or victims) of the aforementioned efforts. The political public is valid in instruction, but in another way. To illustrate this, one must break the framework wide open: from the societal-diaconal basic *of* instruction to the social and sociopolitical themes *in* instruction. For example, there are values produced by decisions made in the political arena that control plural cohabitation. Religious Education, which prepares one for full participation in this society, makes adolescents familiar with questions of life and the world and enables them to develop a position and the ability to argue these positions. It clarifies the dangers tied to a purely consumerist use of the liberties that establish pluralism and justifies the necessity to inform oneself of the criteria to which the continued development of pluralism should be oriented. Pluralism is not considered good from the start; its quality and benefits are derived from the opportunities it provides for the living together of people with different religious and ethnic backgrounds under international responsibility. Education and Religious Education contribute to civic maturity by taking up controversial questions and creating opportunities for students to *learn* how to argue. The specific goal of Religious Education is to help the students develop a set of values – *from* the Christian faith in critical reference *to* traditional faith. Religious Education prepares students of the Christian faith to take part in the public forming of opinions as Christians. Non-believers should at least become familiar with the way that Christians relate themselves in society. This familirization has nothing to do with indoctrination. It is orientated much more on a model of discourse, which in the field of education is called "value communication" (see chapter 8). Empirical findings of the general political interest of young people are humbling. They underline the necessity of anchoring social-political will as an important part of upbringing and education in pluralism. This is what Religious Education wants to do – to perform the function of providing a general education.

Outlook

At the beginning of the chapter, we discussed the role of the public in the process of social differentiation and subsequently provided an example of how each of the three sectors of the public realm affects the field of Religious Education, what effect the field of Religious Education can have on each of these sectors, and how each one of them can become the subject of the learning process. A short consideration stands at the end of this chapter. Its most valuable message reads: *the public is not something separate from the affairs of Religious Education or something to which Religious Education must refer more out of necessity than intrinsically; rather, Religious Education needs a public reference in order to know who it is and what it stands for.* This assurance cannot sufficiently be satisfied b y s elf-reflection. M artin B uber e xpressed this i n a s imilar, e xistentially philosophical way: the I needs the You, and vice-versa.

With the help of some system-theoretical considerations (as developed by Niklas Luhmann), this thesis can be explained and justified. Core terms of the system theory are *system* and *environment*. By system, we understand an "acting entity" or "acting whole" in discussion. A human is, under this terminology, a *personal system*, the Church, an *institutional system*. Environment does not just refer to nature, but rather everything that does not belong to a system. For our purposes, environment can include everything that is included by the word *public*.

The system-theoretical attention applies to both the extensive system and environment, b ut e ven m ore s o t o t he i nterrelation b etween t he two (cf. Z iebertz 1997, 185-213). The system-theory, with its reflections over the relationship between system and environment, has made clear that identity and meaning cannot satisfyingly be produced endogenously, as if to create vertical linkage of unity with tradition, heritage, etc. For example, a look back on the individual Christian tradition is important in order to understand what it is to be Christian today, but this is not sufficient. The consequence is that identity cannot be achieved against or in spite of the environment, but only *in relationship with* it. Therefore, each system must draw its own circle of foundation and stability around itself. If it remains a closed circle, the system itself can dry up because new energy is prevented from entering. This new energy (input) enters the system through its external connections. To help demonstrate, we will take the symbols of a spiral and a circle. The healthy functioning of a system resembles a spiral more than a circle. The circle is closed. Environmental relations take place, if necessary, over determined boundaries, without the opportunity for exchange. The spiral is open to input and output, but at the same time protects, to a certain extent, its continuity, and uses the incoming energy for advancement (transformation).

It becomes clear that Religious Education's concentration on its subject is too limited if it does not consider the public, with which it is in a direct relationship. Cultural development, the socializing effects of media, and the political public are parts of the definition that makes up the subject of what Religious Education is and what it means. Their impact is more incidental than intentional. Even if in no other way, this is evident by the fact that the teachers and the students are all part of it and are influenced by it. The system-theoretical consideration makes equally clear that the inclusion of the public does not mean that the two should be merged together or that it will dictate the agenda from public expectations. That would be like sailing in a ship on the open sea without a compass. The function of R eligious E ducation i s r ather t o b ring t he *reciprocal relationship* between subject and public into view, i.e. to become aware of the interlacing and to decode it in order to arrange it in a precise form.

A positive attitude toward the public does not exclude a strong consciousness of self but instead attempts to direct attention toward the interaction between the public and the closed group. The suitability of this position with pluralism lies in the idea that the public should not be perceived as the source of pressure or distress but rather as a *space of possibility* for *relationship-rich action*, which, if reflection is present, helps in development of Christian identity (see chapter 6). We need the public in order to know who we are and how we should plan our action. Plausibility that is self-produced without being given the chance for public recognition runs the risk of transforming itself into an unrealistic ideology. The churches should not only reflect on their influence on society (in the sense of the effect), but they should not forget to remain forums for critical dispute, to cultivate their own set of *agorae*. In the church itself, public must remain noticeable. The system theory teaches this as well: the public is not only an environment that confronts a church; the public is also deeply integrated in that church. Church members and the clergy themselves are, and in ever-changing configurations, environments for each other. This applies equally for students and teachers in school. To understand the public as a challenge means to take up variety and conflict as well as the domination of opinion and the absence thereof as educational challenges and opportunities.

Part V

Religious Education as a scientific discipline

11

Methodology:
The Empirical Orientation of Practical Theology

In this chapter, the concept of practical theology is used as a header for practical theological sub-disciplines, such as catechesis, Religious Education, homiletics, church development, poimenics, and diaconics. The adjective "practical" is not simply the opposite of "theoretical." More accurately, "practical" refers to the material object of practical theology – the practice of religion. Unlike systematic theological disciplines, practical theology focuses on the real-life human action within religious practice rather than logic. The sub-disciplines mentioned above reflect religious practice within different fields of human action. As a form of *theology*, practical theology is not just looking to describe religious practice but also to understand it, explain it, and lay out possible alternatives for future decisions. The goal of orienting decisions is particularly relevant to normative theology. Some would see the formal objective of practical theology as analyzing the tension between what is, what could be, and what ought to be. This does not mean that theology analyses normative aspects in order to compare these with real-life practice. This would relegate the discipline back to being an applied science. Rather, the goal is to find the theories that define the practice. Practical theology must focus on the practice itself, methodically explaining *how* it focuses and *how* it arrives at conclusions. This definitely requires an empirical emphasis, which may take on different forms: for example, by taking in empirical data or independently doing empirical research within the scope of practical theology. Nowadays, we know that an empirical orientation does not automatically mean a *positivistic* science; it can indeed have very *critical* characteristics.

The following issues will be discussed: first, the subject matter of the research; second, the methodological basis; third, the methods used; and finally, the role played by empirical research within the field of practical theology.

The Material Object of Empirically Oriented
Practical Theology

There are many aspects to religious practice, the material object of practical theology. Several options are available for gaining data about a particular practice that should be supported or encouraged. One could analyze the efficiency of a religious curriculum, the religious and moral attitudes of young people, the teacher-student interaction in religious classes, religious biographies, etc. In Western Europe, one particular topic of research in the empirically oriented practical theology has gained in popularity recently. This topic is change within religion on the macro, meso, and micro levels. The churches and theology in general are becoming ever more estranged in response to the presence of pluralistic religion in our society. At the same time, more and more people are becoming estranged towards religious content as presented by the churches and theology, as well as towards the churches' social structures (cf. Ziebertz 1998a as well as http://www.uni-wuerzburg.de/religionspaedagogik/ forsch.htm).

The demarcation lines between religion, religiousness, church, and belief on one side and society on the other side were fairly clear as long as the process could be explained by the secularization theory, which holds religious degeneration to be inherent to the modern age. Those phenomena that fell outside Christianity as represented by a Christian church were abandoned. As far as the Christian churches' Christianity was concerned, having a monopoly on society's religious needs meant being able to accept the loss of a few believers without considering the need to make any radical self-changes. New modernization theories, however, challenge the notion of a negative correlation between modernity and religion. Their ever-changing relationship is considered, at the very least, *ambivalent*. On the one hand, there is the secularization effect that does influence religion as represented by the churches. On the other hand, the modern age has proved to be a pool of religious creativity and vitality. These two phenomena combined do not necessarily lead to the conclusion that religion is in a crisis or that it is incompatible with the modern age. More exactly, it appears that particular forms of religion are in trouble. In any case, the situation is more complex than the secularization theory makes it out to be (cf. Ziebertz 1999).

According to new modernization theories, religion as such can no longer be exclusively identified with one Christian church or Christianity. Theologians now admit, more or less openly, that the Christian churches have lost their religious monopoly, that the very definition of religion must be stretched (outside of what the churches represent), and, finally, that we are in a competitive religious market where the future of competing religious traditions and institutions is unknown. Moreover, religion is no longer controlled from the top down; rather, the people themselves make the decision as to what and how much and what kind of religion they want.

These phenomena are characteristic of a deep structural change. The roots are to be found within the very process of modernization. With the continuing differentiation processes in modern society, our experience increasingly shows that the Christian churches and culture, theology and religion, theory and practice are moving further and further apart:

- the societal structure is no longer identical to the world view held by the Christian churches;
- contemporary religious styles deviate from the frames of Christian theology; and
- academic dogmatic theology and religious practice are neither identical to nor deductive from one another.

These changes had already been noticed in the 18th century and were considered a serious crisis. One response was the establishment of practical theology as a further department within the theological canon. This new scientific discipline was created to analyze the relationship between theory and practice, explaining why religious plans failed in practice. It would help priests and catechists, who only had knowledge of theology and felt unprepared for education and teaching because of the increasing distance between theological concepts and actual religious attitudes, come to grips with the real world. Historically, practical theology oriented its studies towards the development of concrete instructions for practice; one has to understand the actual practice in order to have an influence on it. On the other hand, understanding religious practice in order to implement religious programs that essentially remain static cannot work in the end. This perspective neglects those subjects who are not necessarily out of tune religiously (M. Weber) but for whom certain religious traditions are simply strange. These traditions are, in fact, becoming increasingly strange today because they were never introduced in a social or family environment. This also means that this group is not just made up of the previously lost but also those who are religiously neutral and open. Quite apart from the instrumental interest in influencing the situation, it has become imperative to understand the changes and the subjects acting within them. This essentially hermeneutical interest is combined with an empirical orientation. Empirical procedures are coupled with hermeneutical thinking and can only be processed though the latter (cf. Ziebertz 1996b; 1998b). For Schweitzer, empirical methods are a continuation of hermeneutical methods (Schweitzer 1993, 39) without concretely abandoning the original concept.

The theories construed are often not enough to understand the religious estrangement. In the field of Religious Education, for instance, the limits of correlating didactics are becoming clear. These assume that there is a fitting Christian interpretation for every event, like a key for every lock. Religious practice, however, is now leaving its church cradle to develop outside of institutional limits. Religious tradition, used to a historical monopoly on the truth, now sees itself confronted by conflict. People who derived their norms more or less naturally from tradition and authority now do so based on their own subjective experiences. Religion and religiousness are now a claim for autonomy, preventing judgment by tradition and authority and subjecting forms and contents of beliefs to the light of subjectivity. What people believe and how they express themselves religiously is unconnected to the Christian religious monopoly. Individual and institutional religion may be identical or simply cross over in some areas, they may coexist peacefully, or they may compete with each other – in the modern era, there are no rules. When people are forced to learn about and practice Christianity (e.g. religious courses in school), there are considerable normative problems and a great need for interactive discussion. This has lead to the development that today, Religious Education begins at a point of didactics of communication. Discussion then ensues, even about truisms. One example thereof is superstition. For schoolchildren (approx. 13 years old) in the 8th grade, it is up for discussion as to what true faith and superstition is. The authors of their schoolbook, however, have no such problems. The only doubters are the children, who miss a certain sense of freedom when exploring different value systems. These are, however, truisms that theologians use everyday as a matter of course. If we do not encourage discussion from the very start, then we just add to the estrangement in progress.

One consequence we must deal with is the dominance of dogmatic thought in practical theological discourse. This, in turn, means that imparting the subject and context of religion becomes the principal task, but the subjects want to play a role in the very definition of religion. This situation is new to most theologians, who have never had to deal with such a myriad of faiths and conflicts. These are now so complex that they cannot be categorized according to church or non-church, Christian or non-Christian, believer or atheist, etc. The ever-changing strangeness itself has become the structure. For the objective sub-disciplines of practical theology, this means the following:

- Practical theology goes beyond churchly theological content and turns towards the socio-cultural presence of religion, which will eventually be constantly confronted through education. Seen objectively, religious practice becomes very loosely defined, going far beyond what Religious Education presumes, be it in the school, church, or in another directed form of learning.

- Practical theology picks up the task of analyzing modern religious styles and trying to understand them on the personal and biographical level as well as on the cultural level. Another goal is to understand both their estrangement from classical religious institutions and the search for existential functionality that leads to their adoption.

- For practical theologians, it is not just about a new religious landscape becoming estranged from tradition and that *estranges tradi-*

tion itself. Estrangement has at least two sides to it. The responsibility carried by e.g. the very social structures propagated by (practical) theology must also be considered.

- Understanding the practice is not just instrumentally interesting for connecting the unchanged programs with the contemporary. It is also important for evaluating the cultural worth of the Gospel today. The practice has a theological dignity all its own.

- As a theological discipline, practical theology has its base within Christian tradition, but it can always take in other points of view as long as neither the contemporary Christian churches and religion nor a particular socio-cultural context is taken as a truism. This also means that a purely theological interpretation of the contemporary situation is insufficient; other points of view must be integrated and theologically developed.

- These other views must be classified empirically. Practical theology as a whole must have an empirical orientation. It is clear from the above that a technical knowledge alone is insufficient; processes for understanding should be the key element.

Methodology: Hermeneutics, Empirical Orientation, and Ideological Criticism

In his discussion of theoretical sciences, the German philosopher Jürgen Habermas pointed out the connection between "knowledge and interest" (1978). He showed that there is no naïve use of method because methods imply a particular view of reality and because methods of knowledge and interest of knowledge are in a dependent relationship to one another. Within the context of a critical, scientific theory, he mentions three relational systems used to define the connection between logical methodical rules and the interests that guide knowledge in the research practice scientifically. He differentiates between empirically analytical, hermeneutical, and critically oriented sciences, and he arranges these types into their technical, practical, and emancipating knowledge interest.

Empirically analytical research is interested in the scientific statements related to experience. The goal is to find rules for the construction and description of theories as well as for their final test. Empirically testable prognoses are gathered from deductive hypothetical connections, which should lead to basic conclusions. Habermas points out that these basic conclusions are not something objectively evident, but rather something drawn out of their preceding perspective (guiding interest) in order to assure and expand successful human action. This is different from the *hermeneutical* method, where formalized language and objective experience remain one and the same. The development of theories is done neither deductively nor with a view to the operational success of systematic experience. Instead of systematically observing and describing facts, the hermeneutical method concentrates on form and meaning. What could be construed as pure theory is, in reality, a developed relationship between the initial comprehension gained from the very start by an interpreter and the hermeneutically produced knowledge applied within the framework of the original comprehension. Habermas finally turns to an *ideologically critical* type of science. Using ideologically critical means, the goal is to turn unanalyzed consciousness into a critical consciousness through self-reflection, thereby freeing the subjects from their dependence on hypostatic forces. Self-reflection is determined by an emancipating knowledge interest (Habermas 1978).

This analytical differentiation shows three different knowledge-guiding interests to be connected to the process of research. First, the production of experienced knowledge, second, adding to our understanding of the purpose and meaning, and third, furthering an emancipation. Should these three issues be understood as "pure types," and if not, should they be ordered next to, above, or below each other? This chapter takes the position, suggested by Van der Ven (1988), that in a practically ordered discipline, the systematic examination of experienced knowledge is of the utmost importance. Without this, theories run the risk of becoming pure speculation. The concept of adequacy would become random, e.g. when developing learning goals or estimating the point of origin for learning processes. A modern science analyzing a complex practice cannot afford to be that inexact. Empirical methods can serve to illuminate the *material* object of practical theology: the present religious practice.

Hermeneutics is also very important, and for three very good reasons. First, Religious Education contains certain concepts that lay down educational goals. Clarity is required to understand which general perspectives, concrete goals, and specific interventions are meaningful. Second, hermeneutically understanding meaning and purpose is necessary within the scope of the experienced knowledge, as this is not completely without theory and as experienced data does not contain its own program that explains what it is good for. According to Habermas, there is a "previous organization within our experience." Its contours must be highlighted to make the inter-subjective reflection accessible. Third, the hermeneutical thought is constantly in line with the dialectics of normativity and factuality, theory and practice. Understanding the meaning and purpose of the *formal* object means using theological hermeneutical thought to reflect on the tension within a practice – what it is and what it ought to be.

Finally, a critical perspective is necessary to set up a forum of ideal meta-communication with both hermeneutical thought and the highlighting of experienced knowledge. It should question new ideas and concepts and search out their implicit presumptions that would hinder the person's own independence and freedom. It should similarly question both the methods used and whether they further the goal of independence. These three perspectives are not exclusive but rather should be seen as complementary to each other. That is what the following theses show.

- Hermeneutics without ideological criticism runs the risk of producing ideology.
- Hermeneutics without empirical orientation runs the risk of losing sight of reality.
- Empirical orientation without hermeneutics runs the risk of being understood in a positivistic manner.
- Empirical orientation without ideological criticism runs the risk of taking factual knowledge at face value and using it as a truism.
- Ideological criticism is inextricably connected to empirical orientation and hermeneutics.

Therefore, practical theology with an empirical orientation will look for a complementary u se o f the three s ystems. E mpirical k nowledge c annot a llow r eligious-educational theories to be based on the personal experience of the researcher. Personal experience should not be drawn out into generalizations, e.g. that all children in the local neighborhood go to church every Sunday. Experienced knowledge must be gathered systematically using empirical methods. Empirical analysis makes correct and result-oriented human action possible, but it is still not enough. These methods are limited by the fact that the actual norm for taking action is indefinable. Therefore, empirical research must be brought into line using a hermeneutical dimension. It should be mentioned that Nipkow argues for the use of a dialectic ideological criticism to gain a meta-theoretical corrective value, thereby keeping the actual social values and connections within reach (Nipkow 1984, 185). This leads to the following conclusion: empirical research is necessary for a factual study of Religious Education, but is not enough in itself. It must be supplemented by hermeneutical and ideologically critical methods in order to gain useful theological theories in regards to Christian socialization, contemporary Christian history, and pedagogic-political history.

Quantitative and Qualitative Orientation in Constructivist Perspectives

The "understand-or-explain controversy" (inspired by Dilthey's quote "we *explain* nature, we *understand* the life of our souls") loses a lot of its significance when one considers the close link between hermeneutical and empirical methods. To explain something was seen as a principle of empirically oriented (natural science) research, related to issues of exactitude and objectivity. The humanities, on the other hand, were reconstructive and interpretative sciences, based on understanding. Dilthey criticized the way methods from natural science were incorporated into the humanities. His reasoning was that it was insufficient (or just plain wrong) to look for firm laws and cause-and-effect scenarios in human action. The humanities were more about the purpose and goals achieved through decisions. To come up with those sorts of results, hermeneutical work was needed. With the subsequent adoption of empirical methods (empirical quantitative procedures, to be exact) in the humanities, the argument arose as to whether this natural science (i.e. foreign) way of thinking and working would not overshadow or simply forget to take into account issues of purpose and goals within human action.

With the increasing use of qualitative methods over the last two decades, the understand-or-explain conflict is no longer one of empirical orientation vs. hermeneutics but rather a discussion *within* the empirical field on the use of qualitative and quantitative procedures. One important argument brought up is that if understanding is defined as "laying something out in terms of something else," then the process of explaining and understanding is nothing more than particular explanations of the world (cf. Uhle 1995). What the world is and what it is made up of would then be questions of how it is laid out. In this case, whether one uses quantitative or qualitative methods is of secondary importance because, whatever it is, the method is just an instrument of precision used to sharpen the image the same way a telescope does. Whether that image actually means anything is by no means guaranteed through the use of the telescope. What is the relationship between object and analysis?

There are several views on how empirically oriented practical theology arrives at its object. Three main positions spring to mind, each with a different take on methodology:

- The first one assumes, quite simply, that empirical orientation is the tool for establishing reality. In other words, those empirical methods guarantee a perfect reproduction of the object the way it really is.
- The second position deals with the method for establishing an object. Certain methods are suitable or correct; others are unsuitable or wrong. This position has sparked a controversy dealing with the use of quantitative and qualitative procedures, first in the empirical social sciences and then, and to a greater extent, in practical theology.

- The third position is based on conclusion theory and highlights the constructive c haracter o f a ll theories – i ncluding e mpirically o ri- ented ones. On the one hand, it rejects the possibility of directly re- lating to an object. On the other hand, the choice of method is seen as secondary, since construction precedes and accompanies meth- odology. T he f ocus is o n the c hanging r elationship betwee n e m- pirical practice and scientific practice.

The first position, where empirical procedures focus immediately on the prac- tice, is not only characteristic of a high degree of consciousness for the every- day but also for empirical studies. It is also common (although often hidden) in those cases where one method is seen as superior to another. One example is the discussion in regards to induction and deduction. In this case, induction is seen as letting the data speak for itself, whereas deduction is felt to push the practice into a system where it does not fit. Accordingly, the practice is more closely defined by induction than by deduction. The third position adds to this argu- ment, since it realizes that both procedures have self-referral elements to them. This would mean that the original question in regards to the practice must be supplemented by what preceded it and by how the use of this method influenced the question.

This assumption is based on the fact that all empirical references are drawn from observations. Observation hones two particular skills: the ability to see differences and the capacity to make sense of those differences. The existence of differences in the real world is not enough for an observation; one also has to be able to recognize them. In other words, conclusions are not drawn from the data itself or from the method with which the data was processed. What are im- portant are the *references* that *were* relevant *before* and *during* the observation and that *are* relevant during later analysis. To recognize something in and through an observation is a very human ability. Because of this, it is also de- pendent on the human historicity and contingency. Observation and self- reference cannot be separated from each other. Self-reference is both a *pre- sumption* and a *consequence* of observation. It is a presumption because there has to be something identical to use as a key, and it is a consequence because observation constantly produces processes of self-reference. This means that the learning subject is itself a large part of the learning process. Every conclusion is tied to his own methods of observing and understanding. There is no method that fully guarantees reporting the object the way it *really* is. The method de- fines the possibilities for observing and establishes *how* something is to be ob- served. Whatever the choice made, it is contingent. The thing being studied can never be seized in its ontological being.

It would, however, be exaggerating if all methical observations were sud- denly labeled "subjective constructivism" with the actual object fading into the

189

background. Obviously, all processes of discovery based on methodical observation attempt to find a fitting explanation for the phenomenon at hand. At the same time, no explanation can claim to be the *real* explanation. The search for truth opens into the future. In this context, objectivity is not an adjective for a particular researcher or research procedure; it is, rather, the overreaching goal of the research. This does not change the fact that every observation reveals at least as much about the logic of the researcher as it does about the object at hand. This is the same for all processes of discovery, whether they use qualitative or quantitative methods. For this reason, the constructivist position questions whether and how scientific practice should become the second priority after the practice itself.

In view of this latter question, a research tradition like Popper's concept of critical rationalism finds itself facing some very serious issues (cf. Ziebertz 2002). This paradigm has made some very noticeable marks within empirical methodology, particularly the so-called quantitative research uses many of Popper's ideas. Within the three-prong approach to a research project, i.e. the context of discovery, the context of justification, and the context of application, critical rationalism focuses intensely on the context of justification. This is where scientific reflection and scientific practice come into play. Theories are then tested against standards of validity and dependability. The context of discovery, where the concrete research problem and question come up, is relegated to the pre-scientific field. This is where the ingeniousness of the researcher and his or her creative spirit and inspiration play their greatest roles. The presumption is that these sorts of variables take away from the scientific core value. The same goes for the eventual use of the results, the context of application, which, in reality, has nothing to do with the actual scientific proofing that preceded it. This is the way, then, to turn off the greatest amount of subjectivity on the part of the researcher. This concentration on the context of justification brought about a picture of an exact research, worthy of (or at least similar to) the precise ideals of the natural sciences. The fact that certain limitations were essential was shown, not just within the context of justification but also in the relationship between the contexts of justification and discovery.

In regards to the context of justification, there is another point to consider. When analyzing the steps that make up the empirical analytical procedure, we see several areas where a decision or interpretation on the part of the researcher becomes necessary. One example thereof is factor analysis. Factor analysis serves to filter out hidden dimensions (a plan, a structure) within a large number of items, thereby reducing the amount of data. This analysis is not just about randomly pushing a key on the computer. Mathematical statistics have produced and keep producing more and better methods for this form of analysis, and only a study of the factor clusters, commonality, and variance can tell us which is the right method. One could opt for a high level of factor discrimination, but that could lead to a weaker variance among other things; one could go with a higher variance, but would then have to accept clustering a single item on two or more factors. The decision as to which result ought to be used for future analysis is not possible without an estimate on the part of the researcher. The result must be meaningful and relevant, as well as interpretable. This also means that both theoretical knowledge gained by deduction and experience gained by induction are essential in order to make a well-founded decision.

If you relate the context of justification to the context of discovery, the subject and individual that is, the researcher becomes a constitutional element of the observation process and its results become an even looser variable (cf. Meinefeld 1995). This influence is not taken into account within the context of justification; it is not even empirically controllable. Classifying this problem as theory steering in empirical quantitative research would be doing too little. Already at the stage of limiting the research field and problem, there is a relevant, albeit not conscious, influence by the researcher. There are the contours of expectation, which structure the perception of the problem, producing a certain perspective (the interconnected selectivity), which, in turn, influences the research. This influence escapes methodological control.

When considering the choice of methods, one realizes that quantitative and qualitative research procedures do not have an impact on the two perspectives above. In both cases, several areas in the critical methodology depend on decisions, value judgments, and interpretations. These may be methodologically controllable to a certain extent. Nevertheless, they do rely on previous experience gained by inductive and deductive reasoning, which cannot be neutralized by any one method. In the case of qualitative procedures, this scenario arises when people are called to an interview and one has to explain what is expected of them, what the purpose of the study is, and what knowledge or results are expected to be gained. The actions of the researcher ought to be kept out of the analytical process (context of justification) since it is not methodologically controllable at that point and because it definitely influences the research and its results. If one then ignores the three-prong approach to the research process and starts to look at the problem from a timeline perspective, it becomes clear that this plays an important role as well. The influence exhibited by this context shows that proofing and justification, the very core of the analytical process, have themselves been dependent on the development of methodological knowledge throughout the course of history (cf. Meinefeld 1995).

On that note, the constructive portion of empirical procedures clearly steps into the spotlight. Between radical constructivism, which holds objectivity to be impossible, and the theory of objectivism, which holds the object to be immediately definable, there is the mixture of the knowledge focus and the knowledge system, of object (practice in the field) and scientific practice. None of these can be allowed to become an absolute value. The question of quantitative or qualitative procedures becomes secondary. The method, from this point of view, is merely one means chosen out of several because it promises to produce a maximum of information and knowledge. It also answers the question as to what the (quantitative or qualitative) research is meant to achieve. In other words, methodological precision must not be allowed to overshadow what the result is based on and what it represents. Knowledge from theories about human conduct is not gained without purpose or simply for its own inherent value. It is gained in order to orient what is going on in the world. On this platform, methods lose their aura of exclusivity that grants them a special place. This aura is based on the assumption that certain methods allow true knowledge and a direct link to the object, whereas others do not. Instead, they ought to be seen as complementary, even though this complementing ("triangulation") will not undo the limitations that come with certain particular methods (Campbell/Fiske 1959; Denzin 1978).

General Functions of Empirical Research in Practical Theology

The goal of empirical research in practical theology is to measure effect and control success. It intends to orient practical human action and take on a critical function in theology, setting it apart from deductive normative theology (cf. van der Ven 1988). These general functions will be dealt with briefly here.

First, empirical research within practical theology will continue to play an important role in *controlling human action in Religious Education*, i.e. research used for a practical purpose. One example is religious didactic material used for education. For all grade levels and forms of curriculum, there are particular learning goals, content, and mediums available. From a certain point of view, these educational materials do what they promise – didactically and effectively guide learning processes. They implicitly answer the questions of what the best content for such and such a goal is, where to begin learning, what knowledge is assumed on the part of the student, where the problems lie, how the content should be structured, what the learning phases are, what means should be used, and how a learning process can be evaluated. One also has to consider what interpersonal learning processes are taking place between the students, what constitution makes up the point of origin, and how educational content relates to the students self-image. Using this example, then, the problem could arise that such educational models are never empirically tested to see whether they have the expected effects – particularly not tested in such a way that more than only a personal experience forms the base of the results. The result is often a mishmash of the hopes and assumptions of teachers and students within their respective learning circumstances. It is clear that, among other things, the concept of education (kerugmatik, problematic, or experience-oriented), the educational style (frontal, multi-media, etc.), the religious attitudes and social background of the students, the quality of the material (additive use of different content, study plan based on increasing difficulty, systematics, etc.) make up a complex network, the effect of which is almost impossible to estimate. Other examples are central theoretical concepts such as "learning through models," "learning through ideals," or "the religion teacher as a witness of the faith," all of which need to be reexamined. What are they capable of, and what are the conditions they need in order to meet the expectations (assuming they do at all) of religious educators? The concepts and models are so important that an empirical evaluation of what they are able to achieve and whether and under what conditions they actually fulfill Religious Education's expectations of them is needed. Such central concepts with regard to the teachers' conduct lack experiential data.

A *second* function of empirical research in practical theology is the production of knowledge needed to *orient human action*. To put it in the words of Max Weber, the goal is to develop empirically based scenarios that give the people in those scenarios the knowledge they need to make decisions responsibly. According to Weber, researchers should use their data to make grounded value judgments possible. Understanding reality in a social setting does not happen in a neutral way or without interest. Gadamer reached the conclusion that the layout of a scenario (*subtilitas explicandi*) is a part of understanding (*subtilitas intelligendi*) and that both are connected to a sense of application (*subtilitas applicandi*) (cf. Uhle 1995). What he is clarifying is that the layout of observations, images, texts, etc. is more than the sum of the implicit meanings of those parts. Processes of understanding and explaining also target a certain judgment, as will be discussed later. Especially for theories about human conduct, it is true that they are difficult to disconnect from the context of their inherent task. Gadamer has defined this context of the task even more precisely. Processes of knowledge (understanding and explaining) serve to rebuild the interrupted accord. Like Habermas points out, this is the understanding of what is strange and what has become estranged. The above introduction pointed out what has become strange for practical theology. In this sense, understanding does not mean the Wittgenstein-type sense of understanding as *knowing a rule* and *participation in a common sense*. Understanding would then mean uncovering every nearby yet hidden cultural truism in a research process. Understanding is the final point of an investigation. Another definition for understanding is finding a meaning that can only be established through interpretational processes. In other words, an investigation that intends to understand does not mirror the true reality but simply adds a scheme for interpreting it. It is, then, the insimultaneousness, the non-identity, etc. that challenge understanding (cf. Uhle 1995).

In-depth interviews with youth have shown that a lot of them see themselves as removed from their church (Prokopf/Ziebertz 2001; Richter/Francis 1998). At the same time, many of them go to church and claim to be touched by the atmosphere there, by the praying, light, candles, music, etc. These young people, who must be classified as on the church fringe, use religious symbols, take part in religious rituals, and incorporate Christian images into their worldview. Even among those who classify themselves as non-religious, the majority want to baptize their future children, get married with a church ceremony, and, of course, be buried by a priest. For religious-educational purposes (church instruction, in particular), deeper knowledge of the religious views of these young people is essential. It is quite possible that a treasure trove of theologization of the real world is waiting to be discovered (cf. Ziebertz 2000).

Obviously, the purpose of such investigations is not the detailed restatement of fact but overcoming an ever-changing estrangement. Understanding social situations is all about forming a will or a judgment – it is not neutral. Because of this, the method for gaining knowledge must not be more important than the knowledge itself. A reference to future application makes it clear that such measures for understanding and explaining have a practical function. Texts, statements, actions etc. must be understood and explained because they serve to create judgments, because they make those scenarios possible that are based on "if" and "then," and because they give the basic information necessary for overcoming difficult life situations and orient human acting. Practical theology is, after all, partly about Religious Education: preaching and announcing, establishing the deaconry and the community.

Third, empirical research in practical theology has a *critical function within theology itself*. Practical theological fields may be seen as "application areas for theological normativity." This is not just true for systematic theology, but also for the practice itself, which has certain expectations. At the same time, it is certainly clear that the practical theological fields must not simply be reduced to deducing theologically developed normativity. In other words, the object field of religious practice is not just a field to be sowed; the field has expectations of the seed. Not everything will grow on this soil, and certain mixtures will not grow at all. The object field practice is more than just an application field; the practice makes demands on the theological reflection.

In the Roman Catholic Church, there is an increasing tendency to deduce theology from top to bottom. The era of new scholastics has clearly shown how dangerous it is when theologians lose their grass-root attachments, creating schemes and concepts that must fit into the actual practice. Today, we ask the question, what are theologians to do with an ever more abstract picture of God?

Is this an effect of secularization, or is it a rejection of a personal model that had always been misunderstood as an anthropomorphic picture of God? Have there truly not been any other theologically justified abstract pictures of God in the 2000 years of Christian history? Should we not see such finds as a call to renewal for modern theology rather than as a danger? Practical theology makes such new issues comprehensible and introduces them to the theological discourse. Practice has another function: the theological concepts and models needed in theology are examined with and through practice. Practice now has a critical function, confronting the theologically normative thoughts and their assumptions with new data. On a theoretical level, this is how ideologies are formed.

Beyond this issue, *sensus fidei/fidelium* is a concept with a lot of theological dignity. Exactly how the people whose practice is being studied shape their faiths is of great theological importance. For this reason, practical theology cannot stay outside the discourse that arises strongly and loudly when tradition and situation conflict in the educational process. Theology as a whole would pass up critical knowledge if practical theology abandons the task of critically judging the terminological and conceptual traditions of religious socialization. It is not enough to study the practice on a speculative level. Practical theology must make use of the procedures of the other theories about human conduct, thereby filling a regulating function necessary for all of theology (van der Ven 1988). Particularly in the case of religious socialization, with all its new and compelling problems, the call for a normative basis for the practical theological fields is getting louder. This tendency should be viewed with a critical eye. This is not just a question of principle, based on a practical theology that has developed its own identity. Rather, it is about a problem of socialization where practical theology, used to extend dogmatism in a downward direction, is losing its grip. An empirically oriented practical theology adds to all theological fields when it uses its studies on practice to develop normative concepts for the conflict between tradition and experience.

Working empirically within practical theology means having both a theological education and knowledge of empirical methods. Empirical thought as a paradigm must be established even further in education and research. The problems faced by religious educators in schools and church communities cannot be resolved without empirical research forming theories and stimulating practice. The basic methodology of practical theology, however, must face up to new questions. The methodological debate cannot be given over to the humanities, leaving practical theology to choose particular procedures eclectically because methodology is the scientific grain of a discipline, and questions of methods and those who use them must decide the methodology. This means, among other things, incorporating methodology into the canon of theological education. In the systematic fields, particularly the historical and exegetic ones, this has been the common practice for quite some time. Students participate in seminars teaching historically critical, linguistic, psychoanalytical, and materialistic methods, giving them the skills they need to analyze texts critically. Are the practical theologians of tomorrow learning the hermeneutical, ideologically critical and (in regards to the practice) empirical skills they will need?

This all points in the direction of a future program of theological education. At their universities, students should learn to analyze religious attitudes, opinions, and learning processes with quantitative and qualitative methods. Such an education not only provides dates; it trains the perception of practice with the ways of science. One cannot intervene in practice if he is not versed well enough in it. Religious Education should especially give attention to searching, researching learning. Learning happens not through the accumulation of knowledge and content alone, but through working on the problems of practice, particularly those in which one is supposed to work later as a professional.

References

Anderson G. L. (1997) (ed.), The Family in Global Transition, St.Paul (Paragon House Publishers).

Astley J./Francis L.J./Crowder C. (1996) (eds.), Theological Perspectives on Christian Formation, Grand Rapids (Gracewing).

Auer A. (1984), Autonome Moral, Düsseldorf (Patmos).

Babin P. (1995), The new Era in Religious Communication, Minneapolis (Augsburg Fortress).

Beck U. (1992), Risk society : towards a new modernity, London (Sage).

Benner D./Peukert H. (1983), Moralische Erziehung. In: Lenzen, D./Mollenhauer K. (eds.), Enzyklopädie Erziehungswissenschaften Bd.1, Stuttgart, 394-402 (Klett).

Berger P.L. (1999) (ed.), The Desecularisation of the World, Grand Rapids (Eerdmans).

Berger P. L. (1988), Zur Dialektik von Religion und Gesellschaft, Frankfurt (Suhrkamp).

Bertram H. (1986) (ed.), Gesellschaftlicher Zwang und moralische Autonomie, Frankfurt (Suhrkamp).

Boeve L./Ries J.C. (2001), The Presence of Transcendence, Leuven (Peeters).

Boys M.C. (1989), Educating in Faith, Kansas City (Sheed and Ward).

Cahoone L. (1996) (ed.), From Modernism to Postmodernism, Malden/Oxford (Blackwell).

Campbell D.T./Fiske D.W. (1959), Convergent and discriminant validation by multi-trait-multimethod matrix; in: Psychological Bulletin 56(1959), 81-105.

Davie G. (2000), Religion in Europe. A Memory mutates, Oxford (Univ.Press).

Denzin N.K. (1978), The Research Act, New York (McGraw-Hill).

Drehsen V. (1991), Praktische Theologie als Kunstlehre im Zeitalter bürgerlicher Kultur. In: Nipkow K.E./Rössler D./Schweitzer F. (eds.), Praktische Theologie und Kultur der Gegenwart, Gütersloh 103-116 (Gütersloher Verlag).

Drehsen V. (1994), Die Anverwandlung des Fremden. In: van der Ven, J.A./Ziebertz, H-G. (eds.), Religiöser Pluralismus und Interreligiöses Lernen. Weinheim/Kampen, 39-69 (DSV/Kok).

Dunne J.S. (1965), The City of the Gods, New York 1965, The way of the All on Earth, New York 1972 (Macmillan).

Durkheim E. (1995), The elementary forms of religious life, New York (The Free Press).

Englert R. (1985), Glaubensgeschichte und Bildungsprozeß, München (Kösel).

Erikson E. (1959), Identity and the Life Cycle, New York (International University Press).

Felderhof M.C. (1985) (ed.), Religious Education in a pluralistic society, London et.al. (Hodder and Stoughton).

Fink H. (1987), Anthropologischer Ansatz und Selbstverständnis der Religionspädagogik. In: Leitner, R. (ed.) Religionspädagogik Bd. I, Wien , 13-29 (Volk und Wissen).

Foster Ch.R./Brelsford Th. (1996), We are Church together. Cultural Diversity in Congregational Life, Valley Forge (Trinity Press Int.).

Francis L.J./Katz Y. (2000) (eds.), Joining and Leaving Religion, Leominster (Grace-wing).

Francis L./Ziebertz H.-G/Kalbheim B./Lewis Ch. (2001), Christlicher Glaube und Glück, In: Religionspsychologisches Archiv 24 (2002), 426-442.

Freud S. (1962), The future of an illusion, London (Hogarth Press).

Green G. (1989), Imagining God. Theology and the Religious Imagination, Grand Rapids (Eerdmans).

Greve W. (2000) (ed.), Psychologie des Selbst, Weinheim (Beltz).

Griffiths P.J. (2001), Problems of Religious Diversity, Malden/Oxford (Blackwell).

Groome Th. H. (1980): Christian religious Education, San Francisco (Jossey-Bass).

Habermas J. (1968), Erkenntnis und Interesse, Frankfurt (Suhrkamp).

Habermas J. (1978), Knowledge and human interests, London (2nd ed.) (Heinemann Educational).

Habermas J. (1981), Die Moderne - ein unvollendetes Projekt. In: id., Kleine politische Schriften I-IV. Frankfurt, 444-464 (Suhrkamp).

Habermas J. (1985), Die Kulturkritik der Neokonservativen in den USA und in der BRD. In: id., Die neue Unübersichtlichkeit. Frankfurt, 30-56 (Suhrkamp).

Habermas J. (1990), Strukturwandel der Öffentlichkeit (1st ed. 1962), Frankfurt (Suhrkamp).

Habermas J. (1997), Die Einbeziehung des Anderen, Frankfurt (Suhrkamp).

Habermas J. (1990), Moral consciousness and communicative action, Cambridge, MA (MIT Press).

Habermas J. (1992), Postmetaphysical thinking: philosophical essays, Cambridge, Mass. (MIT Press).

Hall R. T. (1979), Moral Education: A Handbook for Teachers, Minneapolis (Winston).

Helaas P. (1998), Introduction: on differentiation and dedifferentiation. In: Helaas P. (ed.), Religion, modernity and postmodernity. Oxford/Malden 1-18 (Blackwell).

Hermanns H.J.M./Hermanns-Jansen E. (1995), Self-Narratives: The construction of Meaning in Psychotherapy, New York (Guilford Press).

Hermanns H.J.M./Kempen H.J.G. (1993), The dialogical self: Meaning als movement. San Diego (Academic Press).

Hervieu-Léger D. (2000), Religion as a Chain of Memory, Oxford (Polity).

Hohmann H. (1994), Religion, In: Dunde, R. (ed.), Wörterbuch der Religionssoziologie, Gütersloh, 260-267 (Gütersloher Verlag).

Hole G. (1994), Die depressive Dekompensation – pathologische Endstrecke einer religiösen Anstrengung. In: Klosinski G. (ed.), Religion als Chance oder Risiko, Bern 209-222 (Huber).

Huntington S.P. (1996), The Clash of Civilizations and the Remaking of World Order. New York (Simon & Schuster).

Husserl E. (1973), Experience and judgment: investigations in a genealogy of logic (1st ed. in german 1948), London (Routledge and K. Paul).

Identität und Verständigung (1994), Standort und Perspektiven des Religionsunterrichts in der Pluralität. Eine Denkschrift (im Auftrag des Rates der EKD), Gütersloh (Gütersloher Verlag).

Jugend 2 000 (2000), Deutsche Shell (ed.), 1 3. Shell Ju gendstudie, Opladen (Leske + Budrich).

Kay W.K./Francis L.J. (1996), Drift from the Churches. Attitude toward Christianity during Childhood and Adolescence, Cardiff (Univ. of Wales Press).

Keupp H./Höfer R. (1997) (eds.), Identitätsarbeit heute. Klassische und aktuelle Perspektiven der Identitätsforschung, Frankfurt (Suhrkamp).

Kincheloe J.L./Steinberg S.R. (1997), Changing Multiculturalism, Buckingham (Open University Press).

Klages H. (1988), Wertedynamik. Über die Wandelbarkeit des Selbstverständlichen, Zürich (Interfrom).

Klie Th. (1998): Ecclesia quaerens pädagogiam. Wege zur Semantik heiliger Räume. Einführung. In: id. (ed.): Der Religion Raum geben. Kirchenpädagogik und religiöses Lernen, Münster, 5-16 (Lit).

Knitter P.F. (1985), No other Name? A Critical Survey of Christian Attitudes Toward the World Religions, New York (Orbis).

Kohlberg L. (1981; 1984), Essays on Moral Development (2 Bde.), San Francisco (Harper & Row).

Krauss W. (2000), Das erzählte Selbst. Die narrative Konstruktion von Identität in der Spätmoderne, Herbolzheim (Centaurus).

Kurz W. (1994), Die Bedeutung religiöser Erziehung für die Entwicklung psychischer Gesundheit unter besonderer Berücksichtigung logotherapeutischer Aspekte. In: Klosinski G. (ed.), Religion als Chance oder Risiko, Bern, 187-208 (Huber).

Lee J.M. (1985), The Content of Religious Instruction, Birmingham (Rel.Educ.Press).

Lehmann K. (1994), Vom Dialog als Form der Kommunikation und Wahrheitsfindung in der Kirche heute; Sekretär der Deutschen Bischofskonferenz (ed.), Bonn.

Lickona Th. (1983), Raising good children. Helping your Child through the Stages of Moral Development, New York (Bantam).

Luckmann Th. (1967), The invisible religion: the problem of religion in modern society New York, N.Y. (Macmillan).

Luhmann N. (1977), Funktion der Religion, Frankfurt (Suhrkamp).

Luther H. (1992), Religion und Alltag, Stuttgart (Radius).

Lyotard J.-F. (1984), The Postmodern Condition: A Report on Knowledge. Minneapolis (Univ.of M.Press).

Marino J.S. (1983) (ed.), Biblical Themes in Religious Education, Birmingham (Rel.Educ.Press).

Mead G. H. (1934), Mind, self, and society: from the standpoint of a social behaviorist, Chicago (University of Chicago Press).

Meinefeld W. (1995), Realität und Konstruktion, Opladen (Leske & Budrich).

Mette N. (1978), Theorie der Praxis, Düsseldorf (Patmos).

Mette N. (1983), Voraussetzungen christlicher Elementarerziehung, Düsseldorf (Patmos).

Meyer K. (1999), Zeugnisse fremder Religionen im Unterricht, Neukirchen-Vluyn (Neukirchner).

Moran G. (1989), Religious Education as a second language, Birmingham (Rel.Educ.Press).

Nipkow K.E. (1984), Religionspädagogik Vol I, Gütersloh (Gütersloher Verlag).

Nipkow K.E. (1998), Bildung in einer pluralen Welt (Vol II), Gütersloh (Gütersloher Verlag).

Osmer R.R. (1992), Teaching Faith. A Guide for Teachers of Adult Classes, Louisville (John Knox).

Peukert H. (1984), Über die Zukunft von Bildung. In: Frankfurter Hefte (FH extra 6) 39(1984), 129-137.

Rahner K. (1983), Über den Absolutheitsanspruch des Christentums; in: Schriften zur Theologie XV, Einsiedeln u.a., 171-184 (engl. Theological investigations, New York : Crossroad).

Rahner K. (1957), Über die Erfahrung der Gnade, in: SzTh III (^{2}1957), Zürich/Köln, 105-109.

Raths L. E./Harmin M./Simon S. B. (1966), Values and teaching: working with values in the classroom, Columbus, Ohio (Merrill).

Rémond R. (1999), Religion and Society in modern Europe, Oxford/Malden (Blackwell).

Richter Ph./Francis L.J. (1998), Gone but not forgotten. Church leaving and returning, London (Darton, Longman and Todd).

Riegel U./Ziebertz H.-G. (2001), Images of God in a Gender perspective. In: Ziebertz, H.-G. (ed.), Imagining God, Münster, 229-244 (Lit).

Schillebeeckx E. (1990), Church : the human story of God , New York (Crossroad).

Schlüter R. (1994), Dem Fremden begegnen - eine (religions-) pädagogische Problemanzeige. In: id. (ed.), Ökumenisches und interkulturelles Lernen. Lembeck, 27-53 (Bonifatius).

Schweitzer F. (1993), Praktische Theologie und Hermeneutik: Paradigma - Wissenschaftstheorie - Methodologie. In: Ven van der J.A./Ziebertz H.-G. (eds.), Paradigmendiskussion in der Praktischen Theologie, Weinheim/Kampen, 19-47 (Kok/DSV).

Schweitzer F. (1996), Die Suche nach dem eigenen Glauben. Gütersloh (Gütersloher Verlag).

Schweitzer Friedrich (1987), Lebensgeschichte und Religion, München (Kaiser).

Schweitzer F./Englert R./Schwab U./Ziebertz H.-G. (2001), Pluralitätsfähige Religionspädagogik, Gütersloh/Freiburg (Gütersloher Verlag/Herder).

Schwöbel C. (1996), Pluralismus II. In: TRE Bd.26, 724ff. Berlin/New York (De Gruyter).

Seckler, M./Berchtold, C. (1991), Glaube, in: NHThG II, München, 232-252 (Kösel).

Sennet R. (1976), The Fall of Public Man, New York (Knopf).

Seymour J.L./Crain M.A./Crockett J.V. (1993), Educating Christians. An Intersection of Meaning, Learning, and Vocation, Nashville (Abingdon Press).

Seymour J. L./Crain M. A. (1997): Assessing Approaches to Christian Education, in: Seymour J. L. (ed.), Mapping christian Education, Nashville, 90-93 (Parthenon).

Soeffner H.-G. (1998): Kirchliche Gebäude – Orte der christlichen Religion in der pluralistischen Kultur. In: Klie, Th.(ed.) Der Religion Raum geben. Münster, 44-50 (Lit).

Sterkens C. (2001), Interreligious Learning, Leiden (Brill).

Streib H. (1994), Erzählte Zeit als Ermöglichung von Identität. In: Georgi D. (ed.), Religion und Gestaltung der Zeit, Kampen, 181-215 (Kok).

Swatos W. H./Olson D.V.A. (2000) (eds.), The Secularization Debate, Lanham u.a. (Rowman and Littlefield).

Swidler L. J. (1990), After the absolute: the dialogical future of religious reflection, Minneapolis (Fortress Press).

Taylor Ch. (1992), Multiculturalism and the Politics of Recognition. Princeton (Princeton Univ.Press).

Tillich Paul (^{3}1969), Die verlorene Dimension, Hamburg (Furche).

Torres C. A. (1998), Democracy, Education and Multiculturalism, Boston/Oxford (Rowman and Littlefield).

Türk H.J. (1990), Postmoderne. Mainz/Stuttgart (Matth.Grünewald/Quell).

Turner V. (1982), From ritual to theatre: the human seriousness of play, New York (Performing Arts Journal Publications).

Uhle R. (1995), Qualitative Sozialforschung und Hermeneutik. In: König E./Zedler P. (eds.), Bilanz qualitativer Forschung I, Weinheim, 33-73 (Beltz).

Ven van der J.A. (1988), Practical Theology: From Applied to Empirical Theology. In: Journal of Empirical Theology 1(1988), 7-27.

Ven van der, J.A. (1996), Ecclesiology in context, Grand Rapids, Michigan (Eerdmans).

Ven van der J.A./ Ziebertz H.-G. (1994) (eds.), Religiöser Pluralismus und Interreligiöses Lernen, Weinheim/Kampen (DSV/Kok).

Ven van der J.A. (1985), Vorming in waarden en normen, Kampen (Kok).

Waldenfels H. (1991), Religionsverständnis, In: NHThG IV, München, 412-421 (Kösel).

Watson B. (1992) (ed.), Priorities in Religious Education: A Model for the 1990s and Beyond, London (Falmer).

Weber M. (1984), Die protestantische Ethik (hrsg. v.Winckelmann J.), Gütersloh. (engl.: The Protestant ethic and the spirit of capitalism (2nd ed. 1998), Los Angeles: Roxbury Pub).

Welsch W. (1994), Unsere postmoderne Moderne. Berlin (Akademie Verlag).

Weverbergh R./Ziebertz H.-G. (1999), Collegial reflective Leadership. A self-guided christian community. In:Lukatis I./Lukatis W. (eds.), Education for Leadership. Hemmingen 1999, 104-124.

Wilkerson B. (1997) (ed.), Multicultural Religious Education, Birmingham (Religious Education Press).

Woodhead L./Helaas P. (2000), Religion in modern Times, Oxford/Malden (Blackwell).

Ziebertz H.-G. (2000), God in a modern individualized religiousness, in: Browning D./Häring H./Schweitzer F./Ziebertz H.-G. (eds.), The Human Image of God, Leiden 2000 (Brill).

Ziebertz H.-G. (1990), Moralerziehung im Wertpluralismus, Weinheim/Kampen (DSV/Kok).

Ziebertz H.-G. (1991), Heteronomy and Autonomy. Moralpedagogical conflicting aims of Professionals in Church Youth Work. In: Journal of Empirical Theology 4(1991)1, 39-58.

Ziebertz H.-G. (1992), Sex, love and marriage, the view of RE teachers in Germany. In: British Journal of Religious Education Vol.14., No.3, 1992, 151-156.

Ziebertz H.-G. (1993), Religious Pluralism and Religious Education. In: Journal of Empirical Theology 6(1993)2, 78-98.

Ziebertz H.-G. (1996) Religious in Religious Education. In: Panorama 8(1996)1, 135-145.

Ziebertz H.-G. (1995), Religious Socialization and the Identification of Religion. In: Henau E./.Schreiter R.J. (eds.), Religious Socialization. Weinheim/Kampen 53-67 (DSV/Kok).

Ziebertz H.-G. (1996b), Representations of Church among young Theologians. In: Journal of Empirical Theology 9(1996)2, 5-29.

Ziebertz H.-G. (1997), The Church: Her Image and Her Critics. In: New Theological Review (Chicago) 10(1997)2, 65-82.

Ziebertz H.-G. (1997), Umweltbezug der Gemeinde. In. Id. (ed.), Christliche Gemeinde vor einem neuen Jahrtausend, Weinheim, 185-213 (DSV).

Ziebertz H.-G. (1998a), Continuity and Discontinuity in: International Journal of Practical Theology, 2 (1998)1, 1-22.

Ziebertz H.-G. (1998b), Pluralität und Identität. Religiöse Bildung in der Postmoderne. In: H.-G. Ziebertz, Religion, Christentum und Moderne. Veränderte Religionspräsenz als Herausforderung. Stuttgart (Kohlhammer).

Ziebertz H.-G. (1998b), Types of Curch Leadership in the Context of Catholic Ecclesiology. In: Hansson P. (ed.), Church Leadership. Stockholm 1998, 218-236.

Ziebertz H.-G. (1999), Religion, Christentum und Moderne. Veränderte Religionspräsenz als Herausforderung. Stuttgart (Kohlhammer).

Ziebertz H.-G./Schnider A. (2000) Religiosität und Wertorientierung, In: Porzelt B./Güth R. (eds.), Empirische Religionspädagogik, Münster (Lit).

Ziebertz H.-G. (2001) (ed.), Imagining God. Empirical Explorations from an international perspective, Münster (Lit).

Ziebertz H.-G. (2001) (ed.), Religious Individualisation and christian religious Semantics, Münster (Lit).

Ziebertz H.-G. (2001a), God in modern individualized religiousness? In: Ziebertz H.-G./Schweitzer F./Häring H./Browning D. (eds.), The Human Image of God, Leiden, 329-346 (Brill).

Ziebertz H.-G. (2001b), Religiousness and modernity. In: Ziebertz H.-G. (ed.), Religious individualisation and christian religious Semantics, Münster, 19-47 (Lit).

Ziebertz H.-G./Schlöder B./Kalbheim B./Feeser U. (2001), Modern Religiousness: extrinsic, intrinsic of Quest?, In: Journal of Empirical Theology 14(2001), 5-26.

Ziebertz H.-G. (2002), Normativity and Empirical Research in Practical Theology. In: Journal of Empirical Theology 15 (2002) 5-18.

Ziebertz H.-G./Kalbheim B./Riegel U. (2003), Religiöse Signaturen heute. Ein religionspädagogischer Beitrag zur empirischen Jugendforschung, Münster (Lit).

Zulehner P.M./Denz H. (1993), Wie Europa glaubt, Düsseldorf (Patmos).

Acknowledgments

Some chapters and parts of other chapters in this book have been previously published in either German or English. For this publication, all chapters have been revised. Most of them were streamlined, though some have been expanded. The following publishers have generously given permission to use quotations from copyrighted works in this book:

Chapters 1, 3-6, 8-9 were originally part of the book Religionsdidaktik, edited by Georg Hilger, Stephan Leimgruber and Hans-Georg Ziebertz and published by Kösel (Munich) in 2001.

Chapters 7 and 10 are shortened versions of papers in the book Entwürfe einer pluralitätsfähigen Religionspädagogik, edited by Friedrich Schweitzer, Rudolf Englert, Ulrich Schwab and Hans-Georg Ziebertz and published by Gütersloher Verlagshaus (Gütersloh) and Herder (Freiburg) in 2002.

Chapter 2 was published in English in the International Journal of Education and Religion, Vol. I/1, 2000.

Chapter 11 was published in English in the Volume Religious Education as Practical Theology, edited by Bert Roebben and Michael Warren and published by Peeters (Leuven) in 2001.

The Author

Hans-Georg Ziebertz, Doctor of Theology and Pedagogics, is Professor of Practical Theology / Religious Education at the Faculty of Catholic Theology, University of Würzburg, Germany. His research is focussed on empirical studies about religiousness in the context of pluralism in western societies.

Further information: http://www.uni-wuerzburg.de/religionspaedagogik/

Empirische Theologie

herausgegeben von Prof. Dr. Dr. h. c. Johannes A. van der Ven (Katholische Universität Nijmegen), Prof. Dr. Dr. Hans-Georg Ziebertz (Universität Würzburg) und Prof. Dr. Anton A. Bucher (Universität Salzburg)

Johannes A. van der Ven
Das moralische Selbst: Gestaltung und Bildung
Aus dem Niederländischen übertragen von Thomas Quartier
Moralische Sorgen bezüglich der westlichen Gesellschaft sind ausführlich geäußert worden, sowohl von Experten als auch von "normalen Menschen". Sie beziehen sich auf wesentliche Fragen, wie z. B. die folgenden: Was ist gut? Was ist gerecht? Was ist weise? Was ist zweckmäßig? Es ist nicht das Ziel dieses Buches, zu einer Diagnose zu kommen, was der westlichen Gesellschaft genau fehlt. Vielmehr wird versucht, die weit verbreitete moralische Sorge innerhalb des Westens in die Frage nach einer moralischen Gestaltung und Bildung zu übersetzen. Johannes A. van der Ven interpretiert diese Art moralischer Fragen vom Standpunkt verschiedener Prozesse aus: denen der Entwicklung, des Lernens und des Lehrens, wie sie sich in der Familie, der Schule, in Vereinen und im kirchlichen Umfeld vollziehen. Weiterhin beschreibt, analysiert und evaluiert er diese Prozesse so sorgfältig wie möglich.
Im Verlauf seiner Studie kommt Van der Ven zu einem fundamentalen Verständnis der Prozesse moralischer Entwicklung und der Strukturen der Gestaltung und Bildung, die dabei behilflich sind, sie in Gang zu bringen und zu fördern. Er unterscheidet zwischen zwei Modi informeller moralischer Bildung (Disziplin und Sozialisierung) und fünf Modi formeller Bildung (Übertragung, Entwicklung, Erhellung, Ausprägung der Emotionen und Gestaltung des Charakters). Der gemeinsame Nenner aller sieben Modi ist die "moralische Kommunikation", die als ein fortlaufender Prozeß des moralischen Austauschs und Verständnisses auf der Suche nach der Wahrheit definiert wird. Diese Suche führt schließlich zu einer Gestaltung und Bildung des moralischen Selbst.
Bd. 1, 1999, 440 S., 30,90 €, br., ISBN 3-8258-4169-3

Ulrike Popp-Baier (Hg.)
Religiöses Wissen und alltägliches Handeln – Assimilationen, Transformationen, Paradoxien
In unserer "globalen" Kultur, die durch vielfältige Prozesse der Globalisierung und zugleich Lokalisierung konstituiert wird, verdanken sich die kulturellen Differenzen im Hinblick auf religiösen und spirituellen Orientierungen. Vermutlich ist die vielfach diagnostizierte Wiederkehr des Religiösen bereits dem Umstand zuzuschreiben, daß das Religiöse nun in größerer Vielfalt im Alltag präsent ist. Die in diesem Band versammelten religionspsychologischen und religionssoziologischen Studien einer Amsterdamer Gruppe von ReligionsforscherInnen widmen sich den religiösen Dimensionen einer "globalen" Kultur. An der Leitfrage nach dem Verhältnis zwischen religiösem Wissen und alltäglichem Handeln orientiert, beschäftigen sie sich u. a. mit den Lebens- und Handlungsorientierungen junger Muslimfrauen in der multikulturellen Gesellschaft, dem Zusammenhang zwischen "Spiritualität" und "Körperregime" im New Age oder den spezifischen modernen Orientierungsleistungen christlich-fundamentalistischer Glaubensüberzeugungen.
Bd. 2, 1999, 176 S., 20,90 €, br., ISBN 3-8258-4179-0

Michael Scherer-Rath
Lebenssackgassen
Herausforderung für die pastorale Beratung und Begleitung von Menschen in Lebenskrisen
Lebenskrisen unterbrechen den Alltag. Sie werfen Menschen aus ihrem psychischen Gleichgewicht, da bisherige Ordnungsstrukturen an Bedeutung verlieren und unwirksam werden. Krisen können der Beginn eines Neuanfangs sein. Krisen können aber auch in eine Lebenssackgasse führen, aus der es mit den bisherigen 'althergebrachten' Mitteln keinen Ausweg mehr gibt. Es herrscht Mangel an Handlungsmöglichkeiten, die die Vergangenheit, die Gegenwart und die Zukunft eines Menschen sinnvoll miteinander zu verbinden wissen. Lebenskrisen wie die Suizidkrise werden durch einen solchen Mangel an Handlungs- bzw. Problemlösungsmöglichkeiten gekennzeichnet, der sich allerdings so existentiell zugespitzt hat, daß die Beseitigung dieses Mangels bzw. die Lösung des Problems absolute Priorität genießt. Der Autor geht der Frage nach, wie Menschen in Suizidkrisen auf ein pastorales Gesprächsangebot reagieren und was sie davon erwarten. Darüber hinaus sucht er nach Faktoren, die zum einen die Suizidkrise und zum anderen die Erwartungen an ein pastorales Gesprächsangebot beeinflussen. Konkret werden die Grenzerfahrungen von Tragik, Schuld und Tod untersucht sowie eine Anzahl von Personenmerkmalen und Suizidkrisenaspekten. Wie die Ergebnisse dieser Untersuchung zeigen, stehen die befragten Personen einem pastoralen Gesprächsangebot grundsätzlich positiv gegenüber. Bedeutenden Einfluß haben darauf die Grenzerfahrungen von Tragik und Tod, die für die pastorale Beratung und Begleitung von Menschen

LIT Verlag Münster – Hamburg – Berlin – London
Grevener Str./Fresnostr. 2 48159 Münster
Tel.: 0251 – 23 50 91 – Fax: 0251 – 23 19 72
e-Mail: vertrieb@lit-verlag.de – http://www.lit-verlag.de

in Suizidkrisen eine besondere Bedeutung besitzen. Das Thema Schuld bleibt hingegen außen vor. Es zeigt sich, daß das Ringen der befragten Personen um die eigene Identitätsentwicklung ('Selbst-Behauptung') in den Grenzerfahrungen von Tragik und Tod seinen Ausdruck findet und daß das pastorale Gespräch mit einem Seelsorger oder einer Seelsorgerin als eine Möglichkeit gesehen wird, sich mit diesen 'Lebensbehinderungen' auseinanderzusetzen.

Bd. 3, 2. Aufl. Frühj. 2003, ca. 288 S., ca. 20,90 €, br., ISBN 3-8258-4170-7

Boris Kalbheim
Sinngebung der Natur und ökologisches Handeln
Eine empirisch theologische Untersuchung zu Motiven umweltschützenden Handelns bei Kirchenmitgliedern und Nichtkirchenmitgliedern
Die Verschmutzung der Umwelt ist kein Schicksal, sondern Konsequenz menschlicher Handlungen. Kritiker behaupten, daß das Weltverständnis des Christentums die Umweltverschmutzung verursacht habe. In der vorliegenden Studie wird diese Kritik empirisch untersucht: Welchen Einfluß hat die Mitgliedschaft in einer christlichen Kirche auf die Gründe, umweltschützend zu handeln? Am Beispiel des Handelns im Verkehr wird umweltschützendes Verhalten quantifiziert und die Motive dafür rekonstruiert. Damit wird ein theo logischer Beitrag zur Lösung der Umweltverschmutzung geleistet.

Bd. 4, 2000, 192 S., 20,90 €, br., ISBN 3-8258-4719-5

Norbert Ammermann
Religiosität und Kontingenzbewältigung
Empirische und konstrukttheoretische Umsetzungen für Religionspädagogik und Seelsorge
Religion als Kontingenzbewältigung gilt als das Synonym für Diskursivität von Religionssoziologie, religiöser Entwicklungspsychologie und praktisch-theologischen Arbeitens in Religionspädagogik, Poimenik, Gemeindekybernetik u.a.m. Es bleiben diffizile Fragen und offene Probleme. Eine diffizile Frage z.B.: Die Explorationsmethoden strukturgenetischer Ansätze sind vielfach zu grob gerastert und bieten kaum eindeutige Validitätskriterien. Wie kann ihr empirisches Design verfeinert werden? Ein offenes Problem z.B.: Wie kann der von der praktischen Theologie angestrebte und dringendst benötigte Diskurs mit moderner kogni-tivistischer, konstrukttheoretischer und bewusstseinsphänomenologischer Forschung, die in sich schon ein Paradigma interdisziplinärer Arbeit darstellt, so aufgenommen werden, dass ihr ureigenstes Anliegen, den Menschen in seiner Gottesbeziehung verstehen und thematisieren

zu wollen, adäquat formuliert und zugleich für interdisziplinäres Arbeiten offen evaluiert werden kann?
Die Studie von Norbert Ammermann untersucht empirische und konstrukttheoretische Operationalisierungsmöglichkeiten des Kontingenzbegriffs, um diesen für eine empirische Theologie kritisch zu rezipieren. Ausgehend vom Subjektivitätsverständnis bei Schleiermacher und dessen postulierter Ichhaftigkeit des Menschen in jeder religiösen Erfahrung wird die Diskussion mit kognitivistischen und konstruktivistischen Konzeptionen aufgenommen. Auf der Basis konstruktpsychologischer Methodik wird ein vom Autor am Department for Psychology University of Memphis (USA) entwickeltes, empirisches Verfahren zur Erhebung individueller, religiöse Erfahrung konstituierender Konstrukte vorgestellt. Religionspsychologische, vor allem dem Intro- und Extraversionsmodell verpflichtete Konzeption werden damit kritisch befragt. Ebenso werden strukturgenetische Entwicklungsansätze in ihrer Übernahme durch Religionspädagogik und praktischer Theologie kritisch diskutiert. Abschliessend werden grundsätzliche Überlegungen zur Verhältnisbestimmung von Erfahrung und theologischer Aussage ausgeführt.

Bd. 6, 2000, 424 S., 40,90 €, br., ISBN 3-8258-4822-1

Burkard Porzelt; Ralph Güth (Hg.)
Empirische Religionspädagogik
Grundlagen – Zugänge – Aktuelle Projekte.
Herausgegeben im Auftrag der Ständigen Sektion "Empirische Religionspädagogik" der Arbeitsgemeinschaft Katholischer Katechetikdozent/innen
Empirische Untersuchungen – breit rezipiert, aber häufig nur für "Eingeweihte" nachvollziehbar? Der vorliegende Band der AKK-Sektion "Empirische Religionspädagogik" setzt sich zum Ziel, sowohl fachwissenschaftlich "Versierten" als auch empirischen "Laien" einen Einblick in Möglichkeiten und gegenwärtige Themenfelder religionspädagogisch-empirischer Arbeit zu vermitteln.
Unter drei Stichworten liefert der Band eine Einführung und Zwischenbilanz empirischer Religionspädagogik:

- "Grundlagen": Überblick über Vorgeschichte und gegenwärtige Literatur (A. Bucher) sowie praktisch-theologische Verortung (H.-G. Ziebertz) empirischer Religionspädagogik.
- "Zugänge": Einführung in quantitativ-empirische (A. Schnider) und qualitativ-empirische (B. Porzelt) Vorgehensweisen der Religionspädagogik.

LIT Verlag Münster – Hamburg – Berlin – London
Grevener Str./Fresnostr. 2 48159 Münster
Tel.: 0251 – 23 50 91 – Fax: 0251 – 23 19 72
e-Mail: vertrieb@lit-verlag.de – http://www.lit-verlag.de

- "Aktuelle Projekte": Konkrete Einblicke in die inhaltliche und methodische Vielfalt empirischen Forschens in der Religionspädagogik (A. Bucher, R. Güth, M. Jäggle, H. Mendl, B. Porzelt, A. Prokopf, G. Ritzer, M. Scherer-Rath/J. A. van der Ven, W. Vogel, H.-G. Ziebertz/A. Schnider).

Das Buch legt besonderen Wert auf Transparenz und Verständlichkeit. Es eignet sich nicht zuletzt als Literaturgrundlage für empirisch-theologische Einführungsveranstaltungen und Abschlussarbeiten.
Bd. 7, 2000, 248 S., 20,90 €, br., ISBN 3-8258-4953-8

Hans-Georg Ziebertz et al.
Religious Individualization and Christian Religious Semantics
In the western world, there is a change in religion. Some researchers speak of a general secularisation in the sense of a decline of religion in general. Other researchers claim that religion, represented by the dominant churches in particular, are losing importance. A third group are discovering religious vitality to be an inherent dimension of modernity. The analytical profit might be the greatest if empirical researchers succeed in achieving some sort of balance between functional and substantial dimensions of religion. This is what the authors of this book want to do. It is in this balance that the task of practical theology lies: to reflect on the tension between traditional Christian religion and actual religious practice and to open up perspectives for action in the pastoral practice and teaching.
Authors: Anton A. Bucher (Austria), Leslie J. Francis (Great Britain), Michael Krüggeler (Switzerland), Bert Roebben (The Netherlands), Johannes A. van der Ven (The Netherlands) and Hans-Georg Ziebertz (Germany)
Bd. 8, 2001, 144 S., 17,90 €, br., ISBN 3-8258-4960-0

Hans-Georg Ziebertz (Hg.)
Imagining God
Empirical Explorations from an international perspective
Is the question of God still relevant for our time? Empirical studies from an international perspective show the fact that there are both indications of God's importance and disappearance. The articles deal with questions related to the content, structure and function of images of God. The studies document the actual variety and forms of religious practice and highlight the issues of God present – out of necessity from an ecumenical and interdisciplinary point of view. If and how the question of God is aske d is not only of denominational interest, but is also of a cultural

importance for the individual and public life in Europe. The empirical studies in this collection were discussed at the "Würzburg Research Days – Practical Theology" in December 2000. Contributors: R.Campiche (Lausanne/CH), J.Dreyer (Pretoria/SA), M.Engelbrecht (Bayreuth/D), U.Feeser (Bonn/D), L.J.Francis (Bangor/UK), Z.Gross (Ramat Gan/IL), B.Kalbheim (Würzburg/D), Y.Katz (Ramat Gan/IL), T.Kläden (Bonn/D), E.Klinger (Würzburg/D), E.Pace (Padua/I), W.Pasierbek (Krakow/PL), H.Pieterse (Pretoria/SA), A.Prokopf (Würzburg/D), U.Riegel (Würzburg/D), F.Schweitzer (Tübingen/D), M.Tomka (Budapest/H), J.A.van der Ven (Nijmegen/NL), H.-G. Ziebertz (Würzburg/D).
Bd. 9, 2001, 288 S., 25,90 €, br., ISBN 3-8258-5425-6

Walter Fürst; Walter Neubauer (Hg.) unter Mitarbeit von Ulrich Feeser-Lichterfeld und Tobias Kläden
Theologiestudierende im Berufswahlprozess
Erträge eines interdisziplinären Forschungsprojektes in Kooperation von Pastoraltheologie und Berufspsychologie
Welche Berufe streben Studierende der katholischen Theologie an? Welche Vorstellungen von der eigenen Persönlichkeit und von verschiedenen theologischen Berufsalternativen sind hierbei im Spiel? Wie werden sie im konkreten Berufswahlverhalten umgesetzt?
Diese Fragen waren Ausgangspunkt für das in Kooperation von Pastoraltheologie und Berufspsychologie durchgeführte empirische Forschungsprojekt "Entwicklung des beruflichen Selbstkonzeptes und Berufswahlverhalten von Theologinnen und Theologen", in dem knapp 1000 Theologiestudierende über ihre Berufsvorstellungen und -ziele befragt wurden. Der vorliegende Sammelband dokumentiert Konzeption und Erträge dieses interdisziplinären Forschungsprojektes und stellt sie zur Diskussion.
Bd. 10, 2001, 248 S., 25,90 €, br., ISBN 3-8258-5666-6

Hans-Georg Ziebertz; Stefan Heil; Andreas Prokopf (Hg.)
Abduktive Korrelation
Religionspädagogische Konzeption, Methodologie und Professionalität im interdisziplinären Dialog
In diesem Band wird der aus dem amerikanischen Pragmatismus stammende Begriff Abduktion auf mehreren Ebenen in die Religionspädagogik eingeführt. Ausgangspunkt ist die Diskussion um das Korrelationsprinzip. Die „abduktive Korrelation" weist einen Weg aus der Sackgasse deduktiver und induktiver Konzepte und erweitert

LIT Verlag Münster–Hamburg–Berlin–London
Grevener Str./Fresnostr. 2 48159 Münster
Tel.: 0251–23 50 91 – Fax: 0251–23 19 72
e-Mail: vertrieb@lit-verlag.de – http://www.lit-verlag.de

damit die bisherige Theoriebildung. Abduktives Schließen wird als ein Prozess der Hypothesenfindung vorgestellt. Hypothesen zur Anbahnung von Verständigung und zur Öffnung eines diskursiven Raumes sind nötig, wenn beispielsweise Theologinnen und Theologen sowie christliche Erzieherinnen und Erzieher mit erklärungsbedürftigen Phänomenen oder Äußerungen konfrontiert werden, auf die sie nicht in traditioneller Weise antworten können. Durch abduktives Schließen wird Neues geschaffen.

Der Band beleuchtet interdisziplinär die Möglichkeiten abduktiven Denkens in der Religionspädagogik, klärt grundlegende Fragen einer empirisch-abduktiv orientierten Forschungsmethodologie und beschreibt Abduktion als Element einer zeitgemäßen Professionstheorie.
Bd. 12, Frühj. 2003, ca. 280 S., ca. 29,90 €, br.,
ISBN 3-8258-6264-x

Forum Theologie und Psychologie
herausgegeben von Prof. in Maria Kassel und Dr.
Thomas Meurer (Universität Münster)

Maria Kassel
Das Evangelium – eine Talenteschmiede?
Tiefenpsychologische Revision eines verinnerlichten christlichen Kapitalismus
Die Praxis tiefenpsychologischer, und das heißt erfahrungsbezogener Exegese zeigt, dass es heute anderer Übersetzungsprozesse für die biblischen Überlieferungen bedarf als der üblichen Exegesen. Das Symboldrama mit dem Gleichnis von den Talenten verdeutlicht beispielhaft, wie über eine bloße Analyse der Bibeltexte hinaus die ihnen zu Grunde liegenden religiösen Erfahrungen in die Gegenwart transferiert werden können und wie dabei von Adressaten und Adressatinnen verinnerlichte Wertmuster – z. B. kapitalistische und geschlechtsbezogene – die biblischen Intentionen verändern. Daher – so schlussfolgert die Autorin – muss sich die Bibelexegese grundlegend ändern, um den Zugang zur christlichen Botschaft auch in der Gegenwart offen zu halten.
Bd. 1, 2001, 168 S., 15,90 €, br., ISBN 3-8258-5437-x

Peter Neuhaus
'Erinnerung' als Brückenkategorie
Anstöße zur Vermittlung zwischen der Politischen Theologie von Johann Baptist Metz und der Tiefenpsychologischen Theologie Eugen Drewermanns
Die vorliegende Studie sucht die scharfe Kontroverse zwischen der Politischen Theologie von Johann Baptist Metz und der Tiefenpsychologischen Theologie Eugen Drewermanns, an der

sich gegenwärtig die lange Konfliktgeschichte zwischen Theologie und Psychologie kristallisiert, in einen produktiven Dialog über die gesellschaftlich-therapeutischen Befreiungspotentiale des christlichen Glaubens zu überführen, indem sie den Begriff der "Erinnerung" als verbindende Brückenkategorie empfiehlt: Das geschichtliche Eingedenken der Metzschen Theologie und die therapeutische Anamnetik Drewermanns dienen – so die zentrale These des Buches – dem gleichen Ziel: der Subjektwerdung des Menschen in Geschichte und Gesellschaft. "Die Arbeit leistet einen wichtigen wissenschaftlichen Beitrag zur Diskussion um zwei bedeutende moderne theologische Entwürfe." *(Gotthold Hasenhüttl)*
Bd. 2, 2001, 224 S., 25,90 €, br., ISBN 3-8258-5381-0

Ulrike Schneider-Harpprecht
Mit Symptomen leben
Eine andere Perspektive der Psychoanalyse Jacques Lacans mit Blick auf Theologie und Kirche
Die Verfasserin möchte die von der Wirklichkeitsoptik des frz. Psychoanalytikers J. Lacan ausgehenden Irritationen nutzen, um aufzuzeigen, dass im theologischen Denken der kirchlichen Praxis ein Fehlen fehlt. Lacans kritischer Blick auf das Ich, sein Widerstand gegen zuviel Sinn sowie sein Entwurf der drei Dimensionen des Psychischen laden ein, in der eigenen Theologie und Praxis die kleinen Freiheiten zu entdecken und die eigene Begrenztheit als konstruktiv zu akzeptieren.
Bd. 3, 2000, 344 S., 25,90 €, br., ISBN 3-8258-4887-6

Ruth-Erika Kölsch
Pastoralpsychologie als Suchbewegung und Erfüllung in Begegnung und Verantwortung
Hans-Joachim Thilo – Leben und Werk
Hans-Joachim Thilo ist ein Nestor der Pastoralpsychologie in Deutschland. Nicht nur für das Grenzgebiet der Annäherung von Theologie und Psychologie hat Hans-Joachim Thilo entscheidende Akzente gesetzt, auch für die Berührung von Seelsorge und Ethik, Therapie und Liturgik, Spiritualität und interreligiöser Dialog sind seine Werke wegweisend und wegbereitend.
Das vorliegende Werk folgt den Spuren der Kreativität und Innovationskraft in Hans-Joachim Thilos Leben und verweist in der Auseinandersetzung mit Hans-Joachim Thilos theologischen Grundgedanken auf eine "Theologie der Zärtlichkeit", eine lebbare pastoralpsychologische Perspektive der (Geistes-)Gegenwart.
Bd. 4, 2001, 344 S., 25,90 €, br., ISBN 3-8258-5527-9

LIT Verlag Münster – Hamburg – Berlin – London
Grevener Str./Fresnostr. 2 48159 Münster
Tel.: 0251 – 23 50 91 – Fax: 0251 – 23 19 72
e-Mail: vertrieb@lit-verlag.de – http://www.lit-verlag.de

Daniel Stosiek
Herausfordernde Erinnerung
Gemeinsame Potentiale in Psychoanalyse,
politischer Theologie und Judentum
Bd. 5, 2001, 176 S., 20,90 €, br., ISBN 3-8258-5495-7

Hans-Joachim Thilo
**DIE ANDERE WAHRHEIT: von der
Macht des geistlichen Dialoges**
Bd. 6, 2002, 80 S., 17,90 €, br., ISBN 3-8258-5844-8

Profane Religionspädagogik

herausgegeben von Prof. Dr. Dietrich Zilleßen und
PD Dr. Bernd Beuscher (Universtität Köln)

Dietrich Zilleßen
Experimentelle Didaktik
Ein Diskurs in religiöser Kultur, Bildung,
Ethik
Bd. 1, Frühj. 2003, ca. 368 S., ca. 25,90 €, br.,
ISBN 3-8258-4843-4

Dietrich Zilleßen (Hg.)
Religion, Politik, Kultur
Diskussionen im religionspädagogischen
Kontext
Bd. 2, 2001, 264 S., 20,90 €, br., ISBN 3-8258-4844-2

Dietrich Zilleßen (Hg.)
Markt.
Religion und Moral des Marktes
Bd. 3, 2002, 208 S., 20,90 €, br., ISBN 3-8258-4845-0

Dorothea Bähr
**Zwischenräume – Ästhetische Praxis in der
Religionspädagogik**
Bd. 4, 2001, 264 S., 20,90 €, br., ISBN 3-8258-5200-8

Bernd Beuscher (Hg.)
**Balancé – Gespräche über Theologie, die
die Welt braucht**
Bd. 5, 2001, 170 S., 20,90 €, br., ISBN 3-8258-5677-1

Guido Meyer
Bilder, Bildung und christlicher Glaube
Eine Auseinandersetzung mit den Grundlagen
einer religionspädagogisch verantworteten
Bildtheorie
Bd. 6, 2002, 192 S., 20,90 €, br., ISBN 3-8258-6082-5

Harald Schroeter-Wittke
**Unerhört – Studien zu einer musikalischen
Religionspädagogik**
Bd. 7, Frühj. 2003, ca. 208 S., ca. 19,90 €, br.,
ISBN 3-8258-6089-2

Schriften aus dem Comenius-Institut

herausgegeben von Volker Elsenbast und Christoph
Th. Scheilke (Münster)

Albrecht Schöll; Heinz Streib
Wege der Entzauberung
Jugendliche Sinnsuche und
Okkultfaszination – Kontexte und Analysen
Bd. 1, 2001, 232 S., 20,90 €, br., ISBN 3-8258-4825-6

Dietlind Fischer (Hg.)
Im Dienst von LehrerInnen und Schule
Aufgaben, Konzepte, Perspektiven kirchlicher
Lehrerfortbildung
Bd. 2, 2000, 176 S., 20,90 €, br., ISBN 3-8258-5155-9

Hans-Günter Heimbrock;
Christoph Th. Scheilke; Peter Schreiner (ed.)
Towards Religious Competence
Diversity as a Challenge for Education in
Europe
Bd. 3, 2001, 296 S., 25,90 €, br., ISBN 3-8258-5015-3

Cok Bakker; Olaf Beuchling;
Karin Griffioen (Hg.)
Kulturelle Vielfalt und Religionsunterricht
Entwicklungen und Praxis in vier
europäischen Ländern
Bd. 4, 2002, 176 S., 17,90 €, br., ISBN 3-8258-6275-5

Martin Steinhäuser
**Gemeindliche Arbeit mit Kindern
begleiten**
Empirische Studien zur Entwicklung
der Aufgaben und Strukturen
gemeindepädagogischer Fachaufsicht
Bd. 5, 2002, 248 S., 19,90 €, br., ISBN 3-8258-7341-2

Christoph Th. Scheilke
Von Religion lernen heute
Befunde und Perspektiven in Schule,
Gemeinde und Kirche
Bd. 6, Frühj. 2003, ca. 420 S., ca. 35,90 €, br.,
ISBN 3-8258-7332-3

Peter Biehl; Karl Ernst Nipkow
**Bildung und Bildungspolitik in
theologischer Perspektive**
Bd. 7, Frühj. 2003, ca. 208 S., ca. 19,90 €, br.,
ISBN 3-8258-6558-4

Gert Rüppell; Peter Schreiner (eds.)
Shared Learning in a Plural World
Ecumenical Approaches to Inter-Religious
Education
Bd. 8, Frühj. 2003, ca. 184 S., ca. 19,90 €, br.,
ISBN 3-8258-6571-1

LIT Verlag Münster – Hamburg – Berlin – London
Grevener Str./Fresnostr. 2 48159 Münster
Tel.: 0251 – 23 50 91 – Fax: 0251 – 23 19 72
e-Mail: vertrieb@lit-verlag.de – http://www.lit-verlag.de